modern sportscars

modern
sports cars

ROGER BELL ON THE WORLD'S TOP DRIVING MACHINES

Haynes Publishing

British Library Cataloguing in Publication Data:
A catalogue record for this book is available from the British Library.

ISBN 1 85960 676 8

Library of Congress Catalog Card Number 00-134249

Haynes North America, Inc.
861 Lawrence Drive, Newbury Park,
California 91320, USA

Published by Haynes Publishing, Sparkford,
Nr Yeovil, Somerset, BA22 7JJ, UK.
Tel: 01963 442030 Fax: 01963 440001
Int. tel: +44 1963 442030 Fax: +44 1963 440001
E-mail: sales@haynes-manuals.co.uk
Web site: www.haynes.co.uk

Printed in Great Britain by J.H. Haynes & Co Ltd
While every effort is taken to ensure the accuracy of the information given in this
book, no liability can be accepted by the author or publishers for any loss, damage
or injury caused by errors in, or omissions from, the information given.

Design by Simon Larkin

Most of the photographs in this book have been supplied by *Autocar* magazine,
but the work of Roger Bell, Ian Dawson, Martyn Goddard and Tim Wren is also
featured. The front cover, showing a Porsche 911 GT3, was photographed by
Charlie Magee. Thanks, too, to Richard Heseltine for picture research.

Contents

As a rookie sub on *Motor* magazine, it was my job to fill space earmarked for weekend race reports lost in the ether. For a substitute story, I'd rifle an old wooden filing cabinet housing stock articles. Some of my favourites, filed under 'What is a sports car?', were yellow with age, hinting that the topic had been aired in print since the days of S.F.Edge.

I was reminded of that cabinet, long since gone (*Motor* was absorbed by its weekly rival *Autocar* in 1988), when writing the synopsis for this book. Surely there would be no need to define what a sports cars was. All card-carrying enthusiasts knew that already. It was an instinctive thing, etched on the heart, not gleaned from a spec table – or a dog-eared file.

By common consent, a sports car was a low-slung two-seater with a fabric roof used only by wimps, and a raspy exhaust that evoked power and speed even if there was little of either. Comfort went out with the back seat, practicality and smart hair-dos with the luggage. Masochism came as standard. Or did it?

Half a century ago, this blinkered profile may well have been apt. Not now. Sports cars have moved on. The faster they go, the greater the need to rigidly enclose them. To determine this book's parameters – to decide which cars should be included, and which not – old perceptions would have to go, and new ones evolved.

Introduction

So what is a **sports car?**

While the emphasis would still be on open cars, restricting the list to ragtop two-seaters clearly didn't work, not least because it excluded the enclosed three-seater McLaren F1 – arguably the greatest sports car of them all, certainly the fastest and most expensive. Without the McLaren (a Le Mans winner), rivals like Ferrari's F40 and the ill-fated Jaguar XJ220 – supercars by name, but fixed-head sports cars at heart – would have been summarily dismissed too. More to the point, so would the Lotus Esprit and TVR Cerbera.

Let's deal first, then, with the easy part of the book's title: modern. How recent is modern? Seventies? Eighties? No, these decades are well covered elsewhere. Besides, they were not, with some notable exceptions, vintage years. The focus here is on sports cars *made* during the prolific Nineties and beyond, even though they may have been conceived and launched earlier – in some cases many years earlier.

To cover the last decade of the car's first full century is not quite so arbitrary as it sounds. It was in 1990 that the Mazda MX-5 came to Britain (though as the Miata it had taken the USA by storm the previous year). And the inspirational MX-5 was the ragtop that rekindled the sports car boom – a boom that buoyed the publication of this book. If anything, subsequent newcomers have not so much eroded the Mazda's dominance as expanded the market it originated. Not since the Sixties, the golden age of motoring, have enthusiasts had it so good.

After the sad demise of Britain's mainstream sports cars from Austin-Healey, MG, Jensen, Reliant and Triumph, the lust for funsters was satisfied not by a new generation of open two-seaters – let's call them roadsters, as Jaguar did – but by hot-hatchbacks. And amusingly entertaining little brats some of them were. Despite dazzling alacrity, however, cars like the Peugeot 205 GTi and Renault 5 GT Turbo were not substitute sports cars. As pepped-up family hacks, stronger on practicality than on style and individuality, they had no place here.

Nor, Heaven forbid, did the sports utilities – pick-ups in plain English – that masqueraded as latter-day sportsters in the US. Four-seater convertibles – al fresco tourers, no more – were as easily dismissed. Certain rally-bred saloons, notably those from Mitsubishi and Subaru, got much closer to the mark as driving machines of astonishing pace and ability. But saloons they remained, however exciting dynamically. No room, then, for the Impreza Turbo. Nor for performance-enhanced saloons like those of BMW's M-series.

From another peripheral group, some coupés were easily rejected: down-range Ford Probes and Vauxhall Calibras, for instance, clearly didn't make the grade. But what of the Nissan SX200 and Fiat Coupe Turbo? Should they be included for being so quick and entertaining? Er, no. However loosely one interprets the vague rules, they were arbitrarily too spacious and accommodating to be classed as real sports cars.

You may by now have concluded that it's actually easier to define what doesn't qualify than what does. Properly to cover the 80 or so cars profiled in these pages meant, in the end, resorting as much to subjectivity as specifications, to style as substance.

So, what does make a modern sports car? Size has nothing to do with it, witness the diminutive Ariel Atom at one end of the scale, and the gargantuan Dodge Viper GTS at the other. Both score bull's-eyes. Speed is not an irrelevance, but it's not what counts most; one of the best cars in this book is also one of the slowest. Accommodation? Sports cars can have more than two seats, witness the McLaren F1, but not more than two-plus-two – and here we enter a grey zone because the dividing line between a two-and-a-bit and a full four-seater is often decided by shutting an eye and extending a thumb. It's not scientific, not infallible.

Rail if you wish against the inclusion of Merc's SL, on the cusp of the cabriolet/sports car divide. As a benchmark icon throughout the Nineties, though, the SL roadster muscled its way into these pages as a heavyweight champ. So did the distant rival with plush leather trim, room for two golf bags, air-conditioning and every conceivable driving aid. Doesn't sound like a traditional sports car, but then Ferrari's 200mph 550 Maranello doesn't look like one, either.

So much for analysis. In the end, gut feeling finalised the contents list. Sublime motoring enjoyment, after all, is at the heart of the matter, and all the cars featured in this book strive to provide it – some with much greater success than others.

For easy reference, entries are arranged in alphabetical order. While spec tables follow a standard format, my text – much of it distilled from hands-on driving experience – doesn't. In an attempt to prevent order and consistency numbing a good read, the emphasis, be it technical, historical or anecdotal, varies from car to car. While my head was the source of many expressed opinions, I'm indebted to my archives (and experts on the end of a 'phone) for much of the fine detail.

AC Superblower

Period revival, at a price

AC's Superblower, powered by a 5.0-litre supercharged Ford V8, built like traditional Cobras, with aluminium bodywork. Labour-intensive construction pushed up price.

Judged by the number of flattering fakes it has inspired in the past half century, the AC/Shelby Cobra has eclipsed the title of seminal sports car virtually without challenge. That it epitomises what a raw driving machine should be – imposing, loud, potent, brutish, demanding – goes some way to explain its enduring appeal. But what, you may well be asking, is this golden oldie doing here, up front, in a book about modern sports cars?

True, the Cobra's lineage is almost 50 years old. But the car born in 1953 as the AC Ace (Tojeiro-designed twin-tube ladder-frame chassis, all-independent suspension, Ferrari Barchetta-inspired styling, 2.0-litre six-cylinder AC engine) has evolved through five roller-coasting decades. What's more, it's still in production on both sides of the Atlantic. The car that American race ace Carroll Shelby masterminded in the Sixties – and resurrected in component form in the Nineties – masquerades at AC today under the contrived and far less evocative names of Superblower (which sounds to me like a hair-dryer) and MkIV CRS.

Alan Lubinsky's Pride Group, which bought AC in late '96, could have ditched the best-known model of Britain's oldest surviving car-maker. It chose to rejuvenate it. Recognising that the earlier MkIV (so christened by AC's former owner and saviour, Brian Angliss, when the Cobra name was in dispute), was less than top-drawer excitement, the new team swapped its mild-mannered 225bhp Ford V8 engine for a horny supercharged one.

8

Specification	AC Superblower (2000)
Engine	4942cc, V8, ohv, 16V, supercharger
Engine layout	Longitudinal, front
Power	320bhp at 5700rpm
Torque	385lb ft at 3750rpm
Gearbox	Five-speed manual
Drive	Rear wheel
Front suspension	Unequal length wishbones, coils, anti-roll bar
Rear suspension	Unequal length wishbones, coils
Steering	Unassisted rack & pinion
Brakes	Ventilated front discs, solid rear discs
Front wheels	Alloy 7Jx16
Rear wheels	Alloy 8Jx16
Tyres	225-50VR
Length	4200mm
Width	1746mm
Height	1200mm
Wheelbase	2285mm
Weight	1160kg (2557lb)
0-60mph (97kph)	5.5sec
0-100mph (161kph)	14.0sec
Top speed	155mph (249kph)
Fuel consumption	17-25mpg

Now that was more like it. The 320bhp Superblower, announced in '97, went like a Cobra with real fangs, even if it didn't displace King Cobra. The mighty 7.0-litre Shelby 427 that once catapulted me to 100mph in 9.8 seconds – and a place in *The Guinness Book of Car Records* as the world's fastest-accelerating production car – was decisively quicker. While Cobras in streamlined drag could nudge 180mph (and famously did on the M1 motorway, testing for Le Mans), most of the bluff open-cockpit ones were all out at 135mph. Even the quickies struggled to make 150mph, so the Superblower's claimed 165mph looked decidedly optimistic until AC moderated it to 155.

Although an old pushrod unit, not to be confused with Ford's quad-cam, 32-valver used by Marcos in its supercharged Mantis (and subsequently by AC in its Ace, for that matter), the Superblower's blown V8 was a real powerhouse, if not a richly raucous one. The high-pitched whine of its belt-driven Paxton supercharger tended to dominate exhaust rasp.

Warp-drive to wishbone-suspended rear wheels was through a beefy five-speed manual gearbox from Borg Warner. Nothing wrong with that, given a firm hand and a strong left leg. The gear ratios, though, were so widely spaced that acceleration in intergalactic top was barely discernible, despite the engine's heroic flexibility: 385lb ft is by any yardstick a mountain of torque. No quibbles about the AP racing brakes (strong) or ride (unexpectedly supple). None, either, about the dry grip of generous Cobra tyres (yes, really, made by Cooper's in the States). Wet-road bravura – opposite-lock slides were strictly for the courageous – betrayed the

Highlights of stark cockpit included aluminium-backed central instruments, cranked gear lever for wide-ratio Borg Warner 'box, and minimal weather protection. Hood was a joke.

Bright induction manifold carried AC name-plate, but torque-biased ohv pushrod V8 off-the-shelf Ford. Belt-driven Paxton blower increased power to 320bhp.

sluggishness of unassisted steering that required 3.6 turns lock-to-lock. Worse still was a vintage-size Momo wheel that fouled your knees. Offset pedals didn't help the ache-prone driving position, either. Truth is, the cockpit, dominated by a lovely central set of aluminium-backed black-on-white instruments, was less comfortable than its fine hand-crafted finish suggested. And the billowing hood was a bad joke: AC once conceded that it was likely to take off in tatters above 50mph.

Quick and entertaining though it was, the Superblower needed to be a little more rumbustious, a bit rowdier, like a TVR was rowdy. It may not have needed close-ratio gears, but it would have been all the more entertaining with them. None featured on a year 2000 options list devoted more to cosmetic enhancement than dynamic uplift. At a tad under £70,000 before extras, the Superblower was an extravagant toy.

AC

AC 289 FIA & CRS

The snake proliferates

CRS lighter than Superblower but less powerful, with only 225bhp from normally aspirated 5.0 Ford V8. Even with double-wishbone suspension, handling more retro than modern.

The second Cobra spin-off of AC's Lubinsky era was a replica of the MkII 289 racer. Just seven competition 289s were homologated by the FIA for sports car racing in 1964, according to AC, who pledged to restrict the number of replicas to 25 – an optimistic goal given that the car, first seen at the British Motor Show at Birmingham's NEC in 1998, cost £140,000. That was twice as much as the Superblower. Built to order only on an authentic chassis with 3in side tubes and transverse leaf springs, the Replica 289 was said to be hand-crafted on original wooden bucks.

If the racing Replica was for the dedicated rich, AC's 'Cobra MkIV CRS' (for

Specification	AC MkIV CRS (2000)
Engine	4942cc, V8, ohv pushrod, 16V
Engine layout	Longitudinal, front
Power	225bhp at 4200rpm
Torque	300lb ft at 3200rpm
Gearbox	Five-speed manual
Drive	Rear wheel
Front suspension	Double wishbones, coils, anti-roll bar
Rear suspension	Double wishbones, coils, anti-roll bar
Steering	Unassisted rack & pinion
Brakes	Ventilated front discs, solid rear discs, no ABS
Front wheels	Alloy 7Jx16
Rear wheels	8Jx16
Front tyres	225-50ZR15
Rear tyres	255-50ZR16
Length	4200mm
Width	1745mm
Height	1200mm
Wheelbase	2285mm
Weight	1080kg (2380lb)
0-60mph (97kph)	6.0sec
0-100mph (161kph)	17.0sec
Top speed	135mph (217kph)
Fuel consumption	18-26mpg

Carbon Road Series) aimed to broaden the icon's appeal. Here, on the face of it, was the genuine article that cost little more than the price of a good replica – and there were still some very good replicas around at the turn of the century. The Gardner Douglas GD427, for instance, was said by some to be better than the real thing. But then what was the real thing? Was it built in the USA or Britain? Or both?

The Mk IV CRS was hardly cheap at £38,950, but it was well on the right side of silly money and competitive with it, given that a contemporary Rover-engined Morgan Plus 8 4.6 cost £35,000 before extras. Such was demand that AC had to re-arrange its Brooklands workshops to cope. The secret behind the CRS's massively reduced price lay in carbon-fibre pre-impregnated bodywork, built by Hampshire-based Pro-Tech Motorsport, an offshoot of Kid Jensen Racing, of F3000 fame.

The Superblower's hand-rolled 16-gauge aluminium bodywork was a labour-intensive work of art that cost the earth to produce and took an age to fit. The CRS alternative, using the same laminated carbon-fibre cloth and heat-set epoxy resin as in today's F1 cars, could be made and attached in a fraction of the time. What's more, being a rigid one-piece structure, it didn't require such a complex frame to support it. Result: less weight and considerably reduced manufacturing costs.

Costs were further cut by reverting to the MkIV's naturally-aspirated 225bhp 5.0 Ford pushrod V8, driving through that wide-ratio five-speed Borg Warner gearbox and a Hydratrak limited-slip diff. Even with this modest power, performance was on the muscular side of breezy – AC claimed 145mph and a 0-60mph time of 5.3 seconds. American V8s being so receptive to tuning, considerably more power was available to those who could pay for it. There were even suggestions of swapping Ford's lump for Lotus's twin-turbo quad-cam V8. Why not? What was good for the Ace and Aceca couldn't be bad for the CRS.

AC

Unadorned no-frills cockpit. Traditional instruments set into carbon-fibre dash. Hoops afford roll-over protection, screen 'ears' reduce wind buffeting. Best without hood.

AC **Ace**

Problems with the **problem child**

Despite agonisingly long gestation period, modern AC Ace still seriously flawed when *Autocar* tested it in '99. Base structure made in South Africa, car finished in Britain.

The original Ace – one of the cars with which AC supplemented its invalid trike business – was a classy two-seater based on a race-bred twin-tube chassis designed by John Tojeiro. The Ace's all-independent suspension was considered quite advanced, and its all-aluminium body, which owed much to a contemporary Ferrari, disarmingly pretty. Under the bonnet was AC's ancient 2.0-litre, ohc straight-six, later superseded by Bristol's ex-BMW 2.0 six. When supplies of that ran dry, a humble Ford 2.6 propelled the Ace until it spawned the V8-engined Shelby Cobra.

So much for the uncomplicated tale of the original Ace and the Aceca coupé it sired. The story of its modern namesake is a saga of frustration, blind alleys and unfulfilled hopes. I can think of no other car that has had a more tortured gestation or laboured birth.

The tale started at the 1986 Birmingham Motor Show, where a striking four-wheel-drive prototype powered by a V6 Granada engine attracted much attention. From this stillborn project evolved another, this time with 2.0 Ford Cosworth power and the Cossie's newly developed 4x4 transmission. As joint owners, with Autokraft's Brian Angliss, Ford was now heavily involved in the Ace's development. The purpose-built Brooklands plant it financed to build the car is still AC's headquarters – though, ironically, Ace assembly, using body-in-white units sourced from South Africa, was transferred to Coventry.

In 1991, five years of fruitless endeavour on, came yet another variation on the Ace theme, this one involving the styling expertise of Worthing-based IAD. But after Ford abandoned ship (prompting premature reports of AC's demise), Angliss – by 1992 AC's sole owner – oversaw yet another revamp,

Specification	AC Ace (1999)
Engine	4924cc, V8, ohv pushrod, 16V, supercharged
Engine layout	Longitudinal, front
Power	325bhp at 5700rpm
Torque	385lb ft at 3500rpm
Gearbox	Five-speed manual
Drive	Rear wheel
Front suspension	Unequal length wishbones, coils, anti-roll bar
Rear suspension	Unequal length wishbones, double coils, anti-roll bar
Steering	Assisted rack and pinion
Brakes	ABS-backed ventilated discs front and rear
Wheels	Alloy 8Jx18
Front tyres	235-40
Rear tyres	255-40
Length	4420mm
Width	1930mm
Height	1305mm
Wheelbase	2470mm
Weight	1580kg (3483lb)
0-60mph (97kph)	6.4sec
0-100mph (161kph)	16.5sec
Top speed	148mph (238kph)
Fuel consumption	14-19mpg

with the help of ex-Ford engineer John Mitchell. The Yamaha-developed Ford Taurus V6 engine was ditched for a meatier Ford V8, like that in the MkIV, and the hefty, power-sapping 4x4 transmission replaced by a simpler rear-drive set-up. The styling received a pre-production makeover, too: pop-up headlights gave way to paired recessed ones (looking much like those of a Marcos); an aluminium 'eggbox' grille highlighted the nose; the bonnet acquired a power bulge; and the wings were flared more. Weight distribution was also improved, to a theoretically ideal 50/50.

This was the car that went into small-scale production prematurely in 1993 at a loss-making price of £49,995. It was also the car that South African entrepreneur Alan Lubinsky's operation acquired when it bought AC from the receivers. More work was done on the all-metal Ace, under the supervision of a former Volvo engineer, Jan-Erik Jansson, before its appearance alongside the Superblower at the 1997 London Motor Show.

Alas, the Ace's troubles were far from over. In a hard-hitting '99 road test, *Autocar* still found the car 'seriously flawed'. It singled out for criticism the nervous steering, jittery ride, patchy handling and excessive thirst. Considering the high price, performance was nothing to shout about either. Well made and finished though the aluminium-bodied Ace had become, it barely looked like an £80,000 car. Even allowing for a reassuringly stiff stainless-steel monocoque chassis, an excellent power-operated Karmann hood (now supplemented by a hardtop), strong brakes and (above all) exclusivity, the car wasn't quite special enough.

Undaunted, AC pressed on, boasting 'a host of improvements' for the '99 London show. In a surprise move, it addressed the unspectacular performance of both the Ace and its Aceca sibling by offering Lotus's 350bhp 3.5-litre twin-turbo V8 (good for over 500bhp) as a six-speed alternative to various five-speed Ford V8s. Confusingly, no fewer than three models were listed in 1998: a 240bhp 5.0 with automatic transmission, a 320bhp supercharged 5.0, and the ubiquitous 320bhp, 32-valve quad-cam 4.6 – the latter costing £5,000 less than the premium Lotus engine. By the turn of the century the choice of engines had been trimmed to the 4.6 Ford and the 3.5 Lotus.

The contract with Lotus, supplying its twin-Garrett V8 to another car-maker for the first time, was said to be long-term. AC also hired the man responsible for overseeing the development and production of the Esprit's V8 engine at Hethel. As AC's chief engineer, John Owen had much on his plate.

Smart, hand-tailored cockpit adorned with polished wood and leather. Proprietary switchgear disappointing. Powered hood disappears neatly into lidded well ahead of big boot.

Thirsty blown engine of this '99 Ace is 325bhp, 5.0-litre, 16-valve Ford V8. Later cars had either 4.6-litre 32-valve Ford or – for a hefty premium – twin-turbo Lotus V8.

Alfa Romeo RZ & SZ

il Mostro, the ugly brute

Alfa Romeo RZ open version of more numerous fixed-head SZ, nicknamed Il Mostro (The Monster) when launched in '89. Huge presence of 75-based cars rooted in bizarre slab-sided looks.

Zagato-influenced RZ/SZ driver's delight, with robust performance, glorious exhaust note and terrific handling. Engine 210bhp 3.0 V6, driving de Dion-suspended rear wheels.

Its internal name was ES30, short for Experimental Sports 3.0 litre, but it went on sale as the SZ (coupé) and RZ (roadster), and was endearingly nicknamed Il Mostro (The Monster). The sobriquet stuck, and with good reason. When I first set eyes on this bizarre car, at Alfa's Balocco test track in 1989, I was captivated by its brutal lines, seduced by its audacity. 'The brickbats poured in,' I reported in *Car* magazine. 'And with them came the publicity. Il Mostro made its mark before turning a wheel.' Bull's-eye. Alfa's aim could not have been truer.

Il Mostro was a statement, a symbol of Alfa's resurgence, that cocked a snook at the establishment. It was a piece of frivolous free-thinking that projected glamour, excitement and individuality – traditional Alfa virtues in need of a lift. Above all, it was extrovert, extravagant, over-the-top fun, and none the worse for that. It was the sort of whimsical car that adorned the walls of design studios – but never got made. Well, Alfa

Specification	Alfa Romeo RZ/SZ (1990)
Engine	2959cc, V6, ohc, 12V
Engine layout	Longitudinal, front
Power	210bhp at 6200rpm
Torque	177lb ft at 4500rpm
Gearbox	Five-speed manual
Drive	Rear wheel
Front suspension	Struts, transverse links, coils, anti-roll bar
Rear suspension	De Dion rear axle, Watt links, coils
Steering	Assisted rack and pinion
Brakes	Ventilateded front discs, solid rear discs
Front wheels	Alloy 7Jx16
Rear wheels	Alloy 8Jx16
Front tyres	205-55
Rear tyres	225-50
Length	4060mm
Width	1730mm
Height	1310mm
Wheelbase	2510mm
Weight	1260kg (2778lb)
0-60mph (97kph)	7.0sec
0-100mph (161kph)	Approx 18.0sec
Top speed	152mph (245kph)
Fuel consumption	20-30mpg

made it and the world was all the richer for it.

The basis of the ES30 was a modified 75 floorpan carrying coo-eh plastic bodywork penned by Alfa's Centro Stile with Zagato's collaboration. Why not? Zagato were past masters in outrageous ugliness. The result – a deep-flanked, shallow-windowed, slipper-shaped wedge that was more caricature than car – may not have been a pretty sight, but no-one could accuse it of anonymity. Gawp-factor presence the SZ had in abundance. It was also surprisingly slippery, with a drag factor of 0.30 – no mean achievement for a short, fat, stubby car.

Alfa's mellifluous 3.0 V6, mildly uprated from 190 to 210bhp, drove the rear wheels (gorgeous Speedline alloys) through a five-speed 'box short on shift quality as well as a perfect set of cogs. Front suspension was basically that of the 75, with coil springs instead of torsion bars. At the back was a classic de Dion arrangement. Flick a switch and an engine-driven pump energised a second chamber in the Koni dampers to give two ride heights: low and mind-the-cat's-eyes. Prodigious grip – Alfa spoke of 1.4g, which is what it felt like on Balocco's grippy tarmac – gave the SZ better cornering powers than straight-line speed. Performance enthralled rather than excited, and the car's friendly civility was curiously at odds with its brutal bad looks.

Alfa pledged to create no more than 1,000 of these 'monster' mutations of steel and composites. In the event Zagato made 998, according to Alfa's press office, the bulk of them SV coupés – which makes the open RZ all the more coveted for being so scarce. Alfa officially sold 46 cars in Britain in the 1990-93 period.

Alfa Romeo

Winged seat of Alfa SZ good for strong lateral support when cornering – at up to 1.4g, according to Alfa. Production in 1990-93 totalled 998 cars, ensuring valuable exclusivity.

Alfa Romeo
GTV & Spider
Ragtop to riches

Striking lines of Alfa Romeo GTV spider influenced by swage rising from front wheel to rear deck. Fixed-head coupé stiffer structurally than shaky Spider.

Alfa Romeo stole the 1994 Paris Salon from the French with its spectacular GTV coupé and Spider – the first open two-seater sports Alfa since the Duetto (of *The Graduate* fame). Alfa needed the break. The looks and dynamics of the 145 and 155 mainstreamers had not been particularly well received, so the rakish GTV/Spider had much ground to recover for its down-trodden maker. Nothing less than approbation would do for the new sports cars and the upcoming 156 saloon. Both received it. Alfa was on a roll.

Mechanically, the charismatic GTV/Spider head-turners were identical. Only in body structure, rear-end treatment and headgear did they differ. Shaped by Pininfarina's Enrico Fumia in conjunction with Walter de Silva, director of Alfa Centro Stile, Alfa's new shovel-nosed sportsters refuted the suggestion that there was little flair or imagination left in car design. Here was dramatic individuality in spades without the wackiness of the low-volume RZ/SZ. Alfa's '91 Proteo concept car had had a much stronger influence.

The GTV/Spider owed its bold, distinctive visage to tiny pairs of poly-ellipsoidal lights flanking a heart-shaped grille nestling in a bonnet-swaged vee. A sculpted crease line, slanting upwards from the front wheels to the rear deck, emphasised the car's wedge profile. You didn't go unnoticed in a Spider. From whatever angle the car was viewed, it oozed class and generated lust – which is more than can be said of its predecessor.

Although the previous GTV boasted a traditional front-to-rear drivetrain,

Specification	Alfa Romeo Spider ('96)
Engine	1970cc, 4-cylinder, 16V
Engine layout	Transverse, front
Power	150bhp at 6200rpm
Torque	137lb ft at 4000rpm
Gearbox	Five-speed manual
Drive	Front-wheel
Front suspension	Struts, coils, lower wishbones, anti-roll bar
Rear suspension	Multi-link, coils, anti-roll bar
Steering	Assisted rack and pinion
Brakes	ABS-backed discs, ventilated at front
Wheels	6Jx15 alloys
Tyres	195-60ZR15
Length	4285mm
Width	1780mm
Height	1320mm
Wheelbase	2540mm
Weight	1360kg (2998lb)
0-60mph (97kph)	7.8sec
0-100mph (161kph)	23.0sec
Top speed	130mph (210kph)
Fuel consumption	25-32mpg

it was a disappointing car, a promise unfulfilled. Even the V6 (lovely engine, lousy chassis) fell well short of expectations. Handling was sloppy, driving position poor, gearchange a cruncher, bodywork prone to rust. Its spiritual successor would have to be much, much better in every department. It was.

All Alfas by now had front-wheel drive, so there was no question of reverting to a 'pusher' layout for the new GTV/Spider, even though it may have been the preferred choice for a sports car. The bizarre 75-based SZ of the late Eighties was by now a dead and buried anachronism. As the new twins were to be built in relatively large numbers, at Alfa's Arese plant near Milan, they would have to make use of much existing hardware. It was no coincidence that the wheelbase was the same as that of Alfa's 155 and the Fiat Tipo: all three cars shared the Group's C-type platform.

In the interests of cost-cutting, the use of basic 155 suspension was considered – and quickly rejected as inadequate. Alfa designed instead a bespoke multi-link rear suspension using upper wishbones and twin lower links, all the better to keep the tyres perpendicular to the road. Passive rear steering (the positive rear steer of the Proteo concept didn't make it into production) would contribute to sharp, predictable handling.

The birth of the GTV/Spider Twin Sparks saw the demise of Alfa's classic old twin-cam four, rooted in the Fifties. It was replaced by Fiat's cracking new modular engine that, in Alfa guise, had just about every high-tech accoutrement in the book: twin overhead camshafts (of course), 16 valves (what else?), twin spark plugs per cylinder (if only to uphold Alfa's TC tradition), variable valve control (oomph everywhere), counter-rotating balancer shafts (to kill vibration), and the latest Bosch Motronic management system (for German dependability).

Turbine smoothness – those balancer shafts really did eliminate innate out-of-balance forces – allowed the use of fussless sprint gearing that gave the original 150bhp cars a decent if not spectacular turn of speed. Alfa's

Alfa GTV/Spider aimed at luxury end of the sports car market. Mainstream cabin roomy for two but not adventurously styled. Later cars had six-speed manual.

Ultra-sharp steering responsible for flick-wrist agility and manoeuvrability. Cars run arrow-straight at speed, stop reassuringly. ABS-backed discs too sensitive around town.

new engine was a sweet-running gem, but its raspy performance was blunted by weight: at around 1,350kg, the Spider was no lightweight. Parent Fiat's 1.8 Barchetta had a better power-to-weight ratio, and the turbocharged Fiat Coupé was streets ahead on straight-line speed. Ditto Nissan's formidable 200SX. But then neither was available as a topless roadster.

Objectively, the 2.0's performance was nothing special. Subjectively, it felt quick, flexible and eager. Oh yes, and aurally uplifting. Short gear ratios, crisply swapped, helped foster the impression of liveliness, as did refinement that bordered on the uncanny for a four-cylinder engine. Given the car's low gearing and highish weight, there was no reason to expect good economy, but road-test figures indicated a surprisingly light thirst for unleaded petrol. Bravo.

For real performance, and even more aural appeal, Alfa's wonderfully sonorous 220bhp, 24-valve V6 – 0-60mph in 6.5 seconds, top speed 150mph – was the engine to have. Not that you could initially get it in Britain: right-handed versions did not go on sale in the UK until 1998 – and then only in the fixed-head GTV. Right-handed Spiders didn't get the unblown V6 until early in 2000. The tax-beating 2.0 turbo V6, sold elsewhere in Europe, never did make it across the Channel. No need.

With the front-drive Elan as its benchmark, Alfa aimed high with the GTV/Spider's handling. If not quite in the Lotus league, it didn't disappoint. Sharp steering, giving just 2.2 assisted turns lock to lock, was the key to flick-wrist agility and manoeuvrability. Fears that such responsiveness would make the car nervous at speed were unfounded: it ran arrow-straight at the

Fixed-roof GTV handled better than Spider, as 64 per cent more rigid. Four-cylinder Alfa engine, with twin plugs, counter-rotating balancer shafts and four valves per cylinder, impressive as it looks. Potent V6 option even stronger, aurally sweeter.

130mph maximum. Torque steer, the bane of many powerful front-drive cars, was notable by its absence – and this without any form of traction control, other than that provided by the driver's right foot. The agitated ride, at its jittery worst on pocked urban roads, was just about passable for a firmly sprung, handling-biased sportster.

Despite the lever's long throw, changing gear was once again the indulgence it should be in an Alfa, and the strong all-disc, ABS-backed brakes were marred for me only by excessive servo-assistance.

Aimed at the luxury end of the sports car sector, the Alfa twins were well equipped and appointed. Nicely made, too: you looked in vain for shoddy workmanship. Ditto pared-to-the-bone minimalism, or cockpit cramping; long-limbed drivers could stretch out in comfort behind a wheel that was adjustable for height and reach. Nice touch. Conspicuous by its absence was the old long-arm, short-legged driving position once favoured by the Italians. The Latin Ape, RIP, was dead – and not before time.

What the Spider lacked, and badly so, was structural rigidity, the curse of many roofless cars. On rough roads it wobbled like a jelly. Over potholes it dithered and crashed. You could feel the steering column vibrate, the steering wheel shimmy. The GTV, said to be 64 per cent stiffer, was the better car dynamically, if not the more desirable on a balmy day.

Closed to the wind, the Spider's visually indifferent hood hardly enhanced the car's dramatic lines. Lowering it did. This meant releasing a couple of header-rail levers, clicking two electric switches and getting out to furl the headgear under a rigid tonneau. Press-button operation was to come later, with the Lusso option pack that also included leather seats.

Better by design

The 1998 Turin show marked the launch of improved GTV/Spiders. Visually they were distinguished by new alloy wheels and body-coloured side skirts/bumpers. Inside, the dash was revised and new materials introduced, along with standard-issue air-conditioning, its controls mounted on an extended centre console. By specifying a puncture sealant (complete with powered inflator) instead of a mini-spare, boot space could be increased by 40 per cent.

Using a new variable intake system, first seen in the 156, the power of the 2.0-litre Twin Spark four was increased by 5bhp to 155bhp. Low-speed torque, strong at under 2,000rpm, went up too. What's more, it peaked at lower revs – 2,800rpm instead of 4,000 – giving even better flexibility.

Just as Alfa UK rejected the scorchingly quick 2.0 turbo, sold elsewhere in Europe, so it turned its back on a new 1.8 Spider, which bridged the gap between Fiat's Barchetta and the 2.0 GTV/Spider. Without balancer shafts, the 1.8 lacked the smooth refinement of the quicker 2.0.

Big news on the 3.0 V6 was the option of a six-speed gearbox, promised for the UK by the following year, early '99. Minor changes, which did not affect output or performance, included new oil and water radiators. Suspension refinements were claimed to make the car even more stable and agile.

Minimalist with the most

See how it works. Suspension and wheels on display as minimalist Ariel Atom entertains driver. Naked chassis tubes design feature of funky car built for road and track fun.

And now for something quite different – a raw, affordable, no-frills, in-your-face sports car that owes no allegiance to the Caterham (née Lotus) Seven. And about time, too. I have nothing against Caterhams. Far from it. Love 'em. Even the lowliest are brilliantly uplifting and the seriously quick ones truly breathtaking. But Caterhams and their imitators had been around for a long time, monopolising a market niche that was crying out for a radical alternative. The Light Car Company's Rocket was radical all right, but it was also wildly impractical and horrendously expensive. It wasn't the answer. The Ariel Atom that arrived from Mars in the summer of 1999 seemed much closer to the mark.

The man behind the Atom (in astronomical terms, an explosive speck, which says it all) was design lecturer Simon Saunders, who had long nurtured visions of a minimalist, bare-chassis featherweight. He distances the clean-sheet Atom from the LSC (lightweight sports car) concept that he and Coventry University student Niki Smart created with industry assistance for the '96 British Motor Show. Smart went on the join Ford, but also worked on the Atom.

The growing popularity of track test days, where well-heeled enthusiasts could let off steam without breaking the law, underpinned demand for cheap-to-repair quasi-racers. The basis of the Atom was a powder-coated, bronze-welded spaceframe made by Huntingdon-based Arch Motors, suppliers of chassis to Caterham and other specialist manufacturers. Its curved side members defined a bullet in plan view, and a wedge in profile. The pointed snout looked like that of a single-seater racer, minus its winged nose-cone, and the rump like the business end of, well, a stripped-for-

Specification	Ariel Atom 1.8 (2000)
Engine	1796cc, 4-cylinder, 2ohc, 16V
Engine layout	Transverse, mid
Power	125bhp at 5000rpm
Torque	122lb ft at 3000rpm
Gearbox	Five-speed manual
Drive	Rear wheel
Front suspension	Double wishbones, coils, anti-roll bar
Rear suspension	Double wishbones, coils, anti-roll bar
Steering	Unassisted rack & pinion
Brakes	Ventilated front discs, solid rear discs
Wheels	Alloy 6.5Jx15
Tyres	195-50
Length	3410mm
Width	1800mm
Height	1105mm
Wheelbase	2345mm
Weight	500kg (1102lb)
0-60mph (97kph)	5.8sec
0-100mph (161kph)	16.0sec
Top speed	130mph (209kph)
Fuel consumption	28-36mpg

Atom designers rejected Triumph superbike power for more practical Rover K-series, like that of Lotus Elise. Naked rump leaves pursuers in no doubt about Ariel's business end.

action roadster. No attempt was made to hide the exhaust, never mind the chassis or all-wishbone suspension, centred on racing-style horizontal coil/Koni damper units operated through pushrods and bellcranks. Being able to see it all working was part of the car's fascination.

Originally, Triumph motorcycle power was envisaged for the Atom, complete with six-speed gearbox. Why not, for a projectile that could be seen as a four-wheeled superbike? Ariel, after all, once made four-cylinder motorcycles (remember the Ariel Square Four?), never mind GP cars. But there were cost and practical problems, not least those involving a reverse gear. Saunders chose instead a Rover K-series powertrain, mounted transversely ahead of the back wheels it drove. If the K-series would do for the MGF and Lotus Elise, it would do for the Ariel – especially as the 500kg Atom was much lighter than the featherweight Elise. With at least 120bhp on tap (up to 220bhp was possible with tuning, through 140, 165 and 190bhp stages), the power-to-weight ratio was a scintillating 250bhp per tonne at worst, rising to an awesome 380bhp per tonne. No claims were made for aerodynamic prowess: stability, yes, a low drag factor, no. So a top speed of around 125mph seemed a realistic estimate for the base car. Who would want to go faster without a windscreen?

With its broad track, minimal overhangs, slender build, low centre of gravity and light weight, the Atom was as finely focused on acceleration, braking and cornering as any performance roadster you could name. Generous rubber promised benchmark grip and traction, a high-geared rack (one-and-a-half turns of the quick-release Momo, lock to lock) super-responsive steering, heavyweight MGF discs tireless braking. Competition brakes that could be bias adjusted with a dash knob were an option. So was a close-ratio 'box, race dampers and various wheel and tyre combinations.

As for creature comforts, forget them: there was no bodywork (unless you counted a rear fairing, tight-fitting mudguards and a drain-holed undertray as bodywork). It followed that there were no doors, either. You clambered in over the chassis side-rails and settled into a moulded bucket seat paired as one with the passenger's. Being quite wide, the Atom was not so cramped in the cockpit as a Caterham Seven. Goggles? You needed them. Helmet? Why not? Warm togs, too. If it wasn't essential, the Atom didn't have it. Keeping down weight and costs were over-riding design priorities.

Launch prices started at £14,618 for a base 1.6 track car in component form. There was little to be gained financially through home assembly, but Saunders found, as had Caterham, that some well-heeled buyers welcomed DIY involvement, all the better to empathise with their car. With the optional road pack (which included emission control and quick-release headlights) the 1.6 cost £16,375, the 1.8 £16,992 – cheap compared with, say, Lotus's 340R costing twice as much. If Lotus could sell 340Rs, Ariel's modest target of 75 Atoms a year seemed if anything unduly conservative.

Aston Martin DB7

Ford to the rescue

Styled by Ian Callum (now Jaguar's design chief), Aston Martin DB7 looks great from every angle.

Aston Martin would probably be dead and buried but for Ford and the DB7 it financed. AM's expensive V-cars were virile beasts, like geriatrics on Viagra. Youthful they were not. What AM needed, and fast, was a junior stud, a successor to the much-loved DB series that had ended with the DB6 in 1971. No less desirable than the V8 behemoths it would supplement, the newcomer would have to be appreciably cheaper if it was to be a lot more accessible.

Victor Gauntlett, AM's enthusiastic leader in the Eighties, had had in mind just such a car – one that would sell in comparatively large numbers by Aston Martin's standards. To make it, though, AM needed the protective umbrella and financial clout of a mainstream manufacturer. Enter Ford.

Through Walter Hayes, persuaded out of retirement to run Aston Martin, Ford provided more than cash and expertise. It dished out flair and inspiration, too. Cutting corners to save time, Hayes sanctioned a car that was loosely based on Jaguar hardware. Why not? Cousin Jaguar was one of the family and its TWR-built, XJS-based image-car, dubbed XX, was surplus to requirements. The pragmatic Mr Hayes, one-time journalist and Ford big-wig, saw its potential as a new Aston Martin.

That the DB7 owed nothing to any previous Aston other than its name and style (designer Ian Callum's brief was to take his inspiration from the DB4/5/6) made the car's Jag-in-drag epithet difficult to refute. No-one

22

Specification	Aston Martin DB7 Volante V12 (2000)
Engine	5935cc, V12, dohc, 48V
Engine layout	Longitudinal, front
Power	420bhp at 6000rpm
Torque	400lb ft at 5000rpm
Gearbox	Six-speed manual
Drive	Rear wheel
Front suspension	Double wishbones, coils, anti-roll bar
Rear suspension	Double wishbones, coils, anti-roll bar
Steering	Assisted rack and pinion
Brakes	ABS-backed ventilated discs all round
Front wheels	Alloy 8Jx18
Rear wheels	Alloy 9Jx18
Front tyres	245-40ZR18
Rear tyres	265-35ZR18
Length	4665mm
Width	2035mm
Height	1240mm
Wheelbase	2590mm
Weight	1625kg (3582lb)
0-60mph (97kph)	5.3sec
0-100mph (161kph)	12.0sec
Top speed	165mph (266kph)
Fuel consumption	14-22mpg

seemed to mind. Had the DB7 been Ford-based, it might have struggled for credibility, but there was nothing wrong with its Jaguar ancestry and underpinnings. As if to emphasise the car's clean break from the old dinosaurs, and AM's traditional Newport Pagnell home where they were made, the DB7 was engineered by Jaguarsport and assembled at TWR's Bloxham factory in Oxfordshire, where Jaguar's ill-fated XJ220 supercar had been built.

Power came from a Jag-based 3.2-litre straight-six twin-cam, boosted (at 14psi) by a belt-driven Eaton supercharger to give roughly the same output – 335bhp and 368lb ft of torque – as Jaguar's naturally aspirated 6.0-litre XJR-6 V12. It was enough. Drive to the rear wheels (what else?) was through a five-speed manual Getrag gearbox. As for automatic transmission, that came later.

While some way short of the Vantage's pace, the £78,500 DB7 – built initially only as a fixed-head coupé – was a strong performer, and a vocally exciting one: I loved the spine-tingling high-rev screech of the supercharger, redolent of a pre-war Grand Prix Merc's. The most impressive quality of the DB7's chassis was to combine keen, user-affable handling with a supple deep-pile ride.

In my notes about a pre-production prototype I got to drive, I said that the DB7 'brought exotica down to a practical level – you could live with it as an only car.' I also noted that 'it looks good (but perhaps not £80,000-worth) and goes well (though Toyota's Supra goes harder for half the price).' Because of this, the car 'will depend heavily on quality, character,

Aston Martin

Output of DB7's Jaguar-based straight-six boosted by belt-driven supercharger to 335bhp. Original engine later marginalised by 400bhp V12 that most buyers specify.

handling, exclusivity and individuality to justify its high price.' I also observed that sound quality (notably wind noise) and on-the-limit handling were areas of concern. Both problems were addressed before the car went on sale in 1994.

Quick though it was, and a great drive too, the DB7 beguiled most with its beauty – a simple, unadorned, addenda-free beauty. The coupé looked so spot-on right that cutting the roof off to create a ragtop, which AM did in '96, seemed close to sacrilege. Aesthetically, the folded hood did jar a bit on the gorgeous Volante: it didn't disappear from sight, as a classy hood should (and did on many lesser convertibles), but sat up on the tail as an ungainly backpack, looking clumsy and in-the-way. Pity, because in every other respect the five-layer powered hood was excellent. It enclosed the cockpit with the snugness of a fixed-head coupé.

Being heavier and less slippery than the regular DB7, the Volante was a little slower. That much was predictable. That the topless model should feel almost as rigid and shake-free as its metal-top sibling came as a welcome surprise. In this respect, the Volante had the measure of its Mercedes-Benz SL rival.

Two years on from launch, the DB7 in both guises was all the better for running improvements that included superior seats and a reach-and-rake-adjustable steering wheel, reduced wind noise and an all-over improvement in quality. But there were bigger and better things yet to come.

In 1999 AM's junior bruiser became a fully fledged member of the supercar set with the launch of the mighty 185mph Vantage, powered by a 420bhp Cosworth-developed 6.0-litre V12 engine that had Ferrari looking

Classy dash of AM's DB7 auto. With optional ZF Touchtronic gear selection, conventional gear lever is supplemented by sequential-shift buttons on steering wheel.

over its shoulder. Not surprisingly, demand for the blown 'six', reduced to the role of 'bargain' back-up, dwindled dramatically. The following year, at the 2000 Detroit show – the first international motor show of the new millennium – AM announced the option of press-button Touchtronic transmission. Costing £4,000 extra in Britain, ZF's Touchtronic gave sequential shifting at the touch of wheel-mounted buttons – plus for upward changes, minus for going down. Alternatively, you could shift with the central selector, or leave the 'box to its own devices.

Pity folded hood forms ugly back-pack on rear deck of Aston Martin's Volante.

By the turn of the century the DB7 had become the most popular Aston Martin of all time, with a production run that exceeded 3,000. Even though the V12 Vantage Volante cost over £100,000 with Touchtronic, AM's order books were said to be full early in 2000.

Aston Martin V8s

Brute force versus mass

Aston's traditional V-cars of the Nineties – those made lovingly by hand at Newport Pagnell – were rooted in the William Towns-styled DBS heavyweight, launched in 1967 with a stopgap 4.0 six-cylinder engine. Tadek Marek's much-delayed 5.3-litre V8 was not made available to paying customers until 1970, when the DBS was simply renamed the AM V8.

Three decades and much development later, Marek's howitzers, boasting four valves per cylinder since 1988, were still going strong, yielding (with twin superchargers) more than double the power of the original 275bhp engine.

Although the Virage was unveiled in 1988 at the NEC show – John Heffernan's slippery design beat three other proposals – it didn't go on sale until 1990. Despite efforts to reduce weight (with an aluminium de Dion tube, for instance), the Virage was still grotesquely heavy – too heavy, with 'only' 330bhp to propel it, to turn in much better than a mediocre performance for a £125,000 supercar. In retrospect, the Virage was a lacklustre effort by AM's high standards.

Not until the renaissance in 1993 of the Vantage, powered by a twin-supercharged version of the old 5.4 V8, did AM overcome its V-car's poundage problem. And even then it was by adding oomph rather than reducing weight. The surreal figure to remember was 550 – the engine's output in bhp and lb ft.

Not since the limited-edition Zagato Vantage had Aston fielded anything quite so wild. Provided you tamed off-the-line wheelspin, the new rubber-burning Vantage would hurtle to 100mph in 10 seconds flat and wind itself up to...who knows what? AM reckoned to have lapped Michelin's test track in France at 191mph, which was theoretically possible by over-revving in

Last of the dinosaurs? Mighty Virage-based Vantage 600, monument to outrageous excess, fastest of all Aston Martin's road cars. Top speed nudges 200mph, acceleration awesome.

25

fifth. Sixth gear of the Dodge Viper 'box was strictly for cruising, not maxing.

Even wilder things were to come. The 600bhp Vantage 600 – the fastest road-going Aston ever produced, with a top speed of 200mph or thereabouts – and the 1999 £225,000 Vantage Le Mans it spawned (40 were to be made, to celebrate the 40th anniversary of AM's Le Mans win), were brutally machismo sports GTs nourished on pure testosterone. To call them awesome was to understate their potency – increased by 50bhp (and 50lb ft too) with additional charge cooling. The impression that the V600 was a gargantuan engine, an irresistible force, with a wood-and-leather conveyance attached to it was reinforced by the thunderous V8's gloriously addictive rumble.

The V600 was perhaps the most profligate behemoth of its time, a monument to outrageous excess. If there was a faster four-seater (of the two-plus-two school of accommodation) I could not name it. Despite its girth and weight (nearly twice that of a McLaren F1), this Herculean monster, all mass and muscle, could live with the supercar greats on straight-line speed, even match them on braking. Just imagine what it would have been like hauling half a ton less.

The brute-force V600, however, was the end of the line for AM's old warhorse. Its Vanquish replacement, expected to début at the 2000 Birmingham show, would espouse cutting-edge technology, not just raw muscle, in the quest for even greater performance.

Six months before the new flagship's launch, the motoring press was predicting an Elise-inspired, Lotus-engineered lightweight with an aluminium chassis and carbon-fibre bodywork, based on the fabulous Project Vantage show car penned by Ian Callum. Powered by a Cosworth-fettled V12 yielding over 500bhp, the Vanquish would elevate Aston Martin to the pinnacle of the supercar set. Theme variations were thought to include a 600bhp Vantage, and an open Volante.

Specification	Aston Martin Vantage 600
Engine	5340cc, V8, 4ohc, 32V
Engine layout	Longitudinal, front
Power	600bhp at 6200rpm
Torque	600lb ft at 4400rpm
Gearbox	Five-speed manual
Drive	Rear wheel
Front suspension	Double wishbones, coils, anti-roll bar
Rear suspension	De Dion axle, radius arms, coils, anti-roll bar
Steering	Assisted rack and pinion
Brakes	ABS-backed ventilated discs front and rear
Wheels	Alloy 8.5Jx18
Tyres	285-45ZR18
Length	4745mm
Width	1945mm
Height	1330mm
Wheelbase	2610mm
Weight	1976kg (4354lb)
0-60mph (97kph)	4.4sec
0-100mph (161kph)	9.5sec
Top speed	200mph (322kph)
Fuel consumption	9-16mpg

Profligate V8 engine rooted in Tadek Merak's 5.3 V8 of early Seventies. Twin Eaton superchargers boost output of mighty 32-valve quad-cam to around 600bhp.

Aston's **Z-car misfits**

Virage, Vantage, Volante. Savour the names.
Aston Martin's V cars – V by initial as well as
engine configuration – were its traditional fare.
But what of the controversial Z cars of the late
Eighties and early Nineties? Twixt old V8
(classically muscular) and new Virage
(mainstream sleek), the two Zagatos (plain ugly)
looked like square-peg misfits.

When the stupendously fast but ungainly
Zagato-styled Vantage broke cover to widespread
distaste in 1986, the question on everyone's lips
was this: what had happened to AM's vaunted
elegance of line? The Z-car's saving grace was
that its performance parameters – 0-60mph in
under 5 seconds and a top speed of 185mph –
were met by a 432bhp version of the familiar
5.4-litre V8.

From this 50-off, blunt-ended mutation,
based on the old AM V8, evolved the calmer,
gentler two-seater Zagato Volante – Aston-speak
for open bodywork. If the Patrick Collection's
two-seater ZV (number 12 in a run of 35) I drove
to Wales for *Car* magazine was memorable, it
was for all the wrong reasons, not least a string
of faults and failures – impracticalities, too – that

marred the journey.

Aston's flawed Italian job never looked to me
like a £175,000 car. Nor, with a three-speed
Chrysler auto hooked to its regular 310bhp V8,
did it really go like one. 'The great appeal of
the Zagato Volante,' I wrote, 'is that its design
and engineering is rooted in those muscle-
rippling leviathans of the Sixties...the engine
revs freely and smoothly, its throbby burble
hardening to a rumbustious wail as the revs
rise. And rise they must if the car is to kick grit
at a decent GTi.'

Both Zagatos were disappointing aesthetically
when judged against the car that inspired them –
the fabulous DB4 GT Zagato of the Sixties, the
greatest Anglo-Italian hybrid of them all. Truth is,
the Z-cars' home-grown bits, notably its lusty
engine and well-sorted chassis, deserved better
attire than that provided by Aston's Italian
partners.

With the launch of the more elegant Virage in
1988 came an improved 32-valve version of the
old V8. Two years on, a Volante derivative made
its motor show début, initially as a two-seater,
later as a two-plus-two.

Aston's Zagato Volante
spawned by faster fixed-head
Vantage. Flawed flagship was
not prettiest of Astons,
three-speed auto's
performance indifferent
despite 310bhp V8.

Audi

Audi TT

Trouble for the **wild one**

TT has great presence, however you view it. Styling is strikingly similar to '95 show concept, considered too wild for production.

Dream cars do come true. Audi proved it with the TT, first seen as a wild concept showcase at the 1995 Frankfurt show. Would Audi dare put into production anything quite so bold and mould-breaking without toning down – as Porsche had toned down the Boxster 'twixt show and showroom? It would, and did, largely due to positive public reaction, not all of it complimentary. Audi's marketing people knew that the way-out looks of the TT would polarise opinions, that some people would hate it. They didn't mind so long as others – particularly those with open chequebooks – thought otherwise.

In the event, the original concept changed very little in appearance. What was seen at Frankfurt was pretty well what paying customers got three years later. The most notable visual alteration was the insertion of tiny wedge-shaped rear side windows, which, apart from conforming with Audi's house style, improved visibility. Visually the extra window had the effect of stretching what was a rather dumpy organic lump.

Audi's top brass saw the TT as a 'classic visionary design', as a serious, red-blooded sports car rather than a grand tourer with sporting pretensions. Its prime target was the Porsche Boxster, though BMW's Z3 convertible and Merc's SLK were in the frame too. Ditto Alfa's Spider and the Honda S2000.

The basis of the TT was the chassis platform, shortened by 80mm in the

28

Specification	Audi TT quattro (2000)
Engine	1781cc, 4-cylinder, 2ohc, 20V
Engine layout	Transverse, front
Power	225bhp at 5900rpm
Torque	206lb ft at 2500-5900rpm
Gearbox	Six-speed manual
Drive	All wheel
Front suspension	MacPherson struts, lower wishbones, coils, anti-roll bar
Rear suspension	Double wishbones, coils, anti-roll bar
Steering	Assisted rack and pinion
Brakes	Ventilated discs, front and rear
Wheels	7.5Jx17 alloys
Tyres	225-45ZR17
Length	4040mm
Width	1855mm
Height	1345mm
Wheelbase	2430mm
Weight	400kg (3086lb)
0-60mph (97kph)	6.0sec
0-100mph (161kph)	16.0sec
Top speed	145mph (233kph)
Fuel consumption	21-30mpg

wheelbase, of the Golf and Audi A3 hatchbacks. Nothing wrong with either, of course – for family hacks. But for a serious sports car? Any misgivings were soon dispelled. Only 20 per cent of the TT would in the end be attributable to its more humble siblings.

Audi's claim that chassis reinforcements – taller and broader sills, floorpan cross-beams, stronger rear firewall and a fascia carrier frame – made the Roadster torsionally as rigid as a saloon was borne out by the impressive absence of scuttle shake. No dither and thunk here. Very little in the way of tyre noise, either, especially with the top down. The plus-two accommodation of the Coupé was sacrificed in the Roadster (as was some boot room) to the stowage needs of the hood. Performance was penalised, too, by a weight handicap of over 150lb: complex headgear and chassis strengthening took their toll.

One look at the spec of the flagship howitzer was sufficient to justify Audi's heady ambitions. Beneath the TT's audacious skin, originally penned in Audi's Californian studio by Freeman Thomas (also responsible for VW's new Beetle), was some serious, if eclectic, machinery, based on a 1.8-litre 20-valve twin-cam turbo yielding 225bhp and 206lb ft of torque. New inlet manifolds, a high compression ratio, a KKK blower, Motronic engine management and twin-charge intercoolers helped explain the high specific output of 125bhp per litre. Even the five-speed, 180bhp entry-level front-drive car, capable of 140mph, had 30bhp more than VW's Golf GTi. With the more powerful engine came a six-speed gearbox and quattro four-wheel-drive transmission – a new Swedish Haldex-designed, electronically controlled system, as used in the Golf 4Motion. Its multi-plate clutch could apportion full power to either end, or anything in between.

Although the firmed-up MacPherson strut front suspension owed much to the Golf's, many parts were custom-made for the TT. The quattro got its own special double wishbone arrangement at the back, in place of the usual

Audi

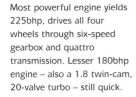

Most powerful engine yields 225bhp, drives all four wheels through six-speed gearbox and quattro transmission. Lesser 180bhp engine – also a 1.8 twin-cam, 20-valve turbo – still quick.

Inside story

The Audi TT was as stylish within as it was bold without. Apart from looking good, the use of brushed aluminium embellishment was symbolic of the lightweight materials used extensively in the car's construction. More to the point, it was cool – super-cool. Anything round – dials, vent outlets, switches, steering wheel boss, gearlever knob and gate surround, for instance – was rimmed with aluminium, the audio cover and console supports made of it.

All this bare, bright metal helped make the cabin a bit special, precious even, certainly a cut above the opposition's, especially with optional 'baseball-glove' stitching. The TT also oozed quality, by now an Audi trademark that even the Japanese admired. It had about it the air of a precision tool without being coldly clinical. The fit and finish was impeccable, the plastic bits unplasticky, the tactile switchgear a pleasure to use. First-class detailing came in for praise, too. The carpets were extra deep, the footwells red-glow illuminated, like the classy part-analogue, part-digital instruments.

The hood – beautifully made, mohair-lined and glass-windowed – sealed out draughts, not to mention wind whoosh, almost as well as the Coupé's fixed head. While not totally automatic in operation – release from (and clamping to) the header rail was done manually – the hood could be furled and erected at the push of a button without getting out. It did not disappear from sight, though, unless you covered it up with a flexible tonneau. In the UK, standard equipment included an electrically powered glass draught deflector that popped up behind your neck at the push of a button. With the (powered) side windows up, there was very little slipstream buffet.

Interior design as bold and adventurous as body styling. Brushed aluminium embellishment symbolises car's lightweight construction. Red-glow instruments classy.

torsion beam. Generous tyres (225/45) and mighty brakes were standard on the quattro. So was cruise control and an anti-lock system that doubled as traction control.

Even when Porsche upgraded its 2.5, 204bhp Boxster to a 2.7 with 220bhp, finally addressing criticisms of indifferent performance, the four-wheel-drive TT was still super-competitive on acceleration (0-100mph in about 15 seconds) if not top speed: an indifferent drag factor of 0.35 (poor for Audi, who invented modern streamlining) restricted the maximum to around 145mph – 10mph shy of the Boxster 2.7's best. Traction off the line was terrific (when was it otherwise with a quattro?) and the absence of lag a noteworthy feature of a strong, torquey engine that disappointed only in aural uplift. Oh for the double-edged yowl of the old five-cylinder quattro coupé!

The TT's handling was a revelation in that it involved and rewarded the press-on driver. With few exceptions, fast Audis had previously impressed rather than beguiled. That the TT did both in spades underscored its ability to entertain. Steering was sharp if not meaty, body control firm, responses keen, grip as tenacious as it got on 225/45 Michelin rubber. There was, however, a potential snag – a nasty sting in the tail – especially for German owners. Following a spate of autobahn accidents involving TT quattros, Audi was compelled to address a high-speed oversteer problem that would probably never have come to light on Britain's restricted motorways.

Audi

In November 1999 Audi issued a press release that acknowledged the problem: 'A number of owners have called into question the handling characteristics...in certain situations at speeds substantially in excess of legal limits in Britain.' The release outlined 'changes which affect both the car's suspension and aerodynamic performance'. These originally consisted of modified anti-roll bars at both ends, revised front wishbones, firmer dampers and a rear spoiler to hold the tail down. ESP traction/stability control was later added to the work list, too. The mods, found on new cars from December '99, would be available as retro fits on old ones from the spring of 2000. The snag for British owners, some 2,400 of them, was that the work was to be undertaken in Germany (at huge cost to Audi), and would take a month. Passive safety features, by the way, included side and front airbags, tubular hoops behind the seats and a reinforced windscreen surround.

For the Goodwood-based UK press launch I attended in November 1999, Audi fielded a fleet of unmodified cars, confident that they would behave impeccably – even when rushed up Goodwood's fast hillclimb against the clock. They did. After 120 miles in a 225bhp car (distinguishable from the lesser one by its twin exhaust pipes) I had no anxieties about the handling. However, I was not the only driver to question whether the flagship quickie, £29,150 at the time, was worth £3,000 more than the 180bhp quattro, which felt almost as fast.

Hood of Roadster furls neatly under push-button power, hoops provide roll-over protection. To improve stability, later cars had rear spoiler.

BMW Z1

Show car to road star

Z1, evolved from one-off showpiece, testbed for multi-link rear suspension. Gave long-nosed, short-rumped sportster terrific handling and grip. Finish below BMW's normal standards.

The Z1 was not the outcome of some well-researched marketing brief. Far from it. Indulgent original thinking by a group of enthusiast engineers at BMW's new Tecnik think-tank spawned a car that promised more than it perhaps delivered. Conceived as a one-off showpiece to display advanced materials and design while remaining true to its 328 and 507 roots, the Z1 was cast in the mould of a modern classic, albeit one that was more retro in character than content.

Press and public reaction, no doubt buoyed in the late Eighties by soaring values for anything exotic, old or new, encouraged BMW to put its concept show car into small-scale production in a very short timescale. The price in Germany was DM85,000, or about £28,000 in Britain, ignoring the crazy premiums paid in both countries by greedy speculators before the bubble burst and sanity prevailed.

In hindsight the Z1 was perhaps not quite so radical and prophetic as BMW made out. It was, in essence, a refined, front-engined, two-seater roadster based on the 325i's mechanicals – 170bhp engine, five-speed gearbox and MacPherson strut front suspension included. At the back was the clever bit, the pièce de résistance – a double-wishbone layout destined for the new 3-series. Dubbed Z-axle, this new multi-link arrangement largely eliminated the tricky camber changes suffered by the outmoded semi-trailing set-up of mainstream BMWs. It also introduced stabilising toe-

Specification	BMW Z1 (1990)
Engine	2494cc, 6-cylinder in line, ohc, 12V
Engine layout	Longitudinal, front
Power	170bhp at 5800rpm
Torque	164lb ft at 4300rpm
Gearbox	Five-speed manual
Drive	Rear wheel
Front suspension	MacPherson struts, coils, anti-roll bar
Rear suspension	Z-axle, double wishbones, coils
Steering	Assisted rack and pinion
Brakes	Ventilated front discs, solid rear discs
Wheels	Alloy 7.5Jx16
Tyres	225-45ZR16
Length	3925mm
Width	1700mm
Height	1245mm
Wheelbase	1440mm
Weight	1335kg (2947lb)
0-60mph (97kph)	8.0sec
0-100mph (161kph)	23.5sec
Top speed	135mph (217kph)
Fuel consumption	22-30mpg

Electrically-powered drop-down doors give new meaning to *al fresco* motoring. Even when lowered, getting in and out awkward. Winged seats strong on lateral support.

Low-volume Z1 powered by stock 2.5 straight-six which makes lovely noise but only 170bhp.

in when it was needed. As a harbinger of the future, the rear suspension was perhaps the Z1's most significant feature, the bit that worked best. Take a bow Ing Rudolf Muller who developed it.

Ground-breaking novelty extended to the chassis – a galvanised steel monocoque strengthened by zinc-infilling between the welds (why not?) and a composite-fibre sandwich underfloor. Scuttle dither? Forget it. Some body panels excepted, the Z1 was immune to the shakes that marred BMW's 3-series convertibles and the subsequent Z3. Trouble is, it was also heavy.

The Z1's rakish bodywork, long in nose, stubby in tail, was assembled from non-load-bearing panels, some of them injection-cast thermoplastics, others less-than-ideally rigid. All these bolt-ons, 15 in all, could be easily removed, facilitating repairs, even a reskin. In the event, none was forthcoming. The finish of the Variflex paint was rather better than some un-BMW-like wide panel gaps.

The trouble with the Z1 was that its fine chassis cried out for a lot more power than BMW's stock 2.5 straight-six could deliver. Despite fantastic off-the-line traction – the Z-axle was in every way a brilliant success – the Z1 was, at almost 1,360kg (3,000lb), perplexingly hefty, and no quicker from rest to 100mph than the like-powered (and lighter) 325i convertible, which cost £7,000 less. Despite the presence of a full-length underfloor, BMW's new two-seater didn't cheat the wind especially well. Its top speed of 136mph was well short of the M3's, never mind that of Porsche's contemporary 911 Speedster. However, canny shaping of the bonnet and transverse exhaust muffler provided high-speed stability without recourse to visible aerodynamic aids.

The best thing about this exclusive BMW was its handling and grip. Here was a car that cornered with the best of them, regardless of mechanical layout. The Z1 proved on the road – as the Panoz sports-racer did on the track a decade later – that a modern front-engined car could corner as well as a mid-engined one. You'd lay bets on the Z1 being nose-heavy. It wasn't, witness the 48/52 weight distribution, largely achieved by mounting the powertrain as far back as possible. Combine this fine balance with a wide track, a low centre of gravity, firm suspension that maximised grip, and generous 225/45 rubber, and the Z1's ability to change direction like a guided missile was easily explained.

So tenaciously did the back end cling on that it was virtually impossible to induce power-oversteer, either indulgently or accidentally. Traction control? There simply wasn't enough power to justify it on dry roads. Even on wet ones, the Z1 was reluctant to relinquish grip or upset the equilibrium that made it so user-friendly stable. Don't assume that front-end grip was sacrificed for rear-end tenacity. It wasn't. The Z1 turned into corners with iron-fisted resolution. Nor was the ride – composed, supple, forgiving – unacceptably compromised.

My only quibble, other than the disappointing performance, concerned sluggish steering that lacked involving feedback. Three turns from lock-to-lock, even allowing for a tight turning circle, underlined the need for a 'quicker' rack. Stronger self-centring would not have gone amiss, either. As you'd expect, the ABS-backed all-disc brakes were well up to the job of arresting what just about qualified as a junior supercar – and a very civilised one at that. There was nothing raucous about the Z1, more's the pity. For a sports car the exhaust was a tad too anaemic, its demure handling too uninvolving. Flawed though it was, Porsche's Speedster was a more exciting car for the serious press-on driver.

Getting in and out of a Z1 was an awkward manoeuvre, particularly with the hood up. Once inside, though, the cockpit – nicely finished and detailed – was snug (too snug for the long-limbed) and comfortable, if not particularly special. Winged seats provided the sort of side support needed in a car that could generate high lateral g, and the dash layout, centred on four, round, reflection-gathering dials, was neat but conservative. Boot accommodation was meagre, restricted by the demands on space of the furled hood, stowed under a rigid flap. Although not powered, the headgear was praised by reviewers for being neat, whoosh-free, weatherproof and easy to manipulate without a struggle. While the Z1 boasted massive side-impact protection from tall sills, the only roll-over bar was that surrounding the screen.

The Z1's zaniest novelty? Bizarre drop-down doors – now you see them, now you don't – operated by electric motors and toothed belts. To get in, you pressed a chrome-ringed, flank-mounted button (also the key lock). First the glass sank into the door, then – in a seamless movement – the door vanished between the outer plastic sill and inner steel structure. Getting in was tricky, getting out no easier – especially for tight-skirted ladies.

Motoring with the doors 'open', so your torso was exposed (a slightly unnerving if invigorating experience), gave new meaning to the term 'driving al fresco'. As the Z1's vertically sliding doors have never been flattered by imitation, they must go down as a gimmicky – and rather impractical – failure.

Innovative monocoque chassis could have handled more power. Fine front-end grip, virtually impossible to induce power oversteer.

Zee-Three tops the pops

The Z3 was always going to be a smash hit, no matter what. How could a stylish new two-seater roadster from BMW with a half-affordable price tag fail to sell like a Big Mac in a famine? Especially in the middle of a ragtop boom. If there was a problem with the Z3 in Europe, particularly in Britain, it had much to do with its American connections. The USA was, for a start, the Z3's main market, its spiritual home, so the car was designed and set up to appeal first and foremost to American tastes. It was even made in the USA (still is), at Spartanburg in South Carolina, which may have had something to do with early quality problems. The Zee-Three, as it was known across the Atlantic, may have been made by BMW, but it wasn't made in Munich.

Between the Z3's 1995 launch in North America and its delayed arrival in British showrooms early in '97, the Alfa Spider, MGF, Mercedes-Benz SLK and Porsche Boxster – never mind Mazda's evergreen MX-5 – had not only made their mark, but had lifted expectations by raising benchmarks. So despite all the good things going for it – the badge, the glamour, the blue-chip image, the sub-£20,000 price (factors that filled BMW's UK orderbooks well in advance of sales) – the Z3 1.9 entered the arena looking a mite under-endowed in the dynamic department. Was it up to the job? Was it really a sports car at all, or simply a family hack in two-seater drag?

Conceptually the Z3 was a simple evolutionary car that owed nothing other than its associated name to the low-volume drop-door Z1 of the late Eighties. BMW sold 8,000 Z1s, which was small fry compared with the Z3's proposed output of 30,000 cars a year (later exceeded). BMW's marketing people were confidently bullish about the newcomer's prospects: it would

US-made Z3 designed to appeal to American tastes. Based on inexpensive Compact platform, car voluptuous mixture of retro and modern.

Uprange Z3s powered by straight-six engines with variable valvegear. In '99, 150bhp 2.0 'six' replaced previous 140bhp 'four'.

Specification	BMW Z3 2.0 (2000)
Engine	1991cc, 6-cylinder in line, 2ohc, 24V
Engine layout	Longitudinal, front
Power	150bhp at 5900rpm
Torque	140lb ft at 3500rpm
Gearbox	Five-speed manual or four-speed auto
Drive	Rear wheel
Front suspension	Struts, coils, anti-roll bar
Rear suspension	Semi-trailing arms, coils, anti-roll bar
Steering	Assisted rack and pinion
Brakes	ABS-backed ventilated discs front and rear
Wheels	7Jx16 alloys
Tyres	225-50R16
Length	4050mm
Width	1740mm
Height	1293mm
Wheelbase	2446mm
Weight	1345kg (2965lb)
0-60mph (97kph)	8.3sec
0-100mph (161kph)	25.0sec
Top speed	130mph (210kph)
Fuel consumption	25-32mpg

displace Mazda's MX-5 as the world's most popular roadster, they forecast. And they were right. With a little publicity boost as James Bond's wheels in *Goldeneye*, it did – though not in Britain. The Z3 was outsold in the UK by the market-leading MGF as well as the MX-5.

The Z3's basis was not a purpose-built monocoque, like the expensive Z1's, but BMW's humble Compact hatchback – the cheapest of its mainstream models. It follows that the Z3 was denied the fancy (and very effective) multi-link Z-axle rear suspension fitted to all other 3-series models. Instead it had the old-fashioned semi-trailing arrangement that once made pretty well all BMWs so tail-happy in the wet. Up front were tried and trusted MacPherson struts, not the pure-bred double-wishbone set-up boasted by some rivals. Still, BMW made good use of them, rear-end adhesion being especially good – too good for extroverts keen to indulge their opposite-lock skills.

Then there was styling – a heady mixture of contemporary (flushed-in headlights, strong visage) and retro (shark-like 507 side grilles, purely cosmetic) – that may have projected a slightly portly mien, but did its stuff as irresistible showroom bait. Bulging wheelarches, necessary to accommodate generous rubber, nicely muscled up the haunches. Few people could say of the Z3 that it looked absolutely right, even if they could not explain exactly why. It still reminds me of a dumbbell – bulbous at the extremities and pinched-in at the middle. Whatever, the two-seater Z3, small though it was for a BMW, was marginally roomier than rivals like the MX-5 and MGF in cabin space, if not in boot. The irony of MG going mid-engined modern, just when BMW was creating a cheap parts-bin special worthy of a traditional MG, was not lost on industry watchers.

Beneath the skin, voluptuously bulgy in the bonnet department, the Z3 was pure Compact, with wide-sill reinforcements, among other things, to provide the sort of structural rigidity normally associated with a fixed-head coupé. Even then, the Z3 tremored slightly on the rough stuff, just as the

3-series convertible did to an even greater degree. Pity. Perhaps BMW should have turned for advice to its Rover subsidiary, who made the MGF feel a whole lot stiffer. Mind you, the F did have a purpose-built monocoque, not a make-do one.

The front-to-rear drivetrain of the Z3 1.9i, powered by BMW's stock twin-cam 16-valver (the lesser eight-valve 1.8 did not make it to the UK until 1999, when the 1.9 four became a 2.0 six) was basically lifted from the Compact 318i. Nothing wrong there, except that 140bhp in a car weighing over 1,150kg (2,535lb) was hardly a recipe for a tyre-smoking zap. Although the 125mph 1.9 broke 9 seconds to 60mph, its performance did not compare too well with the best of the opposition's. Cousin Rover's cheaper MGF VVC was decisively livelier. The BMW's easy delivery, raspy exhaust, close-ratio gearbox and class-leading shift helped camouflage its dynamically challenged test figures.

It wasn't so much indifferent performance, however, as soft, laid-back handling that betrayed the Z3's raison d'être, never mind its simple, rationalised chassis. Safe and tenacious though it was on the corners, the car lacked elan. It wasn't nearly so engaging as, say, a Lotus Elise, even an MGF. As a red-blooded sportster the Z3 1.9 failed to make the grade. But what did it matter? According to market research, most Z3 buyers were

More **Six appeal**

BMW had sold over 170,000 Z3s world-wide before introducing a raft of improvements in 1999. Out went the old 140bhp four-cylinder 1.9, to be replaced by a 150bhp 2.0 six from the 520i. In Britain this move prompted the introduction of a sub-£20,000 entry-level 1.8 that undercut the previous base 1.9 by over £1,500. With only 118bhp on tap, the 1.8 was no fireball. However, counter-rotating balancer shafts made it particularly smooth and refined.

It was the new 2.0 that gave me my first taste of Z3 motoring (better late than not at all). And a pleasant surprise it was, too. I found in the mellifluous 'six' of the second series a car of considerable charm and ability that exceeded expectations. The lusty engine, so smooth and discreetly snarly, was a gem, the cornering powers high, the structure stiffer than I'd been led to believe. If not an out-and-out sports car, the Z3 2.0 was seriously desirable kit that aroused such envy I felt guilty driving the thing. My only gripes concerned the effort (too much for frail arms) needed to clamp the hood, and a mushy shift-marring clutch that may not have been typical.

Double VANOS variable valve timing lifted mid-range punch of the existing 2.8 as well as the new 2.0. All three engines were available with state-of-the-art electronic traction and stability control. Addressing criticisms of the Z3's styling, BMW crispened the tail and reshaped the back lights. It also chrome-ringed the front ones. Inside, various cosmetic and ergonomic improvements – new instruments, switches, clock, materials and colours – lifted the ambience of the roomy cockpit.

Open roadster later
supplemented by oddball
coupé with breadvan lines.

unconcerned about dynamic qualities. All they wanted was a stylish convertible, a user-friendly ego-booster with a name commensurate with the image. In this role, the Z3 was a runaway success.

Comfort was certainly a strong suit, witness the Z3's snug cockpit. You sat low behind a big (too big) fixed-position steering wheel, and a dash that was typically BMW in layout and clarity. The generous seats (no racing-style buckets here) supported well and the driving position was spot on. Criticism, such as it was, centred not on the car's ergonomics but on its ambience. The interior was too mainstream, too Compact-ish for a style-first car of such presence and individuality.

The American Sunroof Corporation was responsible for the design and manufacture of a hood that did the Z3's lines no favours but provided coupé-like civility in inclement weather. Truth is, the Z3 looked far better top-down. It felt better, too, despite (perhaps because of) wind buffeting. In the early days there was no alternative to manipulating the hood manually – an up-and-over process that could be accomplished without getting out. When BMW later offered expensive push-button operation, you still had to throw two stiff (very stiff) levers before electrickery took over. Also to appear on the options list were a snug-fitting hardtop and automatic transmission. More power from bigger engines, too, of course.

Few roadsters have been more eagerly awaited than the Z3 2.8, which made it into UK showrooms in July 1997. The 1.9 was no match for Porsche's 2.4 Boxster, but the 192bhp 2.8, powered by BMW's gorgeous straight-six, 24-valve twin-cam, certainly was – until, that is, Porsche turned the Boxster's 12bhp advantage into a 32bhp one with its new 2.7.

Serious six-cylinder grunt transformed the Z3. While a poor 0.42 drag factor restricted top speed to around 135mph, acceleration was worthy of a junior supercar. Pick-up was at its impressive best mid-range, thanks to strong torque and short gear ratios. Here was a classic rear-drive roadster – an Austin-Healey 3000 in modern drag – that could be steered on the throttle, even kicked into oversteer provided the traction control was switched off. Even so, the 2.8 lacked the poise, precision and, ultimately, grip of the Boxster. The rock-solid integrity, too. Still, with a price advantage of £6,000, the Z3 2.8 could be excused some flaws.

For the majority of Z3 owners, the wacky 321bhp M-roadster that followed was little less than unhinged mayhem, its price of over £40,000 – nearly twice that of the humble 1.9 – plain crazy. Well-heeled speed freaks saw things differently. Here, in the formidable M-roadster, was the fastest accelerating production car BMW had made. For all that, the M failed to arouse unbridled passion.

Original Z3 cockpit smart and well-finished, but not as special in design and decor as later upgrade, shown here. Hoops provide roll-over protection, seats decent side and high support.

BMW Z8

Naughty but nice

BMW waited until the 99th year to reveal its contender for Sports Car of the Century. If the gorgeously hunky Z8 had a passing resemblance to the lesser Z3, nothing was to be read into it. They were light years (and tens of thousands of pounds) apart.

Retro though it was in looks, the Z8 was a seriously quick and trendy roadster pitched not at mass-ranked Z3 rivals like the MGF and Honda S2000, but at much pricier paragons of power, Ferrari's 360 Modena Spider and Porsche's 911 Cabrio among them. Restricted hand-built assembly (of around ten cars a day) and a high price tag (£84,000 in Britain) guaranteed exclusivity.

Based on BMW's Z07 concept car, unveiled at the 1997 Tokyo show, the horny Z8 was an engaging blend of old and new, of trad and trendy. It was clearly the creation of arch enthusiasts, among them Anglophile Bernd Pischetsreider, BMW's former boss with a well-known penchant for classic cars, and his one-time sidekick Wolfgang Reitzle, snatched up by Ford to head its prestige wing, Jaguar and Aston Martin included, following a boardroom coup at BMW.

The Z8's stretched bonnet, far-back cockpit and raunchy wheelarches called to mind golden oldies of the past – Big Healeys, Jaguar E-types, AC Cobras and, more to the point, BMW's own Albrecht Goertz-designed 507 sportster of the Fifties. Hendrik Fiska, Danish chief of BMW's Californian

Specification	BMW Z8 (2000)
Engine	4941cc, V8, 4ohc, 32V
Engine layout	Longitudinal, front
Power	394bhp at 6600rpm
Torque	369lb ft at 3800rpm
Gearbox	Six-speed manual
Drive	Rear wheel
Front suspension	MacPherson struts, coils, anti-roll bar
Rear suspension	Rear suspension Multi-link, coils, anti-roll bar
Steering	Assisted rack and pinion
Brakes	ABS-backed ventilated discs front and rear
Front wheels	Alloy 8Jx18
Rear wheels	9Jx18
Front tyres	245-45ZR18
Rear tyres	275-40ZR18
Length	4400mm
Width	1830mm
Height	1315mm
Wheelbase	2505mm
Weight	1585kg (3494lb)
0-60mph (97kph)	4.5sec
0-100mph (161kph)	11.0sec
Top speed	155mph (250kph)
Fuel consumption	17-24mpg

design studio who headed the team that shaped both Z07 and Z8 – James Bond's wheels in *The World is Not Enough* – acknowledges the 507's inspirational role as a reference design. Only the concept's racy head-fairing failed to make it into production.

In creating the Z8, BMW's design boss Chris Bangle conceded that homage was paid to the low-slung 507 – a gorgeous eyeful of soft curves and sexy bulges. Styling cues echoed by the Z8 included an elongated kidney grille, bright-metal extractor ducts behind the front wheels, humped rear arches and a swage line running through the doors.

If the 507 disappointed it was in promising more performance than it actually delivered – unlike the Z8, which was much faster than its throwback appearance would have you believe. There's another historical irony. The short-lived, low-volume 507 (BMW built just 253 between 1956 and 1959) was a luxury that BMW could ill afford in the late Fifties. With prestige V8s at one end of its range and bubblecar runabouts at the other, BMW stared into the abyss while it addressed the crucial vacuum in between. Forty years on, void well and truly filled, BMW relished the indulgence of a high-performance roadster to ice the cake, not prop it up.

Both cars were powered by V8 engines, but that's it so far as similarity goes. The 507's mild ohv pushrod unit yielded just 140bhp from 3.2 litres. The Z8 had a 394bhp 32-valve 5.0-litre, complete with variable valve control, 32-bit engine management and a drive-by-wire throttle, lifted straight from the M5 saloon. Shoehorning a powerhouse V8 into the nose of a rear-drive, stub-tailed, two-seater lightweight has always been a naughty recipe for rubber-burning performance. And burn it you did. With the traction control disengaged, wheelspin was as easily provoked as opposite-lock slides – and quite right, too.

Driving through a de rigueur six-speed Getrag-sourced manual gearbox, the engine was mounted well back in the chassis to give perfect 50/50 weight distribution of roughly 700kg per axle. And what a chassis. The Z8's monocoque skeleton was fabricated from aluminium extrusions and skinned in stressed aluminium so that the whole body/chassis unit was one-piece, shake-free solid. Aluminium also figured prominently in the suspension – struts up front, a multi-link set-up behind – in a concerted bid to save weight without compromising strength. Inside, the use of decorative aluminium symbolised the car's lightweight construction.

Cockpit retro features of Z07 concept carried over to Z8 include wire-spoke steering wheel, unidentified toggle switches and central instruments that leave sight-line uncluttered.

Rack and pinion steering (left-handed only) replaced BMW's usual recirculating ball arrangement. Then there was Dynamic Stability Control (DSC) and Cornering Brake Control (CBC), ultra-modern electronic aids that protected against indiscreet use of a heavy right foot. Wheels that won't skid or spin (unless you wanted them to) made the Z8 safe in unskilled hands. And it needed to be ultra-forgiving with a claimed 0-60mph time of under 4.5 seconds. Few cars were capable of bettering the Z8's off-the-line getaway, or its raucous, Cobra-like exhaust burble, more Nascar roar than BMW purr. Top speed was electronically restricted to 155mph – though with a drag factor of 0.39 the car's true max was probably no more than 170mph. Fast enough, even on a deserted autobahn, for the fastest-ever production BMW. Not even the mighty, mid-engined M1, bred for track racing, could live with the Z8.

BMW's designers carried the Z8's retro theme through to the colourful cockpit, practically equipped with odds-and-ends stowage to complement a generous boot. Oddball features included unidentified switchgear (another character-building throwback to the past), central instruments (which left the driver with an uninterrupted view of the road ahead), and bright wire spokes for the airbagged steering wheel. There was no skimping on the powered hood, which furled out of sight under a lidded well. No unsightly backpack here, Aston Martin please note. A detachable hardtop was standard equipment, a spare wheel wasn't: the use of run-flat tyres opened up the boot to golf-bag size. Right-hand drive was not in the script, more's the pity.

Design cues for Z8 taken from several sources, including BMW's low-slung 507 of Fifties. Throw-back appearance deceptive. Performance from high-tech 394bhp V8 tremendous.

BMW

Bugatti EB110

The civilised supercar

Bugatti EB110 astonishing
technical *tour de force*.
Styling controversial, cabin
cramped but carbon-fibre
chassis, 3.5-litre, 60-valve
quad turbo V12 and 4x4
transmission impressive.

The trouble with the Bugatti EB110
was that it was too much, too late.
It needed the boom economy of
the late Eighties to succeed, but
was born into a later depressed one
marked by a slump in demand for
outrageous exotica.

Launched in 1991 at a party
that's gone down in industry
folklore for its no-expense-spared
extravagance (recession, what
recession?), the EB110 was an
astonishing technical *tour de force*
created by a top design team
recruited by Romano Artioli, the Italian businessman behind Bugatti's
ambitious revivalist plans. Alas, it didn't last. With sales languishing and
debts accumulating, Bugatti's purpose-built plant on the outskirts of
Modena, Italy, was closed in September 1995 and the assets of the
company auctioned off. It was a sad end to an exciting project. The EB110
deserved a better fate.

Unlike its raw-boned, performance-is-everything Ferrari F40 and Jaguar

XJ220 contemporaries, the Bugatti EB110 (the EB in memory of the great Ettore Bugatti) was designed to convey two people very swiftly in great safety and comfort. User-friendliness, which the F40 and XJ220 patently lacked, was germane to the plot.

Whereas the lightweight Ferrari was bereft of equipment and high-tech systems that might detract from driver involvement, the EB110, based on a carbon-fibre monocoque made by Aerospatiale, bristled with both. Weight suffered, of course, but the engine – a truly fabulous 3.5-litre, 60-valve, quad-turbo V12 – would compensate for that. And it did. Driving all four wheels through a six-speed gearbox and a Torsen diff that split the drive 27/73, the Bug deployed its awesome 550bhp with remarkable aplomb. Performance of the EB110, said by its makers to be capable of 212mph, was terrific by normal supercar standards: Ferrari's 175mph 512TR, for example, was well beaten. McLaren's F1, however, was in another league. So was the uncouth Jaguar.

Smaller than a Ferrari 348 – and therefore nothing like so intimidatingly big as the Jaguar XJ220 – the sophisticated EB110 was of sufficiently manageable proportions to spear down country roads and thread through city traffic without inhibition. With its light and easy controls, it was not physically demanding to drive either.

The Bugatti's handy size did, however, impose upon it one major drawback: its cockpit was cramped to the point of being claustrophobic. Luggage space was on the mean side, too. Of creature comforts, though, there was no shortage: air-conditioning, great seats, timber-embellished leather trim and decent audio came as standard. So did supple, smooth-riding suspension and noise levels on the right side of intrusive. Once heard, the menacing top-end whoosh of the V12 engine was not quickly forgotten. Nor was turbo thrust when the blowers cut in with a ferocity that despatched the 0-100 mph time in 10 seconds flat.

Specification	Bugatti EB110 (1994)
Engine	3500cc, V12, 4ohc, 60V, 4 turbochargers
Engine layout	Longitudinal, mid
Power	553bhp at 8000rpm
Torque	451lb ft at 3750rpm
Gearbox	Six-speed manual
Drive	All-wheel
Front suspension	Double wishbones, coils, anti-roll bar
Rear suspension	Double wishbones, coils, anti-roll bar
Steering	Assisted rack and pinion
Brakes	ABS-backed ventilated discs front and rear
Front wheels	Alloy 9Jx18
Rear wheels	12Jx18
Front tyres	245-40ZR18
Rear tyres	325-30ZR 18
Length	4400mm
Width	1940mm
Height	1125mm
Wheelbase	2550mm
Weight	1560kg (3440lb)
0-60mph (97kph)	4.5sec
0-100mph (161kph)	10.0sec
Top speed	212mph (341kph)
Fuel consumption	14-22mpg

Caterham Seven

No frills, **big thrills**

There's more to a Caterham than an old Lotus Seven cast-off. True, the essence of Colin Chapman's 1957 Seven – keep it simple and keep it light – lives on in the modern Caterham. But note the word modern. In all but looks and concept, turn-of-the-century Caterhams have come a long way since Graham Nearn astutely bought the Seven's manufacturing rights from Lotus in 1973.

Nearly three decades on, Caterhams are still setting dynamic standards by which other sports cars – often much more expensive sports cars – are judged. It was not until the late arrival of raw upstarts like the Ariel Atom and Lotus's bare-boned 340R that the Caterham (and the competitors it inspired) had any real rival as a street-legal track-car. If you wanted sharper responses or a better power-to-weight ratio you either spent silly money beyond the means of all but the super-rich, or you bought a real racer. Talking of which, Caterhams of one sort or another have become an integral part of club racing's backbone.

Nearn established Caterham Cars (at Caterham Hill, Surrey, England) in 1959. Eight years on he became the car's sole concessionaire, then its manufacturer. Nearn's robust

Lusty Vauxhall 2.0 twin-cam engine gave HPC 175bhp and slingshot acceleration. House-brick aerodynamics restrict top speed to 125mph – but car does 0-60mph in 5 sec.

Specification	Caterham Seven VVC ('98)
Engine	1796cc, 4-cylinder, 16V
Engine layout	Longitudinal, front
Power	150bhp at 7000rpm
Torque	128lb ft at 4000rpm
Gearbox	Five-speed manual
Drive	Rear wheel
Front suspension	Double wishbones, coils, anti-roll bar
Rear suspension	De Dion rear axle, radius arms, coils
Steering	Unassisted rack & pinion
Brakes	Discs front and rear, no ABS
Wheels	Alloy 6.5Jx15
Tyres	195-50VR15
Length	380mm
Width	1575mm
Height	1110mm
Wheelbase	2225mm
Weight	550kg (1213lb)
0-60mph (97kph)	5.5sec
0-100mph (161kph)	15.8sec
Top speed	125mph (200kph)
Fuel consumption	25-33mpg

defence of his exclusive rights to the Seven's imprint and design is well known to imitators.

Like Morgan, Caterham has always relied on proprietary power. Many different engines, from Ford, Vauxhall and Rover, have passed through its assembly workshops, Dartford-located since 1987. So have several landmark developments, like the introduction of double-wishbone front suspension, classy de Dion rear suspension, four-wheel disc brakes and a stronger spaceframe, reinforced with honeycomb panels for side protection. Let's not forget Caterham's own six-speed gearbox, either.

By the time this book is published, total Caterham production will be approaching 10,000 (cause for a celebratory model, don't you think?), spread over umpteen iterations. Let's focus here on a couple of Rover-engined ones from the latter half of the Nineties.

The Caterham 1.8VVC, following on from 1.4 and 1.6 K-series variants, was the spiritual successor of the much-loved – and very popular – HPC, axed when supplies of its muscular 2.0 Vauxhall engine ran dry. So how did Caterham's VVC compare with the MGF quickie and the flagship Lotus Elise powered by the same twin-cam, 16-valve, light-alloy engine? Bluntly, it trounced the MG, which was nearly twice the weight, and it left the Elise trailing, at least up to 80mph, before air drag began to even things out.

The 550kg Caterham's massive weight advantage was actually augmented by extra horsepower, increased to 150bhp (from 143) by a more efficient exhaust system. Together, these two assets gave a power-to-weight ratio of some 270bhp per ton – a recipe for manic, ear-rasping acceleration, especially with Caterham's close-ratio, short-shift, six-speed gearbox, costing £1,500 extra in 1998. Even with a Ford Sierra five-speeder, the VVC would sprint to 60mph in a Ferrari-threatening 5.2 seconds, matching the old HPC through the gears if not in mid-range pick-up: the VVC was at its virile best – not to say its most vocal, like an F3 single-seater is vocal – when extended to top-end revs. That the Caterham (drag factor akin to a bungalow's at nearly 0.7) was all out at 120mph says what's necessary about the car's abysmal aerodynamics. No wonder the cleaner MGF VVC (Cd 0.32) was swifter, even though humbled on acceleration.

Compared with the contemporary Superlight, a raw-boned racer that was even more focused on speed and handling, the 1.8VVC was relatively soft in the suspension department and therefore less nervous and darty on the corners, super-responsive and amazingly agile though it was by normal yardsticks. For total involvement, for grip, handling balance and steering feedback, there was nothing quite like a Caterham, even a soft Caterham.

Five minutes at the wheel of a Seven – any Seven – made you realise how blunt were the responses of ordinary cars. It also made you appreciate their civility and comfort. I've always been snugly at ease at the wheel of a Caterham, but you do feel exposed

Obsessive weight-paring brought 230bhp Superlight 500R, with 500bhp per tonne. Capable of 0-100mph in about 8 seconds.

Caterham

Red devil. HPC of early
Nineties one of quickest,
most exciting Sevens. Surfeit
of power over grip
encourages extrovert driving.
Forget about space, comfort
and practicality.

to the slipstream, not to mention adjacent trucks: being hub-high to a 40-tonner is a mite intimidating. What's more, in such a tight-fitting cockpit bereft of creature comforts, you needed to be on intimate terms with your passenger. Better to drive solo if you weren't.

While a leather-trimmed 1.8VVC came as close as a bootless (and doorless) Seven could to everyday transport for the die-hard enthusiast, the Superlight – Caterham's extreme answer to the Lotus Elise – was a raw, undiluted, emotional extravaganza. Weight has always been the performance car's biggest enemy, getting rid of it a key objective. With the uncompromised Superlight, however, weight-paring was not so much a creed as an obsession.

Here was a car bereft of windscreen, trim, carpets, heater, spare wheel, hood, even paint...all in the interests, as the name implied, of lightness. With these and other items on the delete list, Caterham got its featherweight streaker down to an anorexic 470kg (1,058lb). Relate that to the 138bhp output of a tweaked K-series 1.6 twin-cam and you had a power-to-weight ratio nudging a Diablo-threatening 300bhp per ton. Add sprint ratios, a six-speed gearbox and Avon grooved slicks – fitted to the car I drove – and the result is savage acceleration.

I remember the Superlight with as much awe as affection. Writing in *Car*, I said, 'It will out-gun, out-corner, out-manoeuvre and out-brake just about

Caterham

The Seven **comes of age**

The idea was simple. Take a Caterham Super Seven chassis, clothe it in full-width, low-drag aluminium bodywork, add doors, locks, boot, cockpit civility and a decent hood, and hey press-stud, a Seven from heaven, a Caterham 21.

It wasn't quite that simple, of course. The 21's chassis was a stiffer, more complicated affair, and the aluminium body of the prototype, first seen at the 1994 Birmingham show, gave way to one of composite mouldings – high-quality ones, at that, with an excellent surface finish. The cockpit was still tight on room, especially elbow room, but in trim and appointments it was unrecognisable as a Seven's.

Powered by a specially tweaked 1.6 Rover K-series engine, the Supersport version of the 21 was no sluggard. However, while light by normal yardsticks it was, at 670kg (1,477lb), quite heavy by Caterham's. So acceleration was less vicious than that of a traditional Seven with the same power. Nor was the handling and steering quite so sharp.

That the Seven's fine edge should be blunted by additional weight was perhaps inevitable. That it was not offset by a big hike in refinement was regrettable (what, no wind-up side windows?). Although the 21 had the measure of mainstream cars like the MGF, even Mazda's MX-5, it gave best dynamically to its nemesis, the Lotus Elise.

It was Caterham's misfortune that the Elise, ironically conceived as a modern Seven, should hit the road at much the same time as the 21. Starting from scratch, rather than making do with a 40-year-old concept, gave Lotus a head start that Caterham could never make up. Pressing home its advantage, the Elise was also cheaper than the 21 Supersport – a part-finished car requiring 50 hours to complete.

History, perhaps, has been a little hard on the Caterham 21 – a fine driver's car from an enthusiastic team. Had Caterham produced it five years earlier, it would have been greeted with unbounded enthusiasm.

anything on four wheels if you've got the bottle, never mind the lightning-fast reactions, to extend it.' There was, I noted, a fine dividing line between play and panic, huge ability being tempered by intolerance of abuse, even though power-oversteer was as easily corrected as it was induced. 'To overdrive the Superlight in the public domain was to push your luck.' Finesse was the secret to undiluted entertainment, not clumsy bravura. That the Superlight was 10 seconds a lap quicker round Thruxton than an MGF (albeit a standard F) rammed home its dynamic superiority over Rover's mid-engined mainstreamer.

The Superlight was the best short-haul funster, the most thrilling toy, of its day, even if it did oblige the use of goggles and skid-lid. If you didn't vacate the stark cockpit wearing an inane grin, it wasn't your sort of car. Smile? You'd laugh at the subsequent 230bhp 500R (for 500bhp per tonne!), which, in streaking to 100mph in about 8 seconds, punched a big hole in the egos of supercar rivals, and even threatened to topple McLaren's mighty F1 in the sprint to 60mph.

On a performance-per-pound basis, they come no quicker than the R500. Or do they? Honda Blackbird power, all 1147cc and 170bhp of it, reduces weight still more. But not by enough. The R500 – probably the quickest street-legal A-to-B car on the market – has the better power/weight ratio. As a track-day special, it's the one to beat.

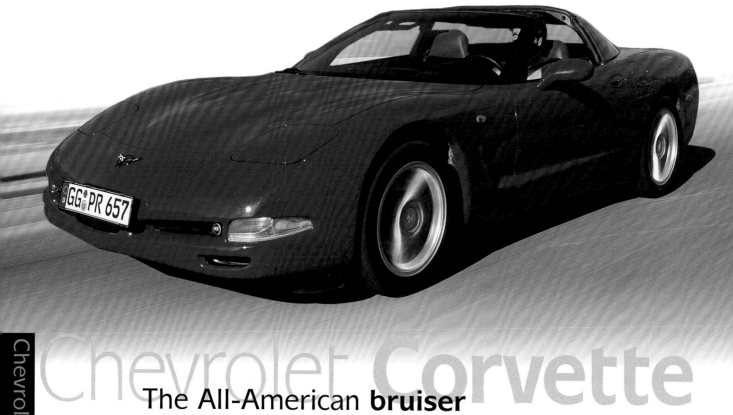

Chevrolet Corvette

The All-American **bruiser**

Corvettes imported to UK in '98 – this is *Autocar's* long-term, fifth-generation automatic displaying secure, wide-track, low-roll cornering. Manuals have six-speed gearbox.

When the first plastic-bodied two-seater Corvette rolled off GM's Flint, Michigan, production line on 30 June 1953, who would have guessed it was the birth of a legend, of America's (and therefore the world's) most popular sports car? Sports car, ha!

The original Corvette, with its toothy chromed grille, asthmatic six-cylinder engine and two-speed (yes, two) Powerglide automatic transmission, may have been the vulgar image-builder that GM sought to put some sparkle into dowdy Chevrolet, but it wasn't Europe's idea of a sports car. If GM's design guru Harley J. Earl really did use Jaguar's XK120 as a benchmark, it's difficult to see what was gained from it, other than a measure for the wheelbase. True, America's new plastic fantasy was low-

slung, eye-catching and a good showroom lure (which was the whole idea), but it steered like a blancmange and ambled to 60mph like it was lame. No, it was no sports car even though impressionable young Americans may have seen it as one.

What the Corvette was initially and what it later became – as a result of an intense muscle-building regime – are two very different cars. The first major uplift was a performance-boosting 265cu in

Specification	Chevrolet Corvette (1998)
Engine	5660cc, V8, ohv pushrod, 16V
Engine layout	Longitudinal, front
Power	339bhp at 5400rpm
Torque	355lb ft at 4200rpm
Gearbox	Four-speed automatic
Drive	Rear wheel
Front suspension	Double wishbones, transverse leaf springs, anti-roll bar
Rear suspension	Double wishbones, transverse leaf springs, anti-roll bar
Steering	Assisted rack and pinion
Brakes	ABS-backed ventilated front discs, solid rear discs
Front wheels	8.5Jx17
Rear wheels	9.5Jx18
Front tyres	245-45ZR17
Rear tyres	275-40ZR18
Length	4565mm
Width	2010mm
Height	1210mm
Wheelbase	2655mm
Weight	1470kg (3240lb)
0-60mph (97kph)	5.8sec
0-100mph (161kph)	13.4sec
Top speed	172mph (277kph)
Fuel consumption	15-23mpg

(4.3-litre) small-block V8 engine, followed by the option of a manual gearbox, first with three speeds, later with four (and currently six). By 1963, when the Corvette had evolved into the Sting Ray – fêted today as a coveted classic – it was taken seriously on both sides of the Atlantic not only as a performance car but also as a track racer. Corvettes first competed at Le Mans in 1960.

If you know what to look for, there are hints of most previous Corvettes in the latest fifth-generation car. Conceptual conformity goes without saying. What else but a plastic-bodied two-seater with a front-to-rear powertrain and a big, torquey V8 making do with ohv pushrod valve gear and two valves per cylinder? And this a new light-alloy engine, too, not a carry-over iron one. When it comes to motive power, the Americans are a conservative lot, preferring tried and trusted measures to fancy new ones. Why risk proven reliability with something unknown? Why go for the expensive option when the cheap one is so effective? Pushrod V8s power 5,000bhp dragsters, so why not 340bhp Corvettes?

Taking a leaf from Ferrari's book (and Alfa's and Porsche's, too, come to that) the gearbox – four-speed automatic or six-speed manual – was shifted away from the engine and mounted at the back as a transaxle, levelling weight distribution to an equitable 50/50. Even with double-wishbone suspension (sprung by synthetic transverse leaf springs, not coils), variable damping (with tour, sport and performance settings), traction control and anti-lock brakes, the fifth-generation car was hardly a ground-breaking tour de force technically. But that was its secret. Corvettes are none the worse for being uncomplicated, all-American muscle-cars, especially when their

Corvette interior smart and colourful, but unadventurous, lacking flair. Fancy dampers are three-way adjustable from cockpit. Compromise setting best. Rumbly tyres mar refinement.

Vette **dream**

If America's favourite sports muscle-car didn't measure up to customer requirements, Callaway Cars has for the past quarter of a century been able to provide that little bit extra – or, in the case of the C12, the company's first all-new Corvette-based supercar for over a decade, a helluva lot extra.

Connecticut-based Callaway has been fettling powertrains (clients include GM, Alfa Romeo, Iso and Aston Martin) since 1976, but it had done nothing quite so comprehensive as the C12 before. President Reeves Callaway said at the car's début in 1998: 'The C12...is the most sophisticated vehicle we have ever produced.'

Built in Germany, in partnership with Munich-based IVM Engineering, the C12 started life as a new, off-the-peg C5 Corvette. This was stripped right down, then rebuilt to a much higher specification and dramatically reskinned. The all-alloy V8, still with only two valves per cylinder, retained the standard 5.7-litre displacement but not much else. Extensive fettling raised output by 25 per cent, from a respectable 345bhp to 911 Turbo-beating 440bhp – sufficient, with wide, low-drag, anti-lift bodywork designed by Paul Deutschman, to push the C12 to Ferrari Maranello-challenging speeds. Callaway's website blurb claimed a zero-to-60 time of under 4.5 seconds and a top speed of 'nearly 200mph'.

A wider track, reworked suspension (which retained the Corvette's unusual composite leaf springs) and uprated brakes helped push the C12's price up to $150,000. So did a cabin makeover that paired rich leather with carbon-fibre embellishment. Even with standard-issue ABS, traction control, a trip computer, air-con, heated mirrors and the rest, the C12 tipped the scales at a respectable (for its size) 1,480kg. Some car.

titanic performance is related to a sub-supercar price.

When the latest Corvette officially went on sale in Britain in 1998 (previous imports were privately arranged), the targa-topped coupé cost just under £40,000, the ragtop convertible just over – pricey by US standards, keen by British ones. Had it not been for the handicap of left-hand drive (right-hookers were not in the script, more's the pity), some of Europe's grandees, Aston Martin, Porsche and TVR included, would have seen the Corvette as a much bigger threat.

Aesthetically, the latest Corvette is perhaps the least distinguished of the series. Eye-catching, yes, mind-blowing, no. Dynamically, however, it's one of the best. That the 'new' 5.7 was as fast as the ZR-1 – a late-Eighties, high-performance evolution of the fourth-generation car – raised some eyebrows. Powered by a Lotus-developed 5.7 quad-cam V8, the ZR-1 was hailed by GM as a Ferrari-eater. Fact is, its exotic 32-valve engine yielded little more power and torque than the simple 16-valve pushrod V8 that followed. Take into account the latest car's weight and aerodynamic advantages, and the similarity in performance is easily explained.

Despite its ancestry, there was nothing retro, even less vintage, about the fifth Corvette. It hauled hard – harder than all but a handful of European exotics – with a deep-chested rumble redolent of a distant Nascar racer high on Daytona's banking. While its chassis may have lacked the sophistication, and ultimately the ability, of pricier rivals, the Corvette handled, steered and stopped almost as well as it reeled in straights. It cosseted, too, through a mainstream cabin notable more for comfort than adventurous design. You sat low, wedged in by a high central divide, behind an impressive array of instruments. Golf bags? The boot carried a pair. Equipment? You name it, the Corvette probably had it. Presence? As a destroyer has presence in a yacht marina. Ride comfort? A lot better than that of the rattly, jittery, crashy Corvette I recall driving in the Eighties. If not a paragon of refinement, the latest iteration of an old warrior does at least show progress.

If size and dependability are priorities, the big, bombproof Corvette has always been a hard act to follow at the price. It was once America's only serious sports car. Many fans still hail it as the best.

Something quite **different**

Sports cars don't come much wackier than the Dare DZ. Built as a gullwing coupé and an open ragtop, the DZ was described by its makers as a showcase for the creative talents of Design And Research Engineering – set up in 1991 by two of the four Walklett brothers, the previous proprietors (and founders) of Ginetta.

Drawing on its experience in designing and building successful race-bred sports cars since the early Sixties, Dare was established as a design consultancy by Ivor and Trevors (plus son Mark). Their attention was soon focused, though, on the extreme DZ, ironically part-funded by Dare's contract to build Ginetta G4s and G12s for the Japanese market.

Dare by name, daring by nature, the DZ was a bizarre mixture of styles – exposed-wheel single-seater up front, Lotus Elise-ish at the back. Whether the two ends united seamlessly in the middle was up to the beholder to decide. That the car had terrific look-at-me presence was not in dispute.

Racing-style double-wishbone suspension carried the steel spaceframe chassis and low-slung, bullet-shaped composite bodywork – exposed at the front so you could see the suspension working from the cosy two-seater cockpit. Relatively soft suspension gave the DZ an unexpectedly smooth ride without introducing unwanted roll when cornering – a DZ speciality, of course. Bodywork was in plastic composites and the interior trimmed to a higher standard than in, say, a Caterham Seven or Lotus Elise. Power came from a Ford Mondeo 2.0 twin-cam slung across the chassis.

Dare's subsequent minimalist TG – again Ford powered – was aimed squarely at Caterham, Westfield and all the other stark featherweights that provided big thrills for modest cash.

Specification	Dare DZ (1999)
Engine	1996cc, 4-cylinder, 2ohc, 16V
Engine layout	Transverse, mid
Power	130bhp at 5700rpm
Torque	128lb ft at 3750rpm
Gearbox	Five-speed manual
Drive	Rear wheel
Front suspension	Double wishbones, coils, anti-roll bar
Rear suspension	Double wishbones, coils
Steering	Unassisted rack & pinion
Brakes	Ventilated discs front and rear, no ABS
Wheels	6.5Jx15
Front tyres	195-50
Rear tyres	205-50
Length	3470mm
Width	1650mm
Height	1030mm
Wheelbase	2235mm
Weight	680kg (1499lb)
0-60mph (97kph)	5.9sec
0-100mph (161kph)	18sec (est)
Top speed	130mph (210kph)
Fuel consumption	28-34mpg

Dodge Viper

Outrageous excess, track success

Viper first US sports car to challenge Corvette. Started as whimsical show concept, developed into serious race-winning supercar. Early roadsters badly flawed, closed GTS superior.

It started as a kite-flying concept – no, not even that, as a whimsical mock-up – at the 1989 Detroit show. Visitors gawked at the audacity of Chrysler's monstrous Dodge Viper, designed in the first place to give a little gee-whizz gloss to America's third-biggest car maker. The company's dull image was in need of a pick-me-up.

Chrysler's president, Bob Lutz, a fast-driving enthusiast, said in 1990 that the Viper's intention was 'to knock your socks off when you looked at it'. Actually to build the car, and sell it to paying customers, was not in the original script. However, public acclaim, and much fluttering of cheque books, persuaded Chrysler otherwise. Lutz was all for it.

Every petrolhead can recall the original Viper's two most memorable features: its outrageously racy looks and the presence under the flight-deck bonnet of a V10 truck engine, initially of 7.0 litres, later of 8.0. Dramatically uniting the two were naughty hot-rod exhaust pipes, poking from the side

Specification	Dodge Viper GTS (1999)
Engine	7990cc, V10, ohv pushrod, 20V
Engine layout	Longitudinal, front
Power	378bhp at 5100rpm
Torque	454lb ft at 3600rpm
Gearbox	Six-speed manual
Drive	Rear wheel
Front suspension	Double wishbones, coils, anti-roll bar
Rear suspension	Double wishbones, coils, anti-roll bar
Steering	Assisted rack and pinion
Brakes	Ventilated discs front and rear, no ABS
Front wheels	10Jx17
Rear wheels	13Jx17
Front tyres	275-40ZR17
Rear tyres	335-35 ZR17
Length	4490mm
Width	1975mm
Height	1195mm
Wheelbase	2445mm
Weight	1555kg (3428lb)
0-60mph (97kph)	5.4sec
0-100mph (161kph)	12.0sec
Top speed	175mph (282kph)
Fuel consumption	12-20mpg

like those of an AC/Shelby Cobra, the Viper's inspiration. Indeed, Carroll Shelby was heavily involved with the Viper's development.

After months of press speculation, Chrysler announced in May 1990 that it would make the Viper to satisfy pent-up demand. Two years later came the first production roadster – still a jaw-dropping eyeful of musclebound metal and plastic, if not quite so radical as the show car had been. Aerodynamic problems dictated prudent changes for stability's sake. The Viper's role as a latterday Cobra, as a minimum frills, maximum thrills projectile, was underlined by the absence of decent headgear, even of door handles and proper wind-up side windows. If ever a car was built for flamboyant fun in America's sunbelt States, the Viper was it.

Recast in aluminium and tweaked by Lamborghini, who worked on the cooling and management system among other things, the Viper's V10 engine may have been low in tech (ohv pushrods, two valves per cylinder) and specific output (a wimpish 50bhp per litre), not to say of dubious lineage. But scorn not. Multiply that 50bhp by eight and you get 400 horsepower. At 450lb ft, torque was even more outrageous. The engine was so flexible, so blisteringly eruptive, you could lug away in third and fourth all day, rendering the other four gears of the Borg Warner 'box largely redundant. If any car has a higher top gear than the Viper's – 51mph per 1,000rpm – I cannot name it.

Although no featherweight, the gargantuan Viper was lighter than, say, Aston Martin's Vantage, even Ferrari's 512TR, which was faster all out than the upstart Dodge but humbled when it came to in-gear hauling. The Viper's party trick was not to scorch from rest to 100mph in 10 seconds,

Mighty V10 engine much improved by development since early roadster. Upwards of 400bhp gives huge performance envelope, 8.0-litre displacement terrific torque and flexibility.

but to accelerate strongly and smoothly from 400rpm – about half the engine's idling speed. And just as well because a stiff and obstructive gearchange did not encourage indulgent shifting. Worse still, a nasty interlock system known as 'skip-shift' prevented low-rev first-to-second changes and dictated first-to-fourth ones instead. Something to do with America's gas-guzzler legislation and therefore not an encumbrance suffered by Europeans.

Dynamically, the Viper was brilliant. Aurally, it was like a falsetto Mr Universe. The characterless drone of the side exhausts failed to convey the car's aggressive power. Tail-piped Vipers, destined for Europe – UK prices in 1996 started at £62,250 – sounded a bit better.

In the interests of equitable weight distribution, the six-speed powertrain was mounted well back in a tubular chassis, suspended by a no-compromise double-wishbone layout at both ends. Plastic composites skinned the monster. Quick steering (just 2.4 turns lock to lock) made the Viper quite agile and darty, nervous even, and the sheer size of it was intimidating, especially with left-hand drive (right-handed cars were never made). Colossal tyres, 335/35s at the back, ensured huge grip. Even so, it was easy to break traction, especially on wet roads in a car notable more for brute force than finesse. Sophistication was not in the roadster's script.

Viper had great handling, agile with quick steering. Huge tyres, especially 335/35 rears, gave fine grip.

As a car for shrinking violets, the butch Viper was a non-starter, a hirsute alien, an escapee from the drag strip. Those who sought first-class comfort were equally repelled. Jitterbugs ruined the ride on poor roads. If it rained you got wet. And to drive fast was to mount a major assault on your scalp and hearing apparatus. Few rivals – if the Viper had any rivals – were quite so raw and uncouth.

A car with little more than side-screen protection was pretty impractical in those parts of the world where you couldn't depend on decent weather. There was clearly scope, then, for a sanitised Viper, for a Viper with an umbrella as well as fangs. Enter, at the 1993 Detroit show, the fixed-head GTS, billed as a design study but clearly destined for production. Three years later, it went on sale.

To describe the GTS as a roadster with a lid would be to sell it short. Over 90 per cent of it was new or extensively modified. Although 60lb lighter than the original roadster, it was 25 per cent stiffer – and more refined, too. On a memorable press trip with former World Champ Phil Hill and sports car ace Brian Redman – who showed us the lines round Spa, Rheims and the Nürburgring – Chrysler's Roy Schoberg (Mr Viper) told me that Ferrari's GTO had been more of an inspiration for the GTS's dramatic beetle-browed styling than Peter Brock's Daytona Cobra had been. In came a double-bubble roof (to allow bone-dome clearance), electric windows (hand-cranked ones were ruled out by space restrictions), doors with electric press-button latches (beware a flat battery), Marcos-like adjustable pedals (so shorties could distance themselves from the wheel), a new dash layout (in funereal black), and a half-decent boot (three cheers from the golfers).

Running changes made previously to the roadster – among them lightweight suspension components and improved geometry – were carried over to the stiffer (and slightly lighter) GTS. The engine got a makeover, too: using the latest computer aids, the blocks and heads were stiffened and lightened – by removing metal. Oil and water content was also reduced.

In the USA the power and torque of the 8.0 V10 were increased, first to 415bhp and 488lb ft, later to 450bhp and 490lb ft. Lower figures prevailed in Europe, however, in order to meet power-sapping noise regulations, among other things. Not that you'd notice. While no paragon of aerodynamic efficiency, the GTS boasted an improved 0.39 drag factor (compared with the roadster's 0.50), which helped increase top speed to something approaching 180mph.

Unless you wanted the exposure of a sun-worship boulevard bruiser, the GTS was in every way a better car that the flawed roadster – production of which was temporarily halted so that Chrysler could clear a backlog of GTS orders. Space was also needed to get the outlandish Prowler off the ground. While it still demanded enormous respect, the inherently understeering GTS was easier and safer to drive quickly. It had a smoother ride, a smarter cockpit, less nervous steering and sweeter handling. Of sophistication, though, there was still little evidence.

Given Chrysler's good track record of spawning production goers from show-stoppers, the GTS-R seen at the 2000 Detroit extravaganza was the likely shape of the next Viper. Billed as a street-legal evolution of the racing Viper, the high-winged GTS-R was lower and more slippery than ever. With 500bhp on tap from its dry-sumped 8.0 V10, it was said to be capable of 200mph. Who's arguing?

Dodge Viper eclipsed Porsche 911 as the car to beat in international GT racing.

Vipers sweep the board
Quick though they were off the shelf, Vipers had huge untapped performance potential. Tuners like Texas-based Hennessy had no trouble raising power to 600bhp – and top speed to 190mph.

Circuit racing was a logical next step. Within a couple of years, Vipers had eclipsed Porsche 911s as the cars to beat in the GT (production-based) category of international sports car racing. Competitiveness improved dramatically as development exorcised teething troubles and raised performance. Top speed rose to 200mph on the faster circuits.

For the Le Mans 24 Hours in 1996 (10th overall) and '97 (14th), the Viper teams were on a steep learning curve. It all came good with class wins in '98, '99 and '00, when Wendlinger, Beretta and Dupuy covered 333 laps to finish seventh overall. The only cars ahead were purpose-built lightweights. In the six-race 1999 American Le Mans series, Vipers won their class in every round – and failed to score a one/two finish only once. Porsche had never had it so bad.

To commemorate its Le Mans victories, Chrysler built a limited run of 100 race-winged, 460bhp GTS-R streakers – pre-empting the like-named 2000 concept.

Ferrari 348

Maranello's flawed gem

Ferrari 348 (for 3.4 litres, 8 cylinders) evolved from 308GT4, successor to the V6 Dino, Ferrari's first mid-engined road car. Engine longitudinal, not transverse. Strong visage centred on dummy grille.

Until quite recently Ferrari wasn't noted for extending the frontiers of technology, even of espousing new-fangled ideas. Mounting the engine amidships behind the driver was pioneered by Cooper and Lotus, not Ferrari. The great man had also been slow to convert from spoked wheels to solid aluminium ones – and for that matter from drum brakes to discs. Even after Enzo's death in 1988, Ferrari continued on its traditional evolutionary course, not a proactive one.

As a major departure from the 328 it superseded, the 348 – Maranello's mainstream model at the beginning of the Nineties – was about as close to revolutionary as Ferrari got.

The 308/328, in its day Ferrari's best-selling model, was always going to be a hard act to follow. It had evolved not so much from the V6 Dino 206/246, Ferrari's first mid-engined road car (named after Enzo's son), but from its successor, the Bertone-styled 308GT4 (1973-80), powered by a new 3.0-litre V8 – hence 308. (Previously Ferrari had identified its cars by the capacity of each cylinder – 250, 275, 365 and so on – so the 206/246/308 was a departure from tradition.)

This tough, high-revving engine, mounted transversely across the chassis, was carried over to the 308 GTB (1975-85) and the 3.2-litre 328 (1986-89). Its lineage ran through to the 348 – but with one major difference. Here the engine was mounted longitudinally in the chassis, not east-west across it, so the five-speed manual gearbox could be moved from an under-engine location to an end-on one, lowering the powertrain by a massive 5in. It followed that the centre of gravity was lowered, too. And the nearer the ground the c of g, the better the handling and stability.

Specification	Ferrari 348tb (1994)
Engine	3405cc, V8, 4ohc, 32V
Engine layout	Longitudinal, mid
Power	320bhp at 7200rpm
Torque	237lb ft at 5000rpm
Gearbox	Five-speed manual
Drive	Rear wheel
Front suspension	Double wishbones, coils, anti-roll bar
Rear suspension	Double wishbones, coils, anti-roll bar
Steering	Unassisted rack & pinion
Brakes	ABS-backed ventilated discs front and rear
Front wheels	5.5Jx17
Rear wheels	7.5Jx17
Front tyres	215-50ZR17
Rear tyres	255-45ZR17
Length	4230mm
Width	1895mm
Height	1170mm
Wheelbase	2450mm
Weight	1465kg (3230lb)
0-60mph (97kph)	5.8sec
0-100mph (161kph)	14.0sec
Top speed	165mph (265kph)
Fuel consumption	17-25mpg

There were other packaging changes besides. The radiators were relocated from front to rear, flanking the engine and moving weight back. And the black-backed grille in the nose? A dummy, would you believe? Not so the Testarossa-like straked inlets slashed across the doors. These really did ram air to the voracious engine and the equipment that cooled it.

The launch of the 348, at the 1989 Frankfurt show, saw the end of the slim-hipped Ferrari and the consolidation of the wide-stance one. With an increase in width over the 328 of 6.5in, the 348 could no longer be described as svelte. Penetratingly obese more like, especially when viewed from behind, the muscular haunches exaggerated in width by the tumble-home of the slender cockpit above.

The first 308 GTBs were clad in corrosion-free glass-fibre bodies – high-class ones at that – before Ferrari reverted to a traditional steel skin. For the 348 steel was supplemented by aluminium (for the boot and bonnet) in an effort to save weight. However, being that much bigger, stiffer and better equipped, the 328's replacement obeyed Colin Chapman's rule about all cars gaining weight. Indeed, the 348 put on nearly 300lb (even more in the States), largely negating a 30bhp increase in power from an engine that was by now a 32-valve, 3.4-litre quad-cam V8. Still, with 300bhp on tap and good cleavage to boot, the 348 (Cd 0.32) was capable in ideal conditions of 170mph.

I have mixed memories of driving Maranello Concessionaires' 348 demonstrator. Ferraris are always mind-numbingly special, and this one was no exception. That said, the 348 lacked the visual drama of the elegantly aggressive 328 that preceded it. On my scorecard it was neither vintage Pininfarina aesthetically, nor Ferrari at its best dynamically. Performance had moved on from the cherished 308GT4 I once owned – but not dramatically so. Startling though its acceleration was by hot-hatch standards, the 348 set no benchmarks in the supercar set. Why, a Lotus Esprit Turbo SE was quicker to 60mph. At the 1993 Frankfurt show Ferrari addressed the matter with a 20bhp hike in power, giving a specific output of 94bhp per litre (for naturally aspirated engines, only McLaren's BMW-powered F1 V12 did better). Even then, Honda's latest NSX – the best supercar ever to come

Spider, popular in USA, lacked rigidity of the fixed-head coupé.

out of Japan – had the Ferrari's measure to 100mph. Indeed, it was Honda as much as Porsche that made Ferrari realise that it would have to try harder and dig deeper technologically for the 348's replacement.

Whatever the figures, they failed to convey the spirit and muscular depth of the Ferrari's engine, even less its glorious wail, which rose to spine-tingling frenzy at the 7,500rpm limit. It was not necessary to stir the sprint-geared 348 along on the gear lever, but it was all the more exciting if you did. When was it otherwise in a red-blooded Ferrari?

Beguiling though it was, the 348 was a flawed gem with more charisma than charm. My notes on Maranello's Berlinetta pinpointed the car's Achilles' heel. I quote: 'There was a knife-edged nervousness about the handling of this highly strung car, which corners like a Le Mans racer – and steps out of line almost as smartly if its staggeringly high limits are breached. With so much power on tap, tail-end breakaway is easily provoked.' I might have added 'especially in the wet'.

What the 348 lacked when driven hard was friendly fluency. While you could map the road surface from the tell-tale feedback of the superb (unassisted) steering, you couldn't totally relax at the wheel. Other than ABS-backed brakes, there were no electronic aids, no active suspension or traction control (not even assisted steering), to protect against over-exuberance.

I was not the only reviewer to be bothered by the 348's disquieting edginess. Mindful of its high price, *Autocar* relegated the 320bhp GTS to third place 'by an appreciable margin' in a head-to-head against Honda's NSX and Porsche's 911.

Ball-topped, spindle-thin gear lever, acting in barred gate, classic Ferrari. Instruments clear, trim quite basic. Prancing horse emblem on wheel constant reminder of car's breeding.

Ferrari 355

A giant leap forward

If the nervous 348 engendered respect rather than lust, its successor, the 355, attracted nothing but unbridled reverence and awe. Where the charismatic but flawed 348 had struggled to justify its premium price against cheaper opposition, the 355 annihilated everything that came within sight. Where the 348 had been a modest onward shuffle from the much-loved 328, the 355 was a giant leap forward from the car it supplanted. Take, for a start, the truly fabulous engine.

In its final form, the 32-valve 3.4 of the 348 yielded an impressive 320bhp. Good but not good enough. The 355's 40-valve 3.5 yielded an astonishing 380bhp at 8,250rpm. Ferrari had experimented with variable valve timing but settled instead on a free-breathing, fuel-guzzling layout of five valves per cylinder – three inlets and brace of exhausts, all the better to breath through. Hydraulic actuation – a first for Ferrari – did away with the need for shim adjustment. Add an almost diesel-like compression ratio of over 11:1, Bosch 2.7 management and a rev limit of 8,700rpm – safely permitted by lightweight titanium con-rods – and the 355's V8 amounted to a new engine rather than an upgrade of the old one. Not even the McLaren F1's V12 could match its specific output of 109bhp per litre.

The transverse gearbox was new, too. Apart from boasting six closely stacked ratios – top gave a motorway-fussy 20.8mph per 1,000rpm – it had engine-heated lubricant (so it warmed up quickly), and double-coned synchromesh on first and second (to facilitate shifting after a cold start – traditionally tricky in a Ferrari). Pugilistic jabs of the 355's chromed lever were still required to snap through seamless changes, but there was little evidence of the baulking that marred the 348. You swapped cogs for the

Pininfarina at its best. Ferrari 355 big advance on 348, aesthetically and dynamically. Front intake real, feeds air to brakes.

59

hell of it in a 355 – and just as well, because the high-revving, power-biased engine was short on low-end muscle, if not flexibility. As for economy, anyone returning more than 17mpg simply wasn't trying.

This time the hike in horsepower was not negated by an increase in weight, kept to around 1,400kg (3,100lb). And this despite the new gearbox, assisted steering, electronic adaptive damping and a monster three-cat exhaust system. Ferrari was catching up fast with modern technology. Lightweight materials – magnesium for the bell-housing and 18in wheels, aluminium for the damper bodies, brake callipers, fuel and coolant tanks, drilled pedals and suspension components – played their part in an effective slimming regime. Result: an even better power-to-weight ratio and truly stupendous performance that not only humbled the (improved) Honda NSX and Porsche 911, but rendered Ferrari's 512TR dinosaur largely surplus to requirements. Why pay so much more for a car that was a couple of seconds slower round Ferrari's Fiorano test track?

Low unsprung weight was one of the keys to improved ride and handling. Another was a Bilstein-made adaptive damping system for the coil-and-wishbone suspension carried over in concept, if not in detail, from the 348. Responding to information provided by various sensors, a 'black box' controller arranged within milliseconds for the dampers to be supple or stiff – or anything in between – providing impeccable body control and a ride free from the harsh jitterbugs of the 348. Chassis reinforcements compensated in the open Spider for the loss of a roof. And effective they were, too; slight dither in the structure was betrayed only when the dampers were set to their stiffest 'sport' mode.

Like 348, 355 was available in three versions. Spider was joined by fixed-head coupé (tb or GTB) and targa (ts or GTS).

Specification	Ferrari 355 (1997)
Engine	3496cc, V8, 4ohc, 32V
Engine layout	Longitudinal, mid
Power	380bhp at 8250rpm
Torque	268lb ft at 6000rpm
Gearbox	Six-speed manual with paddle shift
Drive	Rear wheel
Front suspension	Double wishbones, coils, electronic dampers, anti-roll bar
Rear suspension	Double wishbones, coils, electronic dampers, anti-roll bar
Steering	Assisted rack and pinion
Brakes	ABS-backed ventilated discs front and rear
Front wheels	Alloy 7.5Jx18
Rear wheels	Alloy 10Jx18
Front tyres	225-40ZR18
Rear tyres	265-40ZR18
Length	4350mm
Width	2560mm
Height	1170mm
Wheelbase	2450mm
Weight	1420kg (3130lb)
0-60mph (97kph)	4.8sec
0-100mph (161kph)	11.0sec
Top speed	175mph (282kph)
Fuel consumption	15-26mpg

Together with other developments, including an F1-style stabilising undertray and a diff that limited slip more on the over-run than under power, the handling – sharp yet fluent, no longer nervously edgy – was transformed. The only (minor) criticism voiced by testers was slight loss of kickback 'feel' through the newly assisted steering. Brakes? Fantastic. Noise? Out of this world, the V8's single-plane crankshaft providing, as always, the tearing-calico scream of a true racer, not the booming rumble of a two-plane American V8.

If the 348 was not Pininfarina at its very best, the 355, sensuously bulgy in all the right places, not to say more efficient aerodynamically, certainly was. The front intake, false on the 348, now fed cooling air to the brakes. Beautifully made and finished – and breathtakingly elegant inside – the 355 set new Honda-equalling quality standards for Ferrari. Pity, then, that despite superb seats and an adjustable steering wheel, the driving position was badly flawed by offset pedals that had you sitting awkwardly askew.

Initially the 355 was available only as a conventional stick-shift manual. This was later supplemented (some pundits say rendered obsolete) by Ferrari's F1 paddle-shift system – one of the company's few truly pioneering efforts. F1 shouldn't be confused with other fancy transmissions like Porsche's Tiptronic, which allow you to make clutchless shifts by nudging a lever or pressing a button. Such systems, dependent on a torque converter to take up the drive, are simply automatics offering alternative 'manual' gear selection.

Not so F1, which utilised the same six-speed gearbox – even the same close-coupled sprint gear ratios – as the regular stick-shift car. The same clutch, too – but under electronic control, not muscle power. Gears were swapped by flicking towards you a column-mounted 'paddle' – that on the right for upward changes, that on the left for down ones. Shifts were lightning fast and pretty well seamless, especially if the driver blipped the throttle.

Blipping down through the 'box when braking from speed came as close as you could get to playing at Michael Schumacher. Because there was no loss of power ('sludge pump' torque converters absorb quite a bit), there was no loss of performance either. Unless, that is, you opted to go fully automatic (by pressing a button), in which case the change-up points were restricted to 7,000rpm. Pulling back a tiny lever selected reverse.

Like the 348, the 355 was built in three forms: fixed-head berlinetta coupé (tb or GTB), targa-top (ts or GTS) and open convertible (Spider).

Ferrari 355's 40-valve quad-cam V8 yields astonishing 380bhp from 3.5 litres. Ride and handling better edgy 348's. Six-speed manual came later, with sequential paddle-shift.

Simple elegance of 355 interior, bereft of gew-gaws and superfluous decoration. Offset drilled pedals mar driving position.

Ferrari 360 Modena

The world's best sports car?

The best Ferrari yet? 360 Modena (names are back in vogue at Maranello) did the impossible – improved significantly on the 355.

The 355 was so good, so highly rated, that sceptics feared that Ferrari couldn't significantly better it with the 360 Modena, launched as a fixed-head coupé in 1999, five years on from the 355. It did.

By stirring even more technology into the passion pot, Ferrari produced what's widely regarded as the greatest sports car of the 20th century, certainly one that established a benchmark for the 21st. Not only was the 360 faster in every department than the 355, it was also roomier, safer, comfier, more refined and above all even more uplifting to drive. To cap it all, it cost little more than the outgoing car.

Ferrari started with the basics: adding lightness and stiffness. Out went the old steel-based chassis and bodywork, in came aluminium replacements, following the lead of Honda's pioneering NSX and the Audi A8. (Alcoa, with whom Audi collaborated, was also involved with the 360, by the way.) You could see the naked aluminium flanking the

engine and gearbox – on show through the panoramic rear screen. You could see it in the cockpit, too, symbolically backing the instruments, central switchgear and backbone console. Door trims and classy pedals were made of the stuff as well.

Despite being bigger than the 355, to the benefit of cabin space, the 360M (for 3.6 litres) was actually lighter, by some 80kg – quite an achievement given its greater complexity and size. If not the most striking or eloquent of Pininfarina's designs – criticism centred on the (highly functional) McLaren F1-like front air intakes – the 360 still had absolutely breathtaking presence.

More than that, it was aerodynamically an advance on anything Ferrari had done before. Despite its gumball tyres, the 360 penetrated air with the efficiency of a dart. What's more, it used that air to exert stabilising downforce – 180kg of it at the car's claimed maximum of 185mph. And, look, no wings! It was all done by under-body venturis and clever shaping of the aluminium skin. You could actually feel the car being sucked to the road at speed, instilling a huge sense of security.

The other cause of an improved 288bhp/tonne power-to-weight ratio was an engine – still the familiar 90-degree, 40-valve, quad-cam V8 –

McLaren F1-like intakes part of aerodynamic package. Lightweight aluminium chassis lowers weight despite increase in size.

New Spider said to be 15 per cent stiffer than 355 predecessor, but still not as rigid as closed car.

enlarged from 3,495cc to 3,586cc. With the help of variable-length inlet tracts and dual-phase exhaust timing, power was increased from 380bhp to 400bhp. Torque was up, too. What's more, it peaked at lower revs, making the engine even more flexible, even more tolerant of low-rev lugging.

The 355 had been fitted with a transverse gearbox. For the 360, Ferrari reverted (as in the 348) to a longitudinal end-on six-speeder, either with conventional manual shift or a semi-automatic sequential paddle changer. Although electronic gadgets were still frowned upon by Ferrari boss Luca di Montezemolo, the ASR anti-slip system – a novelty for Ferrari – was by now considered a necessity for those drivers who wanted Ferrari's best but were not up to the job of harnessing its power unaided. Assisted steering and ABS-backed Brembo discs were on the menu, too.

Aluminium construction was not the only way Ferrari flattered Honda by imitation. It also employed acoustic engineers to make its latest V8 engine sound as exhilarating as it went. Anyone uneasy about the on-the-limit nervousness of the 348, even the 355, would have found in the 360 a different car, a car so faithful and viceless that its cornering and braking bordered on the uncanny. Even the moderately skilled could access and exploit all that was offered by the Modena – so named in honour of the town just down the road from Ferrari's Maranello works.

In keeping with tradition, the old 355 Spider – Ferrari-speak for a

Specification	Ferrari 360M (2000)
Engine	3586cc, V8, 4ohc, 40V
Engine layout	Longitudinal, mid
Power	400bhp at 8500rpm
Torque	275lb ft at 4750rpm
Gearbox	Six-speed manual
Drive	Rear wheel
Front suspension	Double wishbones, coils, adaptive dampers, anti-roll bar
Rear suspension	Double wishbones, coils, adaptive dampers, anti-roll bar
Steering	Assisted rack and pinion
Brakes	ABS-backed ventilated discs front and rear
Front wheels	Alloy 7.5Jx18
Rear wheels	10Jx18
Front tyres	215-45ZR18
Rear tyres	275-40ZR18
Length	4475mm
Width	2050mm
Height	1215mm
Wheelbase	2600mm
Weight	1450kg (3197lb)
0-60mph (97kph)	4.4sec
0-100mph (161kph)	9.8sec
Top speed	185mph (300kph)
Fuel consumption	16-24mpg

Cabin more stylish, better equipped than that of previous Ferraris. Gearshift 'paddles' for six-speed gearbox behind wheel. Reach and rake adjustment gives excellent driving position.

convertible – was built alongside the new coupé until the open 360 went into production following its début at the 2000 Geneva show. The new Spider was said to be 15 per cent stiffer than the outgoing one, if not as torsionally rigid as the closed car, even allowing for sill and cross-member reinforcements. Mechanically, Spider and coupé were identical – same engine, same choice of transmissions. The ragtop even retained the coupé's see-through engine cover, so you could admire the red-headed powerhouse beneath without opening up.

The fully automatic, electrically-powered hood needed no manual assistance (other than the press of a button), and stowed out of sight in a clamshell-lidded bay. For safety's sake, a roll-over hoop flanked by a buttress backed each seat. Legroom was not compromised, but luggage space was. With three glass deflectors to keep wind buffeting at bay, drag was increased to the detriment (as if it mattered) of top speed. However, weight – and therefore acceleration – was barely affected. The 360 would rocket to 100mph in under 10 seconds.

As Spiders accounted for the majority of Ferrari's sales in the important US market, over half the 360s made were destined to be ragtops. Ferrari's only problem at the turn of the century was to keep total production down to around 3,500 annually to preserve exclusivity. Even though prices now started at over £100,000, there was no shortage of takers.

Ferrari F40

Enzo's last fling

Ferrari F40 comparatively simple car, built purely for speed. Shovel snout and massive wing reminiscent of Le Mans racer. Popularity extended production well into Nineties.

Central London is not the best place to start your first drive in the world's fastest road car. Harrowingly, it was where I began mine in the Ferrari F40. 'It took no more than the length of Gifford St [where Pink Floyd drummer Nick Mason kept his F40] to appreciate the Ferrari's no-compromise competition heritage,' I wrote in *Car* magazine. 'This is no high-tech showcase like the Porsche 959. The F40 is a comparatively simple car, built simply for speed. Anything detrimental to the dynamics of performance went out with the door handles.'

I remember it well, right down to the cords you pulled to unlatch the doors from the inside. The solid ride, the clonking of metal-jointed suspension, the sizzle of grit on bare wheelarches, the thud and whoosh of Pirelli gumballs, the engine's malevolent snarl, the dreadful bus-hiding

blindspots...these were what first impinged on my memory. The thrill of 480 turbocharged horsepower came later, once the pocked and greasy streets of the capital were left behind. That the F40 coped remarkably well with stop-start city traffic, even though I felt uneasy about it, supported Ferrari's contention that this was the ultimate street-legal hotrod, not an escapee from Le Mans. You wouldn't want to go shopping in an

Specification	Ferrari F40 (1992)
Engine	2963cc, V8, 4ohc, 32V, twin IHI turbos
Engine layout	Longitudinal, mid
Power	478bhp at 7000rpm
Torque	425lb ft at 4000rpm
Gearbox	Five-speed manual
Drive	Rear wheel
Front suspension	Double wishbones, coils, anti-roll bar
Rear suspension	Double wishbones, coils, anti-roll bar
Steering	Unassisted rack & pinion
Brakes	Ventilated discs, no servo assistance
Front wheels	Alloy 8Jx17
Rear wheels	Alloy 13Jx17
Front tyres	245-40ZR17
Rear tyres	335-35ZR17
Length	4430mm
Width	1980mm
Height	1130mm
Wheelbase	2450mm
Weight	1100kg (2425lb)
0-60mph (97kph)	3.9sec
0-100mph (161kph)	9.0sec
Top speed	202mph (325kph)
Fuel consumption	15-20mpg

F40 (where would you put the groceries?) but you could if you needed to.

Aimed at a small number of rich and favoured customers, the 200mph F40 controversially commemorated Ferrari's 40th anniversary as a carmaker. It was at the time the fastest, most expensive production tearaway to leave Maranello. It was also a pure driving machine, bereft of complicated weight-increasing gizmos like four-wheel drive, traction control, active suspension, anti-lock brakes, assisted steering, even a brake booster and glass (front screen apart, the windows were plastic). The only concession to luxury was air-conditioning, considered essential given the proximity of such a raging heat source within inches of your back. The cockpit was otherwise spartan, though none the worse to my eyes for its tasteful simplicity. Nor was it uncomfortable: the winged seats, once you had shoehorned your buttocks into them, embraced with a bear-like hug.

Dynamically, the F40 was way beyond the 288GTO that spawned it. Aesthetically, it was Pininfarina at its brutal best – though a wind tunnel played a vital part in shaping bodywork considerably lightened by all the ducts cut into it, either for scooping air or ejecting it. Considering the size of the stabilising rear wing – a vulgar appendage to some observers – the drag factor of 0.34 was impressively low.

The F40 was based on a lightweight tubular spaceframe, reinforced with

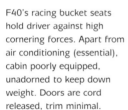

F40's racing bucket seats hold driver against high cornering forces. Apart from air conditioning (essential), cabin poorly equipped, unadorned to keep down weight. Doors are cord released, trim minimal.

Ferrari

bonded carbon-fibre to make it immensely strong and rigid. The wheelbase was the same as the GTO's and the suspension – unequal-length wishbones all round – was pretty conventional, albeit finely tuned. Power came from a 288GTO-based 3.0-litre 32-valve quad-cam V8, boosted by two IHI turbochargers. Drive to the rear wheels was via an end-on five-speed transaxle. So much for the hardware.

Stripped of all superfluous addenda – don't even ask about a radio – the F40 tipped the scales at 1,100kg, wherein lay the secret of its awesome acceleration. As I wrote in *Car*: 'Holy Enzo. Expletives unfit for publication will help preserve the memory of that first burst of eruptive F40 power...it was alarming in its ferocity...to reel in an empty ribbon of tarmac with nearly 500 obedient horses is an unparalleled motoring experience.' I could go on, but you get the drift. The Ferrari F40 was quick – demonically, thrillingly, crazily quick.

It was also hard work. The gear lever, sprouting from a traditional chromed gate, was stiff, the clutch heavy, the brakes heavier still, the steering no pushover. But what delicious responses, what meaningful feedback, what a crescendo of sound – that from the engine of goose-pimple quality, that from the tyres of tiresome intensity. The F40 was not just hard on the ears. More than any other car I've driven, it teased all your senses. I can even remember the way it smelt.

Ferrari intended to make 400 F40s. In the event it built 1,315 to satisfy demand, each and every one a blue-chip collector's item. Because of the extended run, production didn't end in the Eighties, as originally envisaged, but ran until 1992.

Performance of F40's twin-turbo 3.0 quad-cam V8, developed from earlier 288GTO, phenomenal. Top speed nudges 200mph but engine remarkably untemperamental in traffic.

Ferrari **F50**

Formula 1 takes to the road

Built to commemorate Ferrari's half-century as a manufacturer, the mighty F50 was the fastest, most focused road car ever to leave Maranello. Trouble is, it wasn't sufficiently fast or exotic to trump its awesome 230mph McLaren F1 rival. Indeed, it wasn't much of an advance dynamically on its legendary predecessor, the 200mph F40 – in its day undisputed champ of the supercar set and the wildest car I ever drove. Even though the F50 was said to be 4 seconds a lap quicker than the F40 around Ferrari's Fiorano test track, thanks to superior handling and grip, it was no faster in a straight line. So much for progress.

Loosely based on Ferrari's 1990 Formula 1 single-seater, six times a GP winner, the F50 was way out in concept and construction. Here, in effect, was a street-legal escapee from Monza, a hugely impractical super-toy for the super-rich. Nothing wrong with that. Nothing, that is, that another 100 horsepower wouldn't have put right.

With an F1-based V12 engine boasting a staggering 111bhp per litre – 520bhp in all – the F50 was hardly under-powered. But it was no match for the McLaren's 6.1-litre, 627bhp BMW V12. As the ultimate bruiser, as a contender for the title of world's faster car, the F50 was quite simply short on horsepower. All the same, what an engine. What a car!

The old F1 3.5-litre V12, bored and stroked to 4.7 litres, had to be tamed and sanitised for road use. Topping the blocks were purpose-built cylinder heads, each with two chain-driven overhead camshafts operating five valves per cylinder, 60 valves in all, arranged radially in hemispherical combustion chambers. Titanium con-rods allowed a safe 10,000rpm, but the engine was governed to 9,000 for durability's sake. Drive to the rear wheels from

Ungainly F50 built to commemorate Ferrari's half-century as car maker, launched at '95 Geneva. Loosely based on 1990 F1 Ferrari, F50 was contender for title of world's fastest car.

the mid-mounted longitudinal engine – a load-bearing part of the car's structure – was through a six-speed, close-ratio manual gearbox. No push-button gear-changing here.

Carbon-fibre featured strongly in the F50's monocoque chassis and Pininfarina-styled bodywork, redolent through half-closed eyes of past Ferrari sports-racers. Despite the use of exotic lightweight materials, which included Kevlar and Nomex honeycomb, the F50 was no featherweight at 1,230kg. It was, however, light for its size.

If not the most elegant of Ferraris, the F50 was hardly short of dramatic impact. Shaped in a wind tunnel, the bodywork embraced the incompatible needs of built-in downforce (said to be 350kg at 180mph) and clean penetration (Cd 0.37). A black channel, rising from calf height to knee, linked the shovel nose, massively twin ducted, to the high-winged tail section. This hinged forward en masse to reveal the powertrain and racing-style double-wishbone suspension – metal-jointed to eliminate slop. The speed-sensitive, electronically controlled spring/damper units, set transversely across the chassis, were operated through pushrods and rocker arms.

The widespread use of lightweight carbon-fibre didn't extend to the huge, drilled Bembro steel disc brakes. What, no ABS? Certainly not. Ferrari relied on a heavy, easy-to-modulate pedal to prevent skidding. On-board telemetry – a first for a road car – was used for honing the suspension to give understeer-biased handling, for safety's sake. Even so, the F50 was capable of generating 1.4g through the corners.

F50's workmanlike cockpit almost stark in its simplicity. Seats 'winged' for side support, design and decor minimalist. Overlapping instruments easy to read.

Light-alloy inserts bonded to the carbon-fibre tub carried the front suspension and rear powertrain. Because the engine and gearbox were an integral part of the load-bearing structure, there were no isolating bushes to muffle the 65-degree V12's hysterical scream. Ferrari did the only thing it could – cut down on the vibro-massage and turn to its advantage the fact that the F50 was devastatingly noisy. Why not for a road-going racer?

Assisted steering was a definite no-no for the F50. So were cosmetic furnishings for the stark, carpetless cockpit, which emphasised the car's performance role with bare carbon-fibre 'trim' and simple LCD instruments. Other than winged, hip-hugging seats and a surprisingly supple ride (the product of electronically controlled dampers served by 18 sensors), creature comforts were restricted to air-conditioning – essential (as in the F40) to prevent sauna-like cockpit temperatures.

The roadster's joke fabric hood was seen by Ferrari as nothing more than an emergency umbrella – a low-speed one, at that – and the removable carbon-fibre roof a fit-and-forget winter accessory as there was nowhere on the car to stow it for emergency summer use. Not that it was really needed. Even at speed, there was no risk of being scalped by wind rush and turbulence, so well organised was the airflow.

The F50, launched at the 1995 Geneva show, may not have been much of an advance dynamically on the F40, but it certainly had the edge in exclusivity. Over a three-year period production was restricted to 349 cars – a modest total compared to the 1,315 F40s that found paying customers.

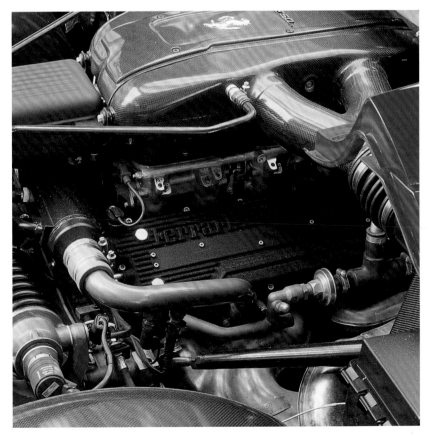

Specification	Ferrari F50 (1995)
Engine	4700cc, V12, 4ohc, 60V
Engine layout	Longitudinal, mid
Power	520bhp at 8500rpm
Torque	347lb ft at 6500rpm
Gearbox	Six-speed manual
Drive	Rear wheel
Front suspension	Double wishbones, coils, anti-roll bar
Rear suspension	Double wishbones, coils
Steering	Unassisted rack & pinion
Brakes	Ventilated discs front and rear, no ABS
Front wheels	Alloy 8.5Jx18
Rear wheels	Alloy 13Jx18
Front tyres	245-30ZR18
Rear tyres	355-30ZR18
Length	4480mm
Width	1985mm
Height	1120mm
Wheelbase	2580mm
Weight	1230kg (2712lb)
0-60mph (97kph)	3.7sec
0-100mph (161kph)	9.0sec
Top speed	202mph (325kph)
Fuel consumption	14-21mpg

F50's 4.7-litre, 60-valve, V12 engine gives 520bhp. That's a specific output of 111bhp per litre. Performance staggering – but beaten by BMW-powered 627bhp McLaren F1 three-seater.

Ferrari
550 Maranello

Back to the **front**

Front-engined 550 Maranello, successor to mid-engined 512M, calls to mind legendary Daytona in spirit if not style. Striking looks but not Pininfarina at its best.

On the face of it, the 550 Maranello, launched by Ferrari in 1996, was a retrogressive car. For all its faults, the superseded 512M, progeny of the Testarossa, distant cousin of the Boxer, was at least mid-engined – and it was etched in stone that no layout was better suited to a sports two-seater. Yet here was Ferrari reverting to a front engine. Had it gone retro-mad in a bid to create a latter-day Daytona, its last front-engined two-seater legend?

Oh ye of little faith! Those who thought Ferrari had gone soft, worse still crazy, were soon devouring their hats. The 550 Maranello spoke for itself. For a start, it was right on the pace, with a top speed nudging 200mph and 512M-beating lap times round Ferrari's Fiorano test track. Ferrari had achieved the impossible, it seemed, and created a front-engined heavyweight that out-handled and out-gripped its lighter mid-engined predecessor. If that wasn't a challenging triumph of development over design, what was?

Specification	Ferrari 550 Maranello (2000)
Engine	5474cc, V12, 4ohc, 48V
Engine layout	Longitudinal, front
Power	479bhp at 7000rpm
Torque	419lb ft at 5000rpm
Gearbox	Six-speed manual
Drive	Rear wheel
Front suspension	Double wishbones, coils, adaptive dampers, anti-roll bar
Rear suspension	Double wishbones, coils, adaptive dampers, anti-roll bar
Steering	Assisted rack and pinion, speed sensitive
Brakes	ABS-backed drilled & ventilated discs
Front wheels	8.5Jx18
Rear wheels	10.5Jx18
Front tyres	225-40ZR18
Rear tyres	295-35ZR18
Length	4550mm
Width	2190mm
Height	1280mm
Wheelbase	2500mm
Weight	1695kg (3737lb)
0-60mph (97kph)	4.5sec
0-100mph (161kph)	10.2sec
Top speed	200mph
Fuel consumption	12-17mpg

Ferrari may have been shy of cutting-edge technology in the past, but it espoused it with relish for the 550 Maranello. The easy bit was to capitalise on the innate packaging advantages – a roomier cabin, better visibility, greater practicality and more refinement – that came with a front-engined layout. Quietness and civility were as much hallmarks of the Maranello as speed and niftiness. It was in consequence a much easier car to live with than the way-out, no-compromise 512. And that was the intention.

Ferrari President Luca di Montezemolo had demanded a flagship that enthusiast drivers could use daily, not just when the mood grabbed them. As it turned out, the 550 was almost too hushed and refined: some reviewers were disappointed that the 5.5-litre, 480bhp engine didn't wail a bit louder. There were no complaints, though, about its performance, even though the 355's 40-valve V8 (never mind the 360's) had a higher specific power output.

If not Pininfarina's most beautiful creation, certainly not its most brutal or aggressive, the Maranello (di Montezemolo decreed that henceforth all Ferraris would have proper names) was a paragon of aerodynamic efficiency: drag was low, lift non-existent. The high-speed stability crucial to a 200mph car was achieved by a fared-in underbody that channelled air through venturis on either side of the transmission.

Mounting the engine well back, and the six-speed gearbox at the rear, as pioneered on the 275GTB (and repeated on the 365GTB/4 Daytona), helped shift weight rearwards to give 50/50 distribution – no mean feat given the size of the engine up front. If there was a surfeit of power over traction (which there was in the wet), three-stage traction control would safely harness it.

Discounting the F40 and F50, the 550 was Ferrari's fastest-ever production road car and, until eclipsed by the 360 Modena, its best handling. Based on a shortened 456GT chassis made the traditional way

Storming performance from 5.5-litre, 479bhp V12 engine, drives through six-speed gearbox. 550 Maranello rockets to 100mph in 10 seconds, does 199mph.

Spacious for two. 512M classic Ferrari inside. Seats modest, no-nonsense dash easy to scan, gear lever guided by metal gate.

512M final iteration of Testarossa, powered by flat-12 engine. Series had huge presence but rendered obsolete by lesser siblings.

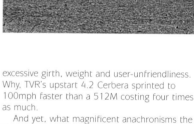

Ferrari's **dazzling redheads**

First there was the eponymous Testarossa, launched at the Paris Salon in 1984. Made for the next eight years, it was strikingly straked and awesomely powered – by a 390bhp 5.0-litre flat-12. No question, the 'redhead' was at the time Ferrari's undisputed flagship, the fastest of the fleet, the ultimate mid-engined supercar. Age, however, did not treat it kindly.

Fast forward a dozen years and basically the same model, by now with 432bhp and badged the 512M (5.0 litres, 12 cylinders, M for Modificato), looked even more of an expensive irrelevance than the in-between 421bhp 512TR (1992-94) had done.

How, then, will history treat the venerable Testarossa and its heavyweight offspring? With reverence, I hope, tinged with cynicism. Humbled by rival hypercars (McLaren F1, Jaguar XJ220 and Bugatti EB110), and rendered obsolete by in-house siblings (first the 355, later the brilliant 360M), the flat-12 redheads never overcame the triple handicaps of

excessive girth, weight and user-unfriendliness. Why, TVR's upstart 4.2 Cerbera sprinted to 100mph faster than a 512M costing four times as much.

And yet, what magnificent anachronisms the Testarossas were. What fabulous engines that booted them. For all its flaws and obesity, the 512TR was not without notable scalps to its credit. In a memorable head-to-head against Lambo's Diablo SE, I concluded in *Car* magazine that 'the half-sensible Ferrari makes for better wheels, if not quite such exhilarating ones.' The daunting Diablo, said to do 200mph, was the swifter car, but the 512TR had the edge, just, on civility. 'After driving the Diablo, the Ferrari feels like a namby featherweight, its controls succumbing to inputs that wouldn't budge those of the Lamborghini.' The size of both cars was at the very least intimidating. 'Sheer girth militates against the sort of wieldiness that would allow, say, a Lotus Elan to outflank both these leviathans...'

from high-tensile tubular steel, it wasn't structurally high-tech. There was no bonded aluminium and little carbon composite. The all-wishbone suspension, stiffened to sharpen responses without seriously jeopardising ride comfort, was basically conventional, too. The clever bit, the secret of uncanny body control, balance and precision, was electronically controlled adaptive damping that, along with ASR traction control, bestowed on the 550 uncanny levels of composure and safety.

A namby-pamby Ferrari, then, bowing to political correctness? Not really. Switching the dampers to 'Sport' cancelled ASR, allowing the driver to indulge opposite-lock skills in the best front-engine/rear-drive tradition. The Maranello's ultra-sharp responses, rooted in flick-quick steering giving just 2.1 turns from lock to lock, seemed to defy the laws of inertia. Received wisdom was that big and heavy cars simply did not change direction with such alacrity. Ferrari rewrote the rulebook to say that they did.

As the softer, roomier 456GT had occasional rear seats, the 550 Maranello was denied them. Instead, it got an open luggage deck in a cabin notable for its sumptuous leather trim and lovely round, chrome-ringed instruments. For its lavish equipment, too. Who said a sports car can't have climate control, powered seats and a CD player?

An open Spider variant, largely to satisfy US demand, was expected in the autumn of 2000.

Europe fights back

Barchetta was first recipient of Fiat's new 1.8-litre, 16-valve, twin-cam four. Produced 130bhp with multi-point injection, boosted to 135bhp in '98. Gearbox five-speed manual.

Bravo Barchetta! Never mind that the name – 'little boat' or 'skiff' – sounds silly in English. This is the roadster that ended Mazda's six-year monopoly in affordable sports cars. Along with the MGF, it led the comeback for Europe, spiritual home of the open funster that the Japanese had eclipsed.

From 1989, when the MX-5 broke cover, to the introduction of the Fiat Barchetta at the 1995 Geneva show, there was no serious competition to the inspired little Mazda. Cash-strapped enthusiasts who wanted a real sports car, rather than a hot-hatch masquerading as one, had no alternative: it was the Mazda or nothing. That rival manufacturers should want a slice of the MX-5's runaway success was hardly surprising. What was amazing is that they all took so long to launch an attack.

The last sports car that Fiat had made was the adventurous mid-engined X1/9. Ironically it was Rover, not Fiat, who chose to emulate it. This time around, the pragmatic Italians – led by Fiat chief Paolo Cantarella, who was keen to get back into the roadster market – eschewed an expensive, bespoke chassis. To keep down costs, the Barchetta was based on the front-drive Punto hatchback, raising questions about the car's pedigree and prowess. Could a Punto in roadster drag really compete with the Elan-inspired rear-drive Mazda, or the MGF with its innately superior mid-placed engine? Any doubts were quickly dispelled, the Barchetta not merely fulfilling expectations but on some fronts exceeding them.

To describe the Barchetta as a two-seater Punto would be to sell it short. For a start, the chassis was shortened in wheelbase by 170mm, over 10in, and the suspension – still MacPherson front struts and rear trailing arms – tweaked and recalibrated to suit a lighter, handling-biased car. Nor was

Specification	Fiat Barchetta (1996)
Engine	1747cc, 4-cylinder, 2ohc, 16V
Engine layout	Transverse, front
Power	130bhp at 6300rpm
Torque	121lb ft at 4300rpm
Gearbox	Five-speed manual
Drive	Front wheel
Front suspension	MacPherson struts, coils, anti-roll bar
Rear suspension	Dead axle, trailing arms, coils, anti-roll bar
Steering	Assisted rack & pinion
Brakes	Ventilated front discs, solid rear discs, ABS optional
Wheels	Steel 6.5Jx15
Tyres	195-55
Length	3915mm
Width	1640mm
Height	1265mm
Wheelbase	2445mm
Weight	1050kg (2315lb)
0-60mph (97kph)	8.5sec
0-100mph (161kph)	25.0sec
Top speed	120mph (193kph)
Fuel consumption	28-38mpg

UK sales of Barchetta restricted by left-handed controls. Cost of right-hand drive too high for limited market. Comfortable seats, driving position, mask firm, jittery ride.

there the faintest hint of Punto in the styling. Designed in-house (there was no inter-studio contest to skin the Barchetta) by Centro Stile's Greek Andreas Zapatinas, the new roadster had a pretty Coke-bottle profile emphasised by a prominent waist-high crease. Plastic-covered headlights and an airdam that drooped at the ends (foreshadowing Ferrari's 360 Modena), gave the Barchetta a friendly, distinctive visage. At the back, paired braces of individual lights set off the rounded, big-booted rump. Unlike the wheelarch-slashed Fiat Coupé, there was nothing controversial about the Barchetta's slightly bulbous looks. Everyone hailed it as a pretty and pleasing shape that held its own against the Mazda's, even the more expensive MGF's.

In power, as in weight, the three cars were pretty evenly matched, the Barchetta being the first recipient of Fiat's new 1.8-litre, 16-valve twin-cam 'four'. With multi-point injection and variable valve timing, it delivered 130bhp (boosted in 1998 to 135bhp by electronic tweaks) and a decent dollop of torque though a five-speed manual gearbox. The Punto's optional six-speeder was not reckoned strong enough for the job, more's the pity. Attractive steel wheels, each served by a disc brake, rendered alloys an expensive extravagance.

Bearing in mind that you sat tall in the upright Punto, Fiat went to some lengths to ensure a low seating position in the ground-hugging Barchetta. Much thought went into the cockpit, too. Whereas the Mazda had an austere, no-nonsense interior, that of the Barchetta was elegant, bordering on the sumptuous and sophisticated. Its black-on-white instruments – Porsche-like, the rev counter got pole position, pushing the speedo to the

left – and Alfa-like venting flaps helped give the dash a touch of class. Another asset was a cracking, easy-to-work (and weathertight) manual hood. True, you had to get out to stow it under (and retrieve it from) a rigid panel, but the neatness of it was worth a few extra seconds of effort.

Fiat's Barchetta was never less than a hoot to drive. I loved it. All right, the ride around town was a little harsh, and the assisted steering – ultra-sharp with just 2.4 turns from lock to lock – wasn't as communicative as that of the unassisted Mazda. A little more exhaust rasp and less under-bonnet whoosh would not have gone amiss, either. In the early days there were also concerns about the ability of the ex-Lancia Maggiora plant near Turin to build Barchettas in relatively large numbers (15,000 annually) to MX-5 quality levels – a tall order for any European factory.

But of the Barchetta's dynamic qualities there were no doubts. There was real substance behind the seductive style. Roadholding was terrific, and the car's fluency and composure when hustling through a bend, better still a series of them, confirmed the Fiat's credentials as a serious driver's car, as a source of endless entertainment. On performance, the eager, rev-happy Barchetta seemed to have a small but decisive advantage over the MX-5. On the other hand, the rear-drive handling of the Mazda was ultimately the more rewarding. So was its peerless gearchange.

Responding to Fiat's challenge, Mazda undercut the £13,950 Barchetta in Britain in 1996 – but only with a spartan 1.6. The comparable 1.8 upgrade cost more – considerably more in its most expensive form. So did the feisty Fiat make any serious inroads into Mazda's territory in the UK? It didn't, and was never likely to because of its left-handed controls – a handicap that also played into the hands of Rover and the MGF.

Sitting on the wrong side of the cockpit did not dilute my enjoyment of the Barchetta, but it deterred most people who might otherwise have been tempted to buy one.

Pretty front-drive Fiat Barchetta ended Mazda MX-5's monopoly in affordable sports cars. None the worse for being based on shortened Punto platform. Car handles, steers well, neat manual hood easy to erect and stow.

Ginetta G33

A promise **unfulfilled**

Where to start with Ginetta? How about at the beginning, in the Fifties, when the Walklett brothers started making race-bred sports cars? The first was a tweaked Wolseley Hornet, the most enduring the Ginetta G4 club racer – still being made at the turn of the century by Dare (founded by some of the Walkletts after they sold Ginetta) as well as by 'new' Ginetta (as the G27). Other models along the way illustrate just how creative little Ginetta really was. They included the G15 (an Imp-powered tearaway), G17 (an FF racer), G20 (stillborn F1 car) and the G26 (a Ford-based sporting saloon). However, the model that caught the eye of the press in the Nineties was the promising G33, perhaps the prettiest open two-seater ever to cradle a Rover V8 engine.

Pitched at British rivals like the TVR S3 and Lotus Elan, the G33 – in size and design clearly inspired by the old G4 – had a classy spaceframe chassis carrying full-width glass-fibre bodywork notable for its long snout and far-back driving position just ahead of a stubby tail. Pop-up lights, integral head fairings (before they became seriously fashionable) and a screen with clipped corners were design features of a car that offered 911 Turbo levels of power to poundage.

Even with a mild-mannered 200bhp 3.9 engine, the five-speed G33 lightweight was junior supercar quick. While there were reservations in the motoring press about the car's handling, driving position, hood and comfort, there was none at all about its looks or performance – and the intoxicating sound effects that went with it.

Alas, the G33 – subsequently made for a while in Sweden with Volvo power – didn't see out 'new' Ginetta's roller-coaster ride.

Specification	Ginetta G33 (1992)
Engine	3946cc, V8, ohv pushrod, 16V
Engine layout	Longitudinal, front
Power	198bhp at 5300rpm
Torque	220lb ft at 2500rpm
Gearbox	Five-speed manual
Drive	Rear wheel
Front suspension	Double wishbones, coils, anti-roll bar
Rear suspension	Double wishbones, coils
Steering	Rack & pinion
Brakes	Ventilated discs front and rear, no ABS
Wheels	Alloy 7Jx15
Tyres	215-50ZR15
Length	3830mm
Width	1625mm
Height	1040mm
Wheelbase	2225mm
Weight	868kg (1913lb)
0-60mph (97kph)	5.5sec
0-100mph (161kph)	14.4sec
Top speed	140mph (225kph)
Fuel consumption	15-24mpg

Honda **CRX**

Looks suffer for **clever lid**

The first CRX, launched in 1984, was a pocket-sized coupé with bags of style and frenzied pizzazz. This no-nonsense brat-pack tearaway, high in spirit and low on room, set the pattern for its raucous sequel – good for 130mph with screaming VTEC engine. Although neither of the first two CRXs were roadsters, both had strong sporting pretensions. So what went wrong with their enigmatic successor?

With only two seats and an opening roof, the third-generation CRX seemed on the face of it more of a sports car than its progenitors. But was

Third-generation CRX denied pert good looks of predecessors, but had instead party-trick targa roof – power operation cost extra. Screaming VTEC engine gives lively performance.

it? Although out-of-the-rut new, it was smoother-riding and more refined. It seemed to be pitched at a market niche adjacent to that occupied by Mazda's MX-5 and Toyota MR2, not on top of it. Being different, however, does not necessarily mean being better.

Although still Civic-based (and therefore one of only a handful of cars in this book with front-wheel drive), the third coming of the CRX had changed for the worse

Specification	Honda CRX (1993)
Engine	1595cc, 4-cylinder, 2ohc, 16V
Engine layout	Transverse, front
Power	158bhp at 7600rpm
Torque	111lb ft at 7000rpm
Gearbox	Five-speed manual
Drive	Front wheel
Front suspension	Double wishbones, coils, anti-roll bar
Rear suspension	Double wishbones, coils, anti-roll bar
Steering	Assisted rack and pinion
Brakes	ABS-backed discs, ventilated at front
Wheels	Alloy 6Jx14
Tyres	195-60VR14
Length	4005mm
Width	1695mm
Height	1255mm
Wheelbase	2370mm
Weight	1100kg (2425lb)
0-60mph (97kph)	8.2sec
0-100mph (161kph)	22.5sec
Top speed	133mph (214kph)
Fuel consumption	23-32mpg

aesthetically. What used to be a beguilingly pretty little car had morphed into an ungainly one. And why? Because instead of being designed from the wheels up it was designed from the roof down.

The car's shape – particularly its long-decked profile – was dictated by the party-trick action of a targa roof panel known as Transtop. On cheap versions this was manually manipulated. Pay extra, though, and at the press of a button the aluminium lid would lift up, slide aft and disappear into the boot. The rear window could also be dropped down, leaving between cockpit and sky only a targa hoop that, being heavily base-buttressed, did nothing for the car's appearance – though it may have been structurally beneficial.

Clever stuff, but there were snags. For a start, the stowed panel halved boot space. As the token rear seats had been dropped altogether, al fresco motoring left little room for luggage. This fancy headgear and its attendant electrickery also imposed a performance-blunting weight penalty of over 100kg. Overall length went up, too.

To spare the CRX's optional bombproof VTEC engine from astronomical revs was to miss the point of its high-tech valve gear. You needed to see at least five-five on the tacho before power burgeoned with a demented wail. All good, clean, intoxicating entertainment for the serious driver, no question about it. Trouble is, Toyota's mid-engined 2.0-litre MR2 had the CRX comfortably beaten on all-out performance as well as on handling, and the MX-5 was a lot more fun. No, the third-generation CRX was not Honda's greatest car.

Honda Beat – small but perfectly formed

No off-road parking space, no car. This was one of the Draconian laws that spawned a peculiarly Japanese sub-species of micro-minis to which the Honda Beat belonged. Small but perfectly formed, the micros were restricted to 130in length and 55in width if they were to qualify for various tax-saving benefits. 'Green' constraints on engine size, power output and performance – 660cc, 64bhp and about 80mph respectively – were added restrictions that encouraged design ingenuity in the interests of environmental amicability.

Working to these tight parameters, the Japanese came up with all sorts of oddball micros, including the pint-sized Nissan Figaro and S-Cargo, mainly for a home market that absorbed 1.8 million of them annually in the early Nineties. The Honda Beat, 1991-94 (including a mid-term break in production), was one of the best.

Imagine a miniature MGF, complete with rounded rump and flank-side intakes feeding a mid-mounted engine, and you have the rhythm of the Beat – cute, curvy, alluring, cheeky. But a serious sports car? As long-distance inter-city wheels, not really: the gear ratios were too short, the cruising too fussy, the theoretical 100mph maximum cut by a governor to 80mph. As an urban tearaway, though, the Beat would have excited Count Basie. Hub-high to a bus, I remember buzzing around London in a personal import (Honda never officially sold the Beat in Britain), and revelling in the car's agility and verve.

The rev-happy little engine – 656cc, three cylinders, single overhead camshaft, 12 valves, electronic injection – sounded like a baby Ferrari when pushing through the gears. No point in slogging it out at low revs: torque was of limp-rag strength at much below 4,000rpm, and the engine (lifted from Honda's Today hatch) wasn't properly into its stride until 5,000rpm. Power peaked at eight-two, would you believe?

Honda NSX

Japan's best supercar

Honda invested heavily in decade-old, high-tech NSX, carried by aluminium chassis years ahead of Ferrari. Dated styling little altered since 1990 launch. Made as fixed-head and targa.

Honda's wonderful NSX has been on sale for ten years. Artist's impressions of its alleged successor, said to be powered by a 500bhp V8, have already appeared in the motoring press. Of more immediate interest, though, are forecasts of an interim reskin, said to feature faired-in lights and a giant rear wing. If anything dated the NSX it was the way it looked.

As the new millennium dawned, production of the evergreen V6 in its original suit of clothes continued, albeit at a trickle, alongside that of the new S2000 sportster at Honda's special Tochigi plant. Such has been Honda's investment in the NSX, before and after its 1990 introduction, that the demise of this Japanese icon is unthinkable.

Nothing like the NSX – one of my all-time favourites – had emerged from the Far East before. The Japanese had mastered most other car categories – micros, minis, superminis, hatchbacks, saloons, even sportsters, coupés and luxury cars. They had also perfected the art – no, call it an exact science – of making mainstream cars that didn't go wrong. When it came to reliability and customer satisfaction, dull but dependable Japanese hacks were the ones to beat, the ones that topped the polls. But supercars? No chance. Where was the tradition, the passion, the flair and emotion to produce cars worthy of Europe's exotica, in particular of Ferrari and Porsche?

At Honda, that's where. It was no surprise that Japan's first – and best – sports supercar came from its most creative and imaginative manufacturer. It was a surprise, though, that Honda made such a good job of it, that its engineers and designers had the necessary comprehension of a concept they'd never tackled before.

Specification	Honda NSX (1998)
Engine	3200cc, V6, 2ohc, 24V
Engine layout	Transverse, mid engine
Power	290bhp at 7000rpm
Torque	224lb ft at 5000rpm
Gearbox	Six-speed manual
Drive	Rear wheel
Front suspension	Double wishbones, coils, anti-roll bar
Rear suspension	Double wishbones, coils, anti-roll bar
Steering	Assisted rack & pinion
Brakes	ABS-backed ventilated disc front and rear
Front wheels	Alloy 7Jx16
Rear wheels	8.5Jx17
Front tyres	215-50ZR16
Rear tyres	245-40ZR17
Length	4425mm
Width	1810mm
Height	1170mm
Wheelbase	2530mm
Weight	1350kg (2976lb)
0-60mph (97kph)	5.2sec
0-100mph (161kph)	11.8sec
Top speed	160mph (257kph)
Fuel consumption	16-25mpg

Six years in the making, the NSX pre-empted Ferrari's 360M by a decade in embracing aluminium construction to reduce weight. It was way ahead of Ferrari, too, in the use of traction control and variable-valve engine timing. In several key areas, in fact, the Honda NSX left the Europeans playing catch-up. Ferrari's 328 was well beaten. Later, after the first of many improving revisions, the NSX trounced Ferrari's 348 (and shaded Porsche's 911) in a three-car confrontation conducted by *Autocar*.

Light weight allowed the use of a modestly sized 3.0 engine. But what an engine – a 24-valver yielding 276bhp with manual transmission, and 256bhp with four-speed auto. If you haven't heard, from inside the cockpit, the glorious wail of the NSX's quad-cam V6, your motoring education is incomplete. In my experience, only McLaren's F1 sounds better. It was no acoustic accident, either: the engine was tuned to bellow gloriously under hard acceleration – and to quieten when light-throttle cruising. Honda rightly recognised that to make the right sort of noise at the right volume was a vital part of the NSX experience. Aurally, the NSX had everything that the Lotus Esprit, four and V8, lacked.

It also had a degree of civility and user-amicability that some observers dismissed as uninvolving, as emotionally vacuous. Supercars should be challenging cars, ran one misguided school of thought. If they made things too easy for the driver, they were lacking in soul and character. Twaddle. I've always loved and admired the NSX as much for its polish as its performance. What's wrong in uniting comfort with charisma, visibility with vim? The only thing that the NSX ever lacked was the heritage of a thoroughbred name, as if it mattered. By supercar standards it wasn't even expensive to run and service – though it has always had a notorious appetite for rear tyres.

Fabulous NSX V6 mounted amidships. Makes glorious wail when charging, muted hum when cruising. Larger 3.2 engine, six-speed gearbox and bigger wheels in 1998.

Honda didn't rest on the NSX's launch laurels. Far from it. As with its great rival, the Porsche 911, continuous development (for which read commitment) has seen Honda's flagship get better and better. The manual gained power steering (the auto already had it) in 1994. In '95 came a targa roof option (the NSX-T), F-Matic fingertip shifting, traction/cruise control and a Torsen limited-slip differential.

NSX's smart cabin criticised for being too mainstream, too conventional. Controls well deployed, driving position fine. Steering electrically assisted, seats comfortable.

The last raft of improvements, in 1998, saw the manual's engine uprated to 3.2 litres and 290bhp. In, too, came a six-speed gearbox, larger wheels (up from 16in to 17in), bigger brakes, a revised front spoiler and power steering with more feel. There's yet more to come.

Honda S2000

Extreme engine, understated car

S2000's air-scooping arrowhead snout most striking aspect of car that celebrated 50 years of motorised Hondas. Some motor! High-revving 2.0-litre screamer 'four' yields 240bhp, feeble torque.

If the wrapping was unspectacular, even a tad understated, the gems it embraced were of memorably high grade. Take, for instance, the S2000's amazing engine – the heart of every Honda and a true paragon of power here. No-one but Honda, a law unto themselves when it comes to making engines, would have attempted to get so much from so little.

A specific output of 100bhp per litre was once considered pretty remarkable for a naturally aspirated production engine. Some exotics – McLaren F1, Ferrari 360 Modena, for instance – were up around the 110bhp/litre mark. Honda's 2.0-litre, four-cylinder twin-cam, designed and built specially for the S2000, yielded an astonishing 120bhp per litre, a resounding 240bhp all told – more than BMW's 2.8 'six' could muster.

No-one doubted Honda's ability to build a lightweight, durable engine that would rev safely to 9,000rpm and satisfy the most stringent emission regulations. After all, its superbike motors whizzed to even dizzier revs. If a frenzied eight-five was needed to get the best from the engine, so be it: VTEC's race cams would deliver. There were, however, misgivings about the ability of a highly stressed 2.0 'four' to perform adequately at less than astronomical revs, given that torque – a more modest 153lb ft – peaked at 7,500rpm. They were justified. Although the engine was quite flexible, low-rev punch was on the feeble side of adequate.

Just to get things in perspective, TVR's 4.0 Chimaera V8 was no more powerful than the S2000, yet it yielded 270lb ft of torque, making it fusslessly fast where the Honda was noisily frenzied. This was no lazy cruiser, but a serious toy for the committed enthusiast. If you didn't like screamers – and they can get a bit wearing – this Honda wasn't for you.

Specification	Honda S2000 (2000)
Engine	1997cc, 4-cylinder, 2ohc, 16V
Engine layout	Longitudinal, front
Power	240bhp at 8500rpm
Torque	153 lb ft at 7500rpm
Gearbox	Six-speed manual
Drive	Rear wheel
Front suspension	Double wishbones, coils, anti-roll bar
Rear suspension	Double wishbones, coils, anti-roll bar
Steering	Assisted (electric) rack and pinion
Brakes	Discs front and rear, ventilated at front
Front wheels	Alloy 6.5Jx16
Rear wheels	Alloy 7.5Jx16
Front tyres	205-55
Rear tyres	225-50
Length	4135mm
Width	860mm
Height	1285mm
Wheelbase	2400mm
Weight	1260kg (2778lb)
0-60mph (97kph)	5.5sec
0-100mph (161kph)	14.5sec
Top speed	150mph (242kph)
Fuel consumption	23-30mpg

For an unblown 2.0, the S2000 was impressively quick. On a closed circuit you could scream its tireless engine all day and enjoy every minute of emulating a racer at full chat. In the public domain, though, habitual top-end play proved a bit wearing on the hearing apparatus and nerves. Although the engine pulled flexibly and sweetly on its VTEC street cams in the lower reaches of its impressive rev range, it did so without the vigour of, say, a torque-optimised TVR V8. Not that snick-snicking the titanium-topped lever of the car's six-speed manual gearbox was anything but unbridled fun. Keeping the revs up and the gears low was part and parcel of the S2000 experience.

Honda described its new sports car, based on the 1995 SSM (Sports Study Model) show car, as a birthday gift, as a celebration of 50 years of motorised Hondas – originally nothing more sophisticated than powered pushbikes, you may recall. Some gift, even if the wrapping was a little unadventurous.

To my eyes the in-house S2000's best aspect was its bold, arrowhead snout, defined by flush light-cluster covers, slinkily trapezoidal in shape, that swept back to unite with fattened wheelarches housing thin-spoked alloy wheels, all the better to cool the brakes. In profile the wedged envelope, defined by a rising waistline, was clean and attractive, but hardly riveting. Underneath was an all-wishbone-suspended steel platform chassis, said to be of immense torsional rigidity – a claim substantiated by the conspicuous absence of scuttle dither and steering shake. ABS-backed disc brakes and electrically powered steering were standard equipment. Traction control was provided by your right foot.

Honda

On the face of it the car's front-engined, rear-drive configuration – Honda's first since the S800 sports car of the Sixties – was unadventurous. A mid-engined layout like the NSX's was considered and rejected for packaging reasons. However, the inclined engine sat so far back in the chassis that it could almost be regarded as mid-mounted – witness the equitable 50/50 weight distribution. Besides, if launch-time rumours were to be believed, the S2000 would be seen in retrospect not so much as a modern-traditional roadster, à la MGB and Lotus Elan, but as a trendily avant-garde one were it to spawn a rear-drive Honda saloon, said to be on the horizon, to challenge BMW's 3-series and the Lexus IS200.

At a launch price in Britain (late 1999) of £27,995, the in-between S2000 split the Mazda MX-5/MGF and Mercedes SLK/Porsche Boxster on price. However, even when upgraded from a 204bhp 2.5 to a 220bhp 2.7, the 82bhp per litre Boxster failed to match the Honda's all-out performance. Ditto the S2000's head-on price rival, BMW's Z3 2.8, which had more accessible oomph but less of it when stretched to the limit.

Black figured prominently in the S2000's neat, no-nonsense cockpit, bisected by a high strength-giving central divide that gave both occupants their own tub-like space, racing-car-style. Even the instrument pod was a lifeless black hole until you turned the key. Then the multi-coloured display lit up to reveal a big digital speedo and bar-chart tacho sweeping above it in a shallow arc. You started the engine in the most evocative way: by pressing a red button, E-type style. Behind the seats – nicely bolstered to support against high-g cornering – were a couple of roll-over bars that

Central backbone divides S2000's smart cockpit into two tub-like cells. Instruments lifeless black hole until activated by ignition. Tacho arched bar-chart, speedo easy-to-read digital in centre.

echoed the shape of the head restraints. A clip-on see-through panel straddled them to reduce slipstream buffet. Although the powered hood didn't sink from sight under a rigid panel, it stowed neatly, without obstructing the mirror view aft.

Driven hard on the right roads – deserted, twisty, demanding roads – the S2000 was a hoot, a driver's dream. Grip was terrific, steering sharp and precise, the brakes strong. Its appeal diminished, though, as the pace – particularly the pace of the rev-happy engine – fell to normal levels. In the clutches of maelstrom traffic, where some sports cars still manage to entertain, the Honda lost its peaky magic. Driving smoothly around town called for delicate footwork if the sharp throttle and unforgiving clutch were not to cause jerkiness. If you preferred the lazy-giant torque of a big V8, the S2000 was flawed by frenzy.

Jaguar XJ220

Technical triumph, PR disaster

All too briefly, Jaguar's mighty XJ220 was the fastest road car in the world. Until eclipsed by the McLaren F1, its alleged top speed of 220mph (hence the name) made rivals like the Lamborghini Diablo, Ferrari F40 and Porsche 959 seem a tad pedestrian. Awesomely quick though it was, however, the XJ220 is remembered not so much for its beauty and speed as its tortured gestation and sales debacle.

As originally mooted by engineering chief Jim Randle late in 1984, Jaguar's technical showcase would have, among other advanced features, four-wheel drive and a 500bhp, 6.2-litre, 48-valve, V12 engine. Beat that, Ferrari.

Four years later, just such a leviathan, designed and built in the spare time of its 'Saturday Club' creators, starred as a concept at the 1988 Birmingham Motor Show. Wow! It was the mother of all supercars, a truly fabulous beast. What's more, it was spot on cue. Against a background of market buoyancy and rising values – prices of thoroughbred classics as well as hot supercars were going through the sunroof – rich must-haves who

Keith Helfet responsible for XJ220's dramatic looks. Car downscaled from all-drive V12 to rear-drive V6 'twixt launch and production. Car sucked onto road at speed.

Rear visibility poor, cockpit trim quite voluptuous, dash nothing special. Engine rough and noisy when ambling, savagely loud when extended. Acceleration phenomenal, roadholding awesome.

wanted a slice of Jaguar's all-action supercar readily parted with the requisite £50,000 deposit.

From there on, things didn't quite go according to the original script, either on the technical front or from a sales standpoint. By the time the definitive version of the XJ220 appeared at the 1991 Tokyo show (two years after Ford had bought Jaguar, seven after the car was conceived), it had lost six cylinders, drive to the front wheels, anti-lock brakes, adaptive suspension, assisted steering, vertically opening doors, several inches in length and wheelbase, and (no bad thing) 400lb in weight.

The XJ220 was still awesomely quick and imposing, but was it what depositors thought they were buying? With recessionary blues in the air, orders were cancelled and solicitors consulted. The thunder-stealing launch of Jaguarsport's V12-powered XJR15 didn't help, either. Technical triumph slumped to PR disaster when the XJ220 – its launch price a wallet-numbing £403,000 (plus VAT) – became the high-profile victim of a messy bursting bubble.

Amidships behind the cockpit was no longer a quad-cam version of Jaguar's evergreen V12, but a compact 3.5-litre, 24-valve, twin-turbo V6 tuned to give an F40-beating 155bhp per litre – and some 400bhp per ton. The V6's origins? TWR's XJR-10 and 11 Le Mans racers, which was said to be powered by an engine based on that of Rover's Metro 6R4 rally car. Power to the 220's huge back wheels was through a five-speed FF gearbox and a viscous limited-slip diff.

Despite fundamental changes beneath its stunning aluminium skin, the 220's shape, wind-tunnel-evolved to reduce drag and create ground-effect downforce, remained pretty faithful to the Keith Helfet original. So did the chassis's aluminium construction, using Alcan's riveting and bonding know-how. Despite the down-graded spec, the XJ220 was, in production guise, no stripped-for-action racer, witness its powered windows, air-conditioning, central locking, plush trim, even a CD player.

On the right road – ideally on a closed track – the 220's savage acceleration and sucked-to-the-road cornering powers were mind-blowing. Wide-eyed and incredulous, I first experienced them alongside Jaguar works driver John Nielsen at the Salzburgring, where 542bhp and 600lb of downforce (not to mention a driver who knew what he was doing) combined to make a memorably thrilling ride. When it was my turn in the hot seat, I found the car to be less intimidating and easier to drive than expected. Its limits were so high that no tyre was likely to approach them, let alone breach them. On the road the 220's huge girth, poor visibility and the raucous timbre of its noisy engine (awful when idling), tended to overshadow huge dynamic ability.

All production XJ220s, the first delivered in the summer of 1992, were built by JaguarSport, a joint Jaguar/TWR enterprise, at a purpose-built plant at Bloxham in rural Oxfordshire (later to become the home of Aston Martin's DB7). Production would not exceed 350 – once insufficient to meet global demand but in the end more than enough for those left in a dwindling queue. Depositors were eventually given the option either of walking away from their contract with another £50,000 payment, or driving away in a new XJ220 for another £100,000 – well below the original asking price. Of the 275 cars eventually completed at Bloxham, some languished unsold for years. It was a sad commercial end to a great technical triumph.

Specification	Jaguar XJ220 (1993)
Engine	3500cc, V6, 4ohc, 24V, twin turbos.
Engine layout	Mid, longitudinal
Power	542bhp at 7200rpm
Torque	475lb ft at 4500rpm
Gearbox	5-speed manual
Drive	Rear wheel
Front suspension	Double wishbones, coils, anti-roll bar
Rear suspension	Double wishbones, coils, anti-roll bar
Steering	Unassisted rack & pinion
Brakes	Ventilated discs all round, no ABS
Front wheels	Alloy 9Jx17
Rear wheels	14Jx18
Front tyres	255-45ZR17
Rear tyres	345-45ZR18
Length	4930mm
Width	2220mm
Height	1150mm
Wheelbase	2460mm
Weight	1450kg, 3197lb
0-60mph (97kph)	3.7sec
0-100mph (161kph)	8.0sec
Top speed	215mph, 346kph
Fuel consumption	9-16mpg

Jaguar XK8 & XKR

Spirits of the E-type

Sublime XKR convertible, powered by supercharged V8. Push-button hood weatherproof but stows untidily on rear deck ahead of joke 'seats'.

Had this book focused on sports cars of the Sixties, Jaguar's E-type – a peerless symbol of style and speed – would have been its star entry. The E's long-running successor, the XJS, was never so revered, but then it was a different sort of feline, more fat-cat GT than seminal sports.

So where does this leave the XJS's replacement, the XK8, its curvy looks inspired more by the sensuous E-type than the hard-edged XJS on which it was based? With its token rear seats and top-drawer refinement, the XK had, on the face of it, dubious sporting credentials. Any doubts about including it in this book were quickly dispelled, though. Of course it should be reviewed. Above all else the XK8 was a great drive. Besides, a sports car tome without a production Jaguar would be like Christmas without turkey.

Launched in the spring of 1996 as the first all-new Jaguar since the XJS in 1975 – and the first, too, under Ford's control – the sublime XK8 was aimed straight at the jugular of Merc's ageing SL series. And in the USA, at Lexus's SC400 coupé, too. First came the fixed-head (at Geneva, on the E-type's 35th anniversary) followed soon after by the convertible (in New York, just to emphasise the importance of the American market to a classy new Jaguar): the E-type (nearly 73,000 made) had sold well there, the XJS (over 112,000) even better. With Ford's marketing muscle behind it, the XK8 was destined to top them both.

Although the floorpan and inner structure were carried over from the XJS

Specification	Jaguar XKR (1999)
Engine	3996cc, V8, 4ohc, 32V, supercharger
Engine layout	Longitudinal, front
Power	370bhp at 6150rpm
Torque	387lb ft at 3600rpm
Gearbox	Five-speed auto
Drive	Rear wheel
Front suspension	Double wishbones, coils, adaptive damping, anti-roll bar
Rear suspension	Double wishbones, coils, adaptive damping, anti-roll bar
Steering	Assisted rack and pinion
Brakes	ABS-backed ventilated discs front and rear
Front wheels	Alloy 8Jx18
Rear wheels	Alloy 9Jx18
Front tyres	245-45ZR18
Rear tyres	255-45ZR18
Length	4760mm
Width	2015mm
Height	1305mm
Wheelbase	2588mm
Weight	1750kg (3858lb)
0-60mph (97kph)	5.2sec
0-100mph (161kph)	12.6sec
Top speed	155mph (250kph) (governed)
Fuel consumption	13-20mpg

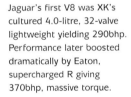

Jaguar's first V8 was XK's cultured 4.0-litre, 32-valve lightweight yielding 290bhp. Performance later boosted dramatically by Eaton, supercharged R giving 370bhp, massive torque.

– as they were by Ford-owned Aston Martin for the DB7 – the new Jag, stiffer than the old and constructed from fewer panels, was a lot more than a reskin, if not so radical as the stillborn F-type, killed off in 1991. Compared with the controversially angular XJS, which lacked the grace of a traditional Jaguar, the XK8 – penned in-house under the guidance of the late Geoff Lawson – looked wonderfully voluptuous, despite the unwanted legacy of a short wheelbase and a long rear overhang. Comparisons with AM's DB7, widely held to be a classic of aggressive elegance, were less favourable. Good though the slightly bloated Jag looked, the Aston – penned by Ian Callum (who was later to become Jaguar's styling chief) – looked even better. Just as well, then, that it cost considerably more.

Apart from wind-cheating curves and dashing good looks, largely free from chrome embellishment, the XK8 also boasted new double-wishbone suspension, speed-sensitive power steering and multiplex wiring. Capping all else, though, came a great new all-aluminium engine – Jaguar's (though not Daimler's) first V8, even though it was made at Ford's Bridgend plant. The days of Jaguar's total independence were gone for good – to the benefit, it has to be said, of build quality and production efficiency. No previous Jag had been quite so well made as the XK8, once initial teething troubles had been resolved.

The cultured engine – a 4.0-litre, 32-valve, quad-cam lightweight yielding 290bhp – was a cracker. So was the ZF five-speed automatic transmission mated to it. Electronically united, engine and 'box were in perfect harmony, each playing to the other's strengths – not least the engine's variable-cam phasing that ensured an even spread of meaty torque.

As in the XJS (except some very early ones) there was no manual alternative. But then Jag's J-gated selector (once known as Randle's Handle, after former engineering chief Jim Randle) gave keen drivers the option of arranging their own ratios in semi-DIY mode. Mind you, more satisfying

clutchless systems were soon to outrank it. Besides, eager responses and seamless shifts made the need for manual over-ride almost redundant.

The smooth, hushed engine's effortless delivery impressed rather more than its outright snort. Truth is, the regular XK8, with a relatively modest 175bhp per tonne, was no faster than a good E-type over 30 years its senior. Not much progress there. That all changed, mind, with the launch of the XKR derivative, powered by an Eaton-supercharged version of the 4.0 V8 engine yielding 370bhp – 80bhp more than the unblown XK8 – and 387lb ft of torque.

If the E-type was an embarrassment to the XK8, the XKR, with 210bhp per tonne, put the old-timer firmly in its place with acceleration times – 12.5 seconds to 100mph – that were now supercar quick. Jaguar claimed that the R would rocket from rest to its governed 155mph maximum in under 40 seconds – less than half the time it took the XK8. No-one was going to feel short-changed by the stonking performance of the R, Jaguar's fastest ever road car, discounting the XJ220.

As a two-time victim of total brake failure in an E-type, I can confirm that the anchors of Sir William Lyon's pride and joy of the Sixties were marginal in extremis. Not so those of the XK8/XKR, which, backed by a three-channel anti-lock system, were beyond reproach. Nor could the E-type, running on relatively skinny tyres, match its progeny's grip, brilliant in the steering and

Black cats. Elegant XK8, launched in '96, aimed at Merc SL. Based on floorpan of old XJS, new XK lacked drama of ancestral E-type. Comfort and refinement great strengths.

Acres of traditional polished timber and bovine hide in XK8's 'classic' interior. J-gate gear selector gives auto shifting to right, manual override to left. Twin airbags are standard equipment.

handling departments though it was for a car made in the Sixties.

Standard XK8s ran on 17in wheels, but 18in alternatives with wider, shallower tyres were also on offer. So was fancy adaptive damping that went under the contrived acronym of CATS (for Computer Active Technology Suspension). From my own experience of the XK8, I reckon most buyers would be more than happy with the base set-up. It did, after all, uphold Jaguar's reputation for maintaining ride comfort without diminishing the driving experience. Enjoyable though the XK8/XKR was to hustle through bends, nose-heaviness, not to mention considerable weight and girth, denied it supreme agility.

I had no complaints about the roomy-for-two cockpit, though some other reviewers thought it lacked adventurous style, despite (perhaps because of) lashings of traditional wood-and-hide decor. Comfort was a design priority for those up front, where they were cosseted – despite indifferent side support – by generous powered seats. The one-touch hood of the roadster was also fully powered. Pity it didn't furl out of sight beneath a rigid cover. In this respect the Jaguar gave best to Merc's much older SL, never mind the latest Porsche 911 cabriolet.

To mark Jaguar's controversial entry into Formula 1 (via the Stewart team that Ford bought), special-edition XKRs, fixed-head and convertible, hit the road in the spring of 2000. Badged Silverstones (before the mud-bath debacle of the April Grand Prix), they had XKR-sourced performance accessories – 20in BBS alloys, stiffer springs/dampers and uprated brakes, for instance – fitted as standard. Minor cosmetic uplifts adorned the cabin, too. The problem of weight (over 1,700kg), wasn't addressed. Nor were the Silverstones – which presaged an XK8/XKR facelift expected at the 2000 Paris Salon – given any more power. For 2001, Jaguar improved the XK series with ultrasonic sensing for the passenger's airbag, adaptive cruise control and new 12-way-adjustable seats.

XK180 & F-type

Jaguar's stunning XK180, inspired by (but not a pastiche of) its Le Mans-winning D-type, stole the 1998 Paris Salon. Alas, it was never destined for production. As a flag-waving exercise by Jaguar's Special Vehicle Operation (SVO) that built it, the XK180 was a technological showcase that doubled as a testbed for, among other things, the 450bhp 4.0 V8 that nestled under its long, louvred bonnet.

With a big boost in power came an appreciable reduction in weight. The wheelbase was shortened, all superfluous fat removed, and the Keith Helfet-designed body hand-crafted from aluminium. If not quite in the same league dynamically as the ill-fated XJ220 – also shaped by Helfet – the XK180 was as seriously fast and exciting as it was inaccessible. Huge 20in alloy wheels, mighty Brembo brakes and sequential push-button shifting pointed the way ahead for SVO – Jaguar's in-house fettling shop to which rich customers beat a path for really special Jaguars, particularly special XKs.

If there's a sequel to this book, Jaguar's compact F-type roadster – displayed as a concept teaser at the 2000 Detroit Motor Show – will surely be one of its stars. While the XK180 was never more than a one-off indulgence, the F-type above was almost certainly destined for production, given favourable public reaction. And the Helfet-styled show car certainly got that.

Jaguar estimated that there was a global market for cars in the Merc SLK/Porsche Boxster class of 200,000 sales annually. The F-type, spiritual successor to the magical E-type, would be launched into this market sector. On the tasty menu were lightweight construction, a choice of engines (topped by a supercharged V8), and six-speed transmission. But don't hold your breath. When this was written in 2000, the F-type was still years away from production.

Jensen S-V8

Renaissance of a classic

Ford's ubiquitous 4.6-litre, 32-valve V8, as used in Mustang Cobra, powers S-V8, upholding Jensen tradition of employing American muscle. Drives rear through five-speed gearbox.

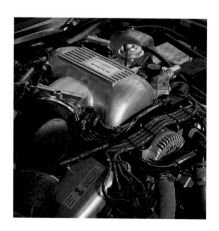

Welcome, Jensen. Good to have you back. Although the new S-V8, first seen as a prototype at the 1998 NEC British Motor Show – and again, in updated form, at the '99 London show – wasn't yet in production when this was written, all the elements necessary for Jensen's renaissance were in place, not least the multi-million-pound funding (much of it from private investors) and a Merseyside plant. Jensen's target was to make 300 cars in the first year, 600 annually thereafter, sold through a select group of dealers with an equity stake in Jensen Motors.

The first car to bear the name of the Jensen brothers – Richard and Alan were keen petrolheads as well as coachbuilders in the Twenties and Thirties – was a Ford V8-powered luxury tourer built in 1937. Hollywood heart-throb Clark Gable is said to have owned one. As it happens, the latest Jensen is Ford V8-powered, too.

Under the aluminium bonnet of the S-V8, driving the rear wheels through a five-speed Borg Warner T45 manual gearbox, was the Mustang Cobra's ubiquitous 4.6, 32-valve, quad-cam yielding 325bhp – several times as much as its plodding side-valve precursor. The Cobra V8, incidentally, is not mass-made. Its blocks and heads are cast by the Italian company Teksid (who also cast aluminium bits for Ferrari) and the engine is assembled (and signed) by a two-man team.

Like most Jensens of the intervening years – the Austin-powered 541, the

94

Specification	Jensen S-V8 (2000)
Engine	4601cc, V8, dohc, 32V,
Engine layout	Longitudinal, front
Power	325bhp at 5800rpm
Torque	300lb ft at 4800rpm
Gearbox	Five-speed manual
Drive	Rear wheel
Front suspension	Double wishbones, coils,
Rear suspension	Double wishbones, coils,
Steering	Assisted rack and pinion
Brakes	Ventilated discs all round
Front wheels	Alloy 7.5x17
Rear wheels	Alloy 8.5x18
Front tyres	225-45ZR17
Rear tyres	245-45ZR17
Length	4165mm
Width	1757mm
Height	1278mm
Wheelbase	2400mm
Weight	1200kg (2645lb) approx
0-60mph (97kph)	4.8sec (est)
0-100mph (161kph)	13sec (est)
Top speed	155mph (250kph) (governed)
Fuel consumption	15-22mpg (est)

ugly CV8 and the Vignale-styled Interceptor – the S-V8 was not short on power. Nor was it lacking in individuality or style: a bland Jensen would have been a failed Jensen. Ditto one without great presence and a fine sense of occasion. In looking the part of a classy roadster, the S-V8 crossed its first big hurdle before turning a wheel.

Seen as a contemporary classic that's true to its heritage – in other words a modern interpretation of past Jensens – the S-V8 was the brainchild of Keith Rauer and Robin Bowyer, owners and joint managing directors of the Creative Group, specialists in design, tooling and production techniques for the car industry. Because of Redditch-based Creative's track record of seeing a design proposal through development into production, expectations of the S-V8's ability and performance ran high. Why not? The people behind Jensen's revival, not least chairman Graham Morris, formerly boss of Rolls-Royce, have impeccable credentials.

The new car was based on a welded steel-sheet, box-frame chassis carrying aluminium bodywork styled by Design Q – the company of ex-Jaguar designers Howard Guy and Gary Doy, working within Creative's premises. Between its show appearances, the S-V8 acquired light-coloured slats to soften the black-hole prominence of the front grille.

With 325bhp to propel around 1,250kg, Jensen were predicting a sub-5-second 0-60mph time and a top speed governed to 155mph. Wide-based, all-wishbone suspension – metal jointed on the prototypes in the interests of pin-sharp responses, uncorrupted by rubber bushing – promised fine handling and grip. So did the development input of Derek Gardner (designer of Tyrell's six-wheeled F1 car) and Martin Stretton (who raced one).

Half-leather trim for the plush and roomy cockpit was listed as standard equipment in early sales literature. Active damping, air-conditioning, GPS navigation, powered seats and a hardtop were options.

Jensen

Finish and equipment of lush cockpit places S-V8 at luxury end of sports car market. Early sales literature listed active damping, air-con and sat-nav as options.

Lamborghini

Lamborghini
Diablo

Hot and hellish

The devil incarnate. Dramatic
Diablo in its final Audi-
influenced 6.0-litre VT form is
ultimate head-turner. Lines
cleaned up but great girth
and restricted visibility still
deter everyday use.

When it comes to devilish things, to outrageous excess, few cars can match
Lamborghini's fearsome flagship. Consider the limited-edition, race-bred
GT of the late Nineties – the craziest, wildest, fastest Diablo of them all.
Playing the numbers game, how about 6.0 litres, 12 cylinders, 48 valves and
570bhp for starters? For the main course, try four-wheel drive (but,
surprisingly, only five manual gears), 0-100mph in under 9 seconds, and a
top speed comfortably in excess of 200mph. Oh yes, and a price tag
nudging £200,000 – cheap compared with McLaren's defunct F1 (from
which the Diablo GT contentiously inherited the title of world's fastest road
car), but a tad pricey even for a Latin exotic.

The Diablo was launched in 1980 as an evolution of the crazy Countach,
progeny of the bad but beautiful Miura. I never took to the outrageously
noisy and uncomfortable Miura. And the Countach that I once thrashed
around Scotland I loathed as passionately as I loved. The performance,
demented wail and tenacious grip were memorably uplifting, the awful
visibility, crackpot driving position and hellish heat distressing. Air-
conditioning partially resolved the sticky-shirt problem, but the Diablo
otherwise carried on where the Countach left off. If Ferrari's wildest was
not wild enough, the Devil from the one-time tractor-maker probably was.

As the thrust of this book is towards open cars, let's focus briefly on what

96

Specification	Lamborghini Diablo ('95)
Engine	5703cc, V12, 4ohc, 48V
Engine layout	Longitudinal, mid
Power	492bhp at 6900rpm
Torque	428lb ft at 5200rpm
Gearbox	Five-speed manual
Drive	All-wheel
Front suspension	Double wishbones, coils, anti-roll bar
Rear suspension	Double wishbones, coils, anti-roll bar
Steering	Assisted rack and pinion
Brakes	Ventilated discs all round, no ABS
Front wheels	Alloy 8.5Jx17
Rear wheels	Alloy 13Jx17
Front tyres	235-40ZR17
Rear tyres	335-35ZR17
Length	4460mm
Width	2040mm
Height	1105mm
Wheelbase	2650mm
Weight	1650kg (3638lb)
0-60mph (97kph)	5.0sec
0-100mph (161kph)	11.0sec
Top speed	202mph (325kph)
Fuel consumption	12-18mpg

at the time was the world's fastest four-wheel-drive convertible – the Diablo roadster of the mid-Nineties. Going topless did nothing for the appearance of a car so bizarre that it looked in profile like a squashed pick-up. Marcello Gandini has created prettier shapes. Convertible? Well, not really. Above your head was a large, lightweight panel held in place by four catches. Manual labour was required to release them and heave the lid back to an alternative position above the rear deck. No push-button operation here, despite the £175,000 price tag. By all accounts Lamborghini's efforts to preserve the structure's integrity – in short, to prevent the shakes – were singularly successful.

Decapitation did more than expose your scalp to a violent slipstream. It also amplified the glorious wail of the magnificent 492bhp V12 engine. Devilish indeed. Deploying so much power was never a problem with Lambo's all-wheel-drive VT (viscous traction) transmission. Normally, only the back wheels were driven. Any hint of slip, though, and torque – up to 30 per cent of it – was transferred by VT to the front wheels. So far so good. The trouble with all-wheel drive, however, is that it increases weight and frictional losses. Add tall gearing to the equation, and the Diablo's less than sensational off-the-line acceleration – inferior to that of a Lotus Esprit V8, just to get things into perspective – was easily explained. Still, 0-100mph in 10 seconds isn't bad going for a five-speed heavyweight.

Audi's stewardship and influence made the last incarnation of the Diablo – 6.0 litres, 550bhp, 475lb ft, four-wheel drive – the best made (and most desirable) of a series that came to epitomise gross excess. Without

Exotic V12 of 2000 Diablo far cry from Lamborghini's preceding tractors. Race-bred engine develops 550bhp from 6.0 litres, drives all four wheels. Top speed said to exceed 200mph.

World's fastest four-wheel-drive convertible? Awkward-looking Diablo Roadster of mid-Nineties had clumsy roof panel, manipulated manually despite car's £175,000 price.

diminishing the car's visual impact, various appendages were sliced away, all the better to appreciate Gandini's original shovel-nosed masterpiece. Rigidity was improved (and a little weight saved) by introducing carbon-fibre to the body structure, never mind to the redesigned cabin as symbolic decoration. Although still very heavy, the 6.0 had awesome acceleration and a top speed of over 200mph, making it the world's fastest production car, post-McLaren F1.

Would Audi's cool Teutonic approach smother the Diablo's burning Latin passion? Seems not. The last of the great supercars was none the worse for a host of Audi-instigated improvements – classier cabin, more comfortable driving position, improved air-conditioning, wider front track, fettled suspension, refined exhaust and so on. No, the Diablo's swansong was its finest hour.

Light Car Company
Rocket

Minimalist with the most

Tiny Rocket street-legal racer with exposed wheels and suspension, carbon-fibre sprayguards. Passenger sits squashed up behind driver.

It was well-named, the Rocket. Perhaps the most focused firebrand of all time, it was designed for but one purpose: fast entertainment. Arriving in a Rocket was almost an anti-climax, despite the interest it would arouse. The adrenaline rush came while getting there. According to its makers, The Light Car Company, this diminutive demon was not so much a means of transport as 'pure driving pleasure'.

The brainchild of racer Chris Craft, accomplished Le Mans ace, and Gordon Murray, the man behind some of McLaren's most successful Formula 1 single-seaters (and later its fabulous 230mph F1 supercar), the

Rocket was up-yours daring in its singular approach to performance through minimalism. The figure uppermost in Murray's mind was the one that related power to weight – 360bhp per tonne, as it turned out.

As a funster, first and foremost, the Rocket was as short on civility and space as it was strong on performance and grip. There were no doors, hood, boot, heater or

Specification	Light Car Company Rocket (1992)
Engine	1002cc, 4-cylinder, dohc, 20V
Engine layout	Transverse, mid
Power	143bhp at 10,500rpm
Torque	77lb ft at 8500rpm
Gearbox	Five-speed manual with two-speed axle
Drive	Rear wheel
Front suspension	Double wishbones, coils
Rear suspension	Double wishbones, coils
Steering	Unassisted rack & pinion
Brakes	Unassisted drilled discs all round, ventilated at front
Wheels	Alloy 6Jx15
Tyres	195-50VR15 (no spare)
Length	3645mm
Width	1580mm
Height	950mm
Wheelbase	2400mm
Weight	400kg (882lb)
0-60mph (97kph)	5.0sec
0-100mph (161kph)	12.5sec
Top speed	135mph (217kph)
Fuel consumption	28-37mpg

Yamaha superbike engine in tail had four cylinders, 20 valves, 143bhp. Rev limit was sky-high 11,500rpm.

conventional trim. Not even a fuel gauge or a proper windscreen; you drove at your peril without helmet and visor. The bare-boned cockpit, reduced to essentials, carried only one proper seat, centrally mounted in a torpedo-shaped glass-fibre body wrapped around a classy spaceframe chassis. Your intimate passenger, brave soul, rode 'pillion', legs akimbo, staring at the anorak ahead, as on a motorcycle. Rockets were best ridden solo.

The sobriquet 'four-wheeled superbike' was worn with some conviction. Seating apart, the Rocket was powered by a peaky, power-mad, four-cylinder, 20-valve Yamaha engine that whacked 143bhp to the back wheels through a sharp, multi-plate clutch and a special Weismann transmission that mated five-speed box with two-speed transaxle. Result, 10 forward gears (and five in reverse), selected by a one-back, four-forward switch-like lever. In the lower range, the Rocket would sprint with a demented 11,500rpm scream to 60mph in under 5 seconds. In the upper one it would exceed 140mph, if you could withstand the mechanical mayhem. For a car of such performance, economy was remarkably good. And just as well, as the fuel tank was puny.

To emphasise its racing roots, the beautifully made Rocket had exposed wheels and see-how-it-works front suspension (a classic coil-and-wishbone arrangement). So intimately did the black carbon-fibre sprayguards hug the low-profile tyres that you could barely see them through the camouflage. It needed little imagination to see in the Rocket an F1 Cooper, Jack Brabham's head cocked to one side. Not that there's anything retro about its design.

Light weight (a mere 400kg, which is half the weight of a mini hatchback), was the key to scorching performance. Ditto telepathic handling like that of no previous road car. Pre-Rocket, Caterham's Seven was about the ultimate in agility. Post-Rocket, even the former Lotus felt a mite clumsy. As *Autocar* put it in 1992: 'The Rocket elevates driving to an altogether higher and more exhilarating plane beyond the reach of even the extraordinary Seven.'

So why did the Rocket not endure? How come it never outsold the Caterham Seven? In a word: price. In another: impracticality. At just under £40,000 in 1992, the Rocket was a horrendously expensive toy costing twice as much as Caterham's Seven HPC, which was almost as quick and miles more practical. Commercially, the Rocket barely recorded a blip in motoring history. Dynamically, it was one of the highlights of the Nineties.

Lotus Elan

Heroic failure

Front-drive Elan radical departure for Lotus. Car very wide in relation to length, giving appearance of squat cockleshell. Cornering powers high, handling friendly but rather uninvolving.

Colin Chapman, founder of Lotus, would probably not have endorsed the second-generation Elan. Launched seven years after his death, it hardly conformed with the maestro's edict about keeping things light and simple. Chapman was driving Lotus firmly up-market, away from the low-cost, low-profit sportsters that were the company's roots, when he was persuaded to develop a Toyota-powered sportster (the stillborn M90), cast in the mould of the original front-engined, rear-drive Elan.

It was not until after Chapman's death in 1982 that front-wheel drive was mooted at Lotus's think-tank. Anticipating that many buyers would be trading up from their GTis, post-Chapman Lotus reasoned that the market was ready for a FWD roadster. Although it had never before made such a car, it understood the nuances of 'puller' technology from consultancy work undertaken for clients.

While the logic was sound, Lotus knew that it was taking a gamble in denying traditionalists indulgent rear-wheel-drive play. Much soul-searching took place at Hethel before a decision was reached. Lotus assured pre-launch sceptics that the Elan would be as much fun to drive as it would be user-friendly. Protecting occupants would be a design priority.

Following the demise of M90, attention switched to the FWD X100, born under the regime of BCA's David Wickens and killed under the following GM one. These were troubled times for the roller-coasting Lotus, destabilised by frequent changes of ownership.

Dissatisfied with the X100 package as well, MD Mike Kimberley replaced it in 1986 with the GM-blessed M100 – a clean-sheet FWD design scheduled to go public in 1989. It did, as the Elan, at London's October

100

Specification	Lotus Elan SE (1991)
Engine	1588cc, 4-cylinder, dohc, 16V, turbocharger
Engine layout	Transverse, front
Power	165bhp at 6600rpm
Torque	148lb ft at 4200rpm
Gearbox	Five-speed manual
Drive	Front wheel
Front suspension	Double wishbones, coils, anti-roll bar
Rear suspension	Double wishbones, coils, anti-roll bar
Steering	Assisted rack and pinion
Brakes	Discs all round, ventilated at front
Wheels	Alloy 6.5Jx15
Tyres	205-50ZR15
Length	3085mm
Width	1735mm
Height	1230mm
Wheelbase	2250mm
Weight	1020kg (2249lb)
0-60mph (97kph)	6.6sec
0-100mph (161kph)	17.7sec
Top speed	138mph (222kph)
Fuel consumption	23-31mpg

Motorfair, fulfilling Kimberley's ambition to see a small, open two-seater Lotus once more. The press clamoured. A star was born. Or was it? Doubts were to temper early enthusiasm.

The new Elan was very different from its smaller, rear-drive progenitor. Exceptional torsional rigidity, necessary to maintain accurate suspension geometry (never mind to stop the scuttle from shaking), was achieved through a complex chassis built around a traditional steel backbone strengthened by a bonded composite platform. Rear suspension – upper links and lower wishbones – was like that of the Excel. The coil and wishbone front suspension, however, incorporated patented Lotus tweaks that gave very precise wheel control while maintaining the compliance needed to minimise harshness. This was achieved by mounting the stiffly bushed 'interactive' wishbones on a separate aluminium 'raft'. Another advantage was that torque steer – corrupting steering wheel tug that marred many FWD cars – was virtually eliminated.

Power came from a Lotus-developed four-cylinder twin-cam made by Isuzu, GM's Japanese subsidiary. Keep-it-in-the-family nepotism? No doubt, but the engine – particularly the turbocharged SE that everyone wanted – served the Elan well, even though the lighter Elan Sprint of the Seventies was almost as quick. Some reviewers contended that Isuzu's sweet-running 1.6 – a gem by any standards – was the car's best feature, so crisply and effortlessly did it deliver 165bhp through an end-on five-speed gearbox. What's more, it was reliable – and reliability was crucial. While Lotus was determined to dispel its reputation for shoddy build quality with the Elan, it still allowed into production a leaky hood supported by an unsightly metal

GM ownership of Lotus influenced decision to use 'in-house' Isuzu engine. Turbocharged version sweet and lively, arguably Elan's best feature. Delivers effortless 165bhp.

Wide cockpit conservatively mainstream in design and decor. Instruments neatly clustered, switchgear sound, gearchange a gem. Series 2 cars have better hood, firmer damping, less power.

frame, and doors that failed to shut with a satisfying clunk.

Not everyone was enthusiastic about the car's tubby styling, the work of Peter Stevens, who had brilliantly reskinned the Esprit. The Elan's odd dimensions – short in wheelbase but unusually wide – gave rise to a cockleshell appearance that tended to polarise opinions. To my eyes, the car looked pert and pretty from the side, but bulbously pregnant head on. Aerodynamic stability was the main concern during wind-tunnel development, which is why the Elan's hood-up drag factor was an indifferent 0.35 (and far worse al fresco).

Although the bathtub cockpit was quite roomy – and boot space generous – there was nothing uplifting, nothing charismatic about its design and decor. The oh-so-conventional dash could have come from any mainstream hatchback. Ditto the seats, switchgear and orange-on-black instruments. It was ergonomically sound, pleasing to the eye and nicely finished – GM saw to it that the Elan was the best-made Lotus to date – but where was the flair and inspiration? It was in the radical chassis, that's where.

The Elan was a sensation to drive. Sceptical hacks (me among them) attending the first press drive at Lotus's Hethel headquarters revelled in the car's scorching performance, impeccable composure, brilliant handling, rock-solid stability and astonishing grip. It was, without question, the world's best-handling FWD car – Alfa Romeo used it as the benchmark for its GTV/Spider twins – and it covered ground more quickly than most super-exotics with twice as much power. What's more, it did so while smoothing away bumps with supple suspension.

As Lotus testers had promised, the car was super-friendly even when driven close to its high limits. And there, perversely, lay the flaw. 'Lotus has denied the car the sort of wristy, telepathic wieldiness of its predecessor, never mind the Mazda MX-5,' I wrote in March 1990. It was a view echoed by most of the hard-driving tearaways from the specialist press. Great car, they all agreed. Pity it's so uninvolving, so characterless.

Even if the Elan had been a paragon of perfection, fate would have been no kinder to it. Lotus had geared up to make 3,000 cars a year, so when demand fell short of plan the company began stockpiling cars – and the bottom-line went red. A world-wide recession, compounded by the introduction of a luxury tax in the US, were blamed for the sad debacle. While outside forces beyond Lotus's control helped to scupper the tricky-to-make Elan, high development and production costs also contributed to its demise. Lotus's most sophisticated sports car deserved a better fate.

Elan's wide stance better for stability than looks. Korea's Kia version, below, was never sold in UK.

GM could have baled out its loss-making subsidiary from the petty cash tin, but it didn't. After 30 months production was halted at number 3,857 – and the Elan was no more. No more, that is, until its reincarnation 18 months later, this time under the wing of Romano Artioli's doomed Bugatti, purchasers of punch-drunk Lotus from GM in 1993. The world's biggest car-maker, which had sunk £36 million into the Elan, had had enough of its troubled minnow.

Colin Chapman may not have approved of the Elan, but he'd have applauded the opportunism behind its resurrection. With 'free' tooling and 800 crated Isuzu powertrains to use up, Lotus developed a Series 2 limited-edition car that addressed many of the original's shortcomings, such as they were. It had a better hood, firmer damping, more communicative steering, larger wheels, lower-profile rubber, a crisper gearchange, a new wiring loom – all told, the S2 embraced about a hundred changes.

Among them was a cat-cleaned exhaust, by now obligatory. While exhaust rasp was up slightly, all the better for aural stimulation, power was down by about 10bhp. Although performance suffered – the 0-100mph time increased by about 4 seconds – the S2 handled and gripped even better, prompting demand for suspension upgrades from S1 owners.

The stopgap S2 was a nice little earner for cash-strapped Lotus while it developed the Elan's successor, the mid-engined Elise. Although Lotus's affair with front-wheel drive was short-lived and controversial, its legacy was nearly 5,000 durable, easy-to-drive sports cars that hold their value exceptionally well. The Elan may have its critics, but owners love 'em.

The Kia connection

One resurrection is unusual, two must be unique. The third coming of the front-drive Lotus resulted from the purchase by Korea's Kia of the defunct Elan's manufacturing rights, production line and tooling. Rocky Lotus, going through one of its most troubled periods, needed the cash. Kia wanted the kudos of a pedigree sports car, especially for its Pacific rim market. So a deal was done. Trouble is, in the metamorphosis from Lotus to Kia, the Elan lost some of its magic and breeding.

The turbocharged Isuzu powertrain gave way to a normally aspirated, Mazda-derived 1.8 in-house unit of adequate (151bhp) rather than exciting performance. In the interests of rationalisation, various components – rear lights, steering wheel, switchgear, instruments and so on – were swapped for Kia ones. Cosmetic tweaks included sharpening the bonnet line and extending the front bumper.

On copy-cat Minilite wheels, raised suspension and Korean tyres, the new Elan didn't steer, grip, brake or handle quite so well as the old one. 'Anyone expecting the Kia to replicate the driving manners of the Lotus Elan will be at best disappointed and at worst shocked by the way this car behaves...' So said *Autocar* in July 1997, anticipating that sales would soon start in the UK at prices well below those of the S2 Elan. They never did. The Kia Sport (called an Elan only in Korea) was never made with right-hand drive and therefore never exported to its spiritual home.

And just as well, perhaps. In Britain, all Elans remain real Elans.

Lotus

Lotus Elise

The sports car **redefined**

Inspired Elise returned Lotus to its roots. Chunkily styled, mid-engined and very light, Elise huge success as seat-of-the-pants entertainer. Minimal creature comforts, hood joke.

Colin Chapman may not have endorsed the overweight, underwhelming front-drive Elan, but the following Elise, launched at the 1995 Frankfurt show, would surely have won his approval. Small, light, imaginative, innovative and focused, the mid-engined Elise, spartan but speedy, proved that Lotus hadn't lost its touch, that the spirit of Chapman, who died before the car was a glimmer in anyone's eye, lived on.

Chapman's minimalist philosophy was brilliantly espoused by the Elise, which took Lotus back to its roots while eschewing the retro route to stardom. The Elise was a watershed in Lotus's history – in the history of the sports car, come to that, even though hard-nosed economics dictated a lesser proprietary powertrain than that used in the controversial Elan.

Lotus's traditional backbone chassis (which in the original Elan provided no side-impact protection whatsoever) was ditched. In came instead a state-of-the-art monocoque designed by Richard Rackham. Built by Hydro Aluminium in Denmark, it consisted of

Specification	Lotus Elise 111S (2000)
Engine	1796cc, 4-cylinder, dohc, 16V
Engine layout	Transverse, mid
Power	143bhp at 7000rpm
Torque	128lb ft at 4500rpm
Gearbox	Five-speed manual
Drive	Rear wheel
Front suspension	Double wishbones, coils
Rear suspension	Double wishbones, coils
Steering	Unassisted rack & pinion
Brakes	Ventilated discs all round
Front wheels	Alloy 5.5Jx15
Rear wheels	Alloy 7.5Jx16
Front tyres	185-55ZR15
Rear tyres	225-45ZR16
Length	3725mm
Width	1820mm
Height	1200mm
Wheelbase	2300mm
Weight	770kg (1698lb)
0-60mph (97kph)	5.5sec
0-100mph (161kph)	15.0sec
Top speed	132mph (212kph)
Fuel consumption	20-32mpg

aluminium extrusions (think of them as beams squeezed out of a shaped nozzle) bonded together (yes, glued) to form a structure even stiffer – and very much simpler – than that of the committee-designed Elan. The Elise programme, headed by Tony Shute, encouraged individual flair.

Apart from providing a flex-free, weld-free structure for the suspension – basically classic coil-and-wishbone all round but with Lotus magic thrown in – the tub-like chassis, weighing a mere 68kg, afforded excellent crash protection. Comparisons were inevitably made with Renault's contemporary aluminium-based Sport Spider, which even without windscreen weighed 930kg. That the Elise tipped the scales at an anorexic 700kg explains its dynamic superiority over the Renault with less power.

Lotus aimed to make the Elise as predictably user-friendly as the Elan, but without the personality by-pass that flawed the front-drive car. The Elise was to be a seat-of-the-pants entertainer, a communicative companion that rewarded the skilled without punishing the inept. The rear-biased weight distribution of a mid-engined configuration helped here. So did rear-wheel drive (what else?) and a wide track. What elevated the Elise to another plane, though, was the detail design of its suspension. Soft springs, stiff dampers, low roll centres, restricted camber changes, low castor and kingpin inclination...getting these and other variables spot-on through a combination of inspiration and hard-graft trial-and-error testing are what made the Elise extraordinary.

It didn't end there. There was no need to assist the quick steering as the modestly shod front wheels were lightly laden and took little effort to swivel. No PAS, no steering corruption, no dulling down of feel. By the same token, no servo, no sloppy brake pedal to activate the cool-running, fade-free aluminium disc brakes (later to give way to conventional steel ones with a consequent increase in unsprung weight). By doing away with both steering pump and brake booster, Lotus saved on cost and weight.

Slung transversely behind the cockpit was Rover's respected (and reliable) 1.8 dohc twin-cam four, as used in lesser versions of the MGF (a much heavier car that was not nearly so lively) mated to a five-speed manual gearbox operated by a central lever through cables. The F's more powerful VVC engine (variable valve control) Rover at first kept to itself. Three years elapsed before the Elise got it as well.

Julian Thomson's in-house design team beat off some worthy opposition (including Zagato, IDEA and Peter Stevens, who had shaped the Elan) in the competition to style the Elise – named, incidentally, after a niece of Romano Artoli, boss at the time of Lotus-owning Bugatti. It was a lucky coincidence that the name began with an E, as in Elite, Elan, Europa, Esprit and Excel: quite fortuitously was a tradition upheld.

In the beginning the Elise's styling was not greeted with universal acclaim. Critics (me among them) thought it looked unimaginative, even kit-car-ish. Seen on the road, though, the Elise captured hearts with its muscular prettiness. What's more, the finish of its composite body panels, none of them load bearing (facilitating a partial or total reskin in the future), withstood close scrutiny.

In the interests of lightness and purity of purpose, the low-slung cockpit – difficult to access over wide crash-protecting side sills – was stripped of all unnecessary cosmetic embellishment, even of soundproofing. Why cover up beautiful anodised aluminium? Simple though it was, the cockpit

No superfluous decoration in bare-bone cockpit. Elise at its entertaining best open to the wind on twisty secondaries that exercise brilliant handling. Later cars more comfortable.

Lotus

Rover K-series twin-cam 16-valve engine mounted transversely in lightweight chassis. Output up to 200bhp, according to state of tune. Even base car quick, with 0-60mph in 5.5 sec.

heightened the sense of drama when clambering aboard. The arm's-length steering wheel was specially made. Ditto the thin, fixed-back seats (more supportive than they looked and later padded up), gear knob and gorgeous pedals – also exquisite aluminium extrusions, not hunks of bent iron. The narrow strip dash, stark in its elegant simplicity, was viewed from a driving position that was spot-on for long-limbed drivers, if not short ones.

Creature comforts? Not many. This, remember, was a driving machine, not family transport. Wind-up windows scraped into the specification. So did a joke hood. Oh yes, and there was a very powerful heater for those who liked to drive al fresco in winter. Is there another way? Luggage space was confined to a small well aft of the engine.

On the move, you tapped into a rich seam of raw entertainment. Lotus aimed to improve on the benchmark Caterham Seven's handling, while also smoothing out the ride. It succeeded magnificently. Responding eagerly to light and delicate inputs – this was no car for the clumsy – the Elise vividly communicated to sensitive hands (and backsides), drawing you into the action as surely as a mainstream Japanese hatchback distanced you from it. It was not just amazing agility and grip that rewarded press-on driving. It was also the total involvement, the feeling of being a component part of a car that seemed to skim the ground, its supple suspension shrugging aside surface irregularities.

Considering the modest powertrain, performance of the regular Elise was surprisingly strong. The secret? A power-to-weight ratio of 163bhp per tonne. While there was nothing special about top-end acceleration, blunted by an indifferent drag factor, pick-up to the legal limit of 70mph was sparkling, witness a 0-60mph time of 5.5 seconds. Pity that the exhaust note did not convey more aural excitement – a disappointment addressed in the raspier Sport 135, of which more later. The sloppy gearchange came in for some mild criticism, too. Objectively, the brakes were up to the job. Subjectively, they failed to match the feeling of invincibility conferred by the anchors of some rival sports pedigrees.

Lotus hit the spot with the Elise. It was the car that serious enthusiasts really wanted and clamoured to get. What's more, it was not crazily expensive. Running costs were quite modest, too, the fuel consumption up to about 30mpg. Keenly priced at £18,950 in July 1996 – about the same as the MGF 1.8 VVC – many early ones fell into the hands of speculators interested only in turning a quick profit. Premiums of several thousand pounds above list were asked for – and given.

So successful was the Elise that production forecasts were revised

upwards (to around 3,000 a year) and plans for an extended V6 Coupé dropped. During the course of normal development, Lotus addressed some of the original car's weaknesses – seats, hood, window operation, rattles – making later versions even better.

Quick though it was, the 118bhp Elise cried out for greater power. Ignoring the 190bhp track-only VHPD racer, launched in March 1998, the first listed upgrade was the limited-edition, metallic-silver Sport 135, its Rover engine tweaked to give 135bhp. The interim Sport's package included a terrific short-shift, close-ratio gearbox, sports seats with more padding, and lowered suspension. Larger front discs – cast iron now, not aluminium – and wider 225/45 rear tyres were thrown in, too. While the Elise's fabled ride suffered, and the hike in performance was relatively modest, handling, grip and entertainment soared to new heights.

Three years on from its launch the Elise finally got the engine that everyone wanted – Rover's acclaimed K-series 1.8 VVC, its variable valve timing boosting top-end power without seriously compromising flexibility. Also on the menu for the 111S were close-ratio gears and a lower final drive to make the most of the engine's 7,000rpm limit.

Disappointingly, the 111S, priced at £29,000 in March 1999, was no quicker to 60mph from rest than the standard car, which had shorter getaway gearing. Slug it out in fourth or fifth, and the S was actually slower. The peaky nature of the engine meant using the gears to the full and keeping the revs up. Then, and only then, did the 130mph S display any worthwhile advantage in straight-line speed. Still, many reviewers questioned whether a couple of seconds off the 0-100mph time (now under 15 seconds) was worth such a hefty price premium, even though it did include bespoke Pirelli 225/45 P-Zero rear tyres (the fronts were unchanged), a ducktail rear wing (said to give downforce), six-spoke alloy wheels, carbon-fibre dash trim and better seats – by now fitted to all Elises.

Exige – a racer for the road

The anticipated road-legal version of the competition Elise broke cover in the spring of 2000 as the Exige (above). Great car, pity about the name. Although wilder than either of the two previous limited-edition roadies (the 135 and the 160), the Exige – a fixed-head coupé, not a roadster – was not quite so radical or uncouth as the Sport racer that spawned it. The front apron/splitter assembly, for instance, was raised to a more sensible ramp-avoiding height, and the rear wing reduced in size to maintain aerodynamic balance, not to mention conformity with the law.

Lotus also stuck to a conventional two-abreast seating plan, rejecting the trackster's central solo arrangement as too impractical. Besides, show-off owners would want to share the Exige experience with a passenger, wouldn't they? To improve visibility aft, there was a see-through polycarbonate rear roof panel that doubled as a hatch to the diminished boot.

Creating downforce didn't significantly increase drag, witness the claimed top speed of nearly 140mph. A snorkel air intake atop the roof fed air to a tweaked version of Rover's regular 1.8 twin-cam, not the variable-cam job: Lotus found the extra urge – 179bhp rising to 200bhp, according to tune – through conventional means. Bulging wheelarches accommodated wider alloy wheels carrying bespoke Yokohama rubber – 225/45 at the back – all the better to despatch the bendy bits on fettled suspension tuned for road and track. The lightweight Exige (0-100mph in a claimed 12.3 seconds) went on sale in the summer of 2000 at just under £33,000, distancing it from Vauxhall's upcoming VX220 to be made at the same Hethel site.

The popularity of the Elise and its derivatives can be gauged from the 3,164 cars Lotus made in '99. Sometime during 2000, total production exceeded 10,000.

P58 OAH

Lotus Esprit

The evergreen geriatric

Effective mid-life reskin gave Esprit, launched '75, new lease of life. Of many iterations, 240bhp GT3 one of best.

The Esprit was never made by Lotus as a convertible, though bespoke soft-top conversions exist. No-one, though, would challenge the credentials of Lotus's long-serving flagship as a pedigree sports car. When this book went to press, 24 years on from the Esprit's launch in 1976, the evergreen Lotus was still the fastest, most expensive model in Hethel's line-up. Still its sporting superstar.

To trace its lineage we need to rewind to 1972, to the Giugiaro-styled, Europa-based concept exercise that appeared at the Turin show that year. As a result of favourable feedback, dream car became real car three years later when the productionised Esprit, its screen less acutely raked than that of the showpiece (but otherwise a pretty faithful replica), was previewed at the 1975 Paris Salon.

Whereas the superseded Europa had rather ungainly 'bread van' lines, its wedge-shaped, shovel-nosed successor, penned for Lotus by Giugiaro's Ital Design, was fashionably angular, and striking with it. As with so many two-seater coupés, it was a case of looks before practicality: poor rear visibility, gruesome packaging and a girth that bordered on the obese were always to dog the Esprit in close-quarter driving. But who's complaining? Ferrari-challenging presence was what counted here, and the Esprit always had that in spades.

Like most of its siblings, the Esprit was based on a stiff, steel backbone chassis, not properly rust-proofed (by galvanisation) until 1980. It was dramatically clothed in GRP bodywork that had a top and a bottom – hence the prominent waistline where the two met in the middle.

Power came from Lotus's own Type 907 2.0-litre, 16-valve, twin-cam, as used in (and debugged by) the Jensen Healey, never mind the world championship-winning Sunbeam Lotus rally car. Expediently evolved from the light-alloy block of a Vauxhall Victor (the last all-new car Vauxhall designed before the UK wing of GM turned to badge-engineered Opels), the 907 had humble roots. It just so happened that Vauxhall's slant-four, which allowed a low bonnet line and the possibility of a doubled-up V8, was exactly what Lotus also had in mind, right down to the bore centres. The evolution of this tough, simple, naturally aspirated engine, mated to a Citroën-Maserati SM five-speed gearbox (and very nice too), is the story of the four-cylinder Esprit.

First came the raw S1 that handled and gripped as a Lotus should, but didn't perform as swiftly as claimed, according to press tests. The revised S2 (Speedline wheels, integrated airdam, intakes aft of the rear windows) spawned the lovely black and gold limited-edition JPS specials that commemorated Mario Andretti's F1 championship win in the like-liveried Lotus 79. The S2 (1978), still with a 160bhp 2.0 engine, turned in better performance figures, and the subsequent torque-enhanced S2.2 (1980), which soon gave way to the S3, was quicker still. Development had by now made a decent car of the Esprit, if not a particularly durable one.

No-one who attended the extravagant party at London's Royal Albert Hall will forget the 1980 launch of the Esprit Turbo, the first 100 in the garish red and blue livery of Essex Petroleum, Lotus's F1 sponsors. With its 2.2-litre, 210bhp blown engine, the Turbo was by far the fastest road car Lotus had built. As chassis and suspension tweaks kept pace with those made to the engine, the Turbo joined the supercar set with real authority, though quality problems were still to dog it as a Porsche competitor.

Eagerly anticipated V8 disappointing, engine uncouth, bit rough. Handling and grip Esprit's great strengths. Steering too.

The Esprit's only major change of clothes came in 1987 with a brilliant Peter Stevens reskin that softened the car's hard edges without fundamentally changing its profile. Updating a design already in its teens was quite an achievement. With the new body came improvements in finish and quality – not least through the use of VARI (Vacuum Assisted Resin Injection) body construction. Lotus also switched to a Renault GTA transaxle to transmit the normally aspirated car's 172bhp and the Turbo's 215. This was increased in 1989 to 264bhp in the Turbo SE (later to become the S4, by now with standard-issue power steering), which had a claimed top speed of 164mph.

The JPS and Essex specials were the precursors of several sales-boosting, limited-edition Esprits

GT3 cockpit utilitarian, rather than stripped. Gear lever emerges from body-coloured composite decoration. Footwells cramped, Recaro seats hug intimately.

down the years. The one I best remember was the 1993 Sport 300, a street-legal version of Lotus's X180R racer, its engine tweaked to give 302bhp in a pared-to-essentials shell. Pitched against Porsche's 911 RS 3.8 (also with 300 horsepower) in a head-to-head for *Car* magazine, the ultimate four-cylinder Esprit had the pace to eclipse its much pricier German rival on the old Nürburgring, but not the ground clearance. Every stomach-crunching dip was accompanied by a nasty graunch and a shower of sparks.

On the road – particularly on super-smooth German secondaries, which suited the 300's stiff suspension – the Lotus was sensational, provided you could tolerate the noise and lack of refinement. To quote from my story: 'It's the two gs – grip and grunt – that command attention. Road cars do not corner or handle better than the Sport 300, exotica's yardstick by a metric furlong. Steering is wonderfully precise and linear...roadholding is prodigious...the car's ability to change direction like a fleeing gazelle a revelation.'

There was nothing wrong with the engine's performance, either. 'Overtaking is ferociously brief, short straights are despatched in a fleeting frenzy. If anything disappoints it's not so much the engine's peaky delivery as the cosmic gaps in the Alpine Renault gearbox. The Sport 300 would be all the better for a close-ratio gearset...and a six- or eight-cylinder engine, if only to generate superior sound effects. Lotus's sloper-four may be a giant-killing technological marvel, but after a cold start it clatters with the metallic decorum of a cement mixer.'

Ah yes, the V8 – often mooted but hitherto seen only in the one-off, stillborn Giugiaro-styled Etna show car, displayed at the 1984 London Motor Show. Lotus did indeed double up its old slant-four to make a 4.0-litre V8, but it never got beyond the experimental stage. The V8 that broke cover at the 1996 Geneva show was an all-new 3.5-litre, quad-cam, twin-turbo lightweight, said to weigh only 15 per cent more than the old 'four' it supplemented. Lotus had hit the big time, or so it seemed.

En route to Norfolk – to the former Lotus F1 team's base at Ketteringham Hall to be exact – to drive the V8, I had keyed myself up to expect something extra special. Those expectations were rudely dashed. The new Esprit V8 was certainly quick, but it sounded no better (some said worse) than the old four-cylinder car, and the stiff and obstructive gearchange was a real cruncher. Nor was there any advance visually, inside or out. The Esprit we had all waited so long to savour was, at its first showing, a big disappointment subjectively, even allowing for huge levels of grip, deft handling and a wonderful ride.

Lotus

110

Reviews of subsequent upgrades suggested that uncouth noise and poor shift quality were ongoing problems. The 1998 V8GT had a power hike to 350bhp and was lighter by 40kg because it had less equipment, cheaper furnishings and minimal aerodynamic addenda. It was cheaper, too, by a considerable margin, which made its performance – from rest to 100mph in under 10 seconds, top speed over 170mph – barely credible. But though the gearchange was better, it still wasn't good. And the sound and timbre of the flat-plane engine failed to match its charismatic delivery. What the V8GT did was objectively impressive. How it did it was not.

The subsequent limited-edition Sport 350, described by Lotus as 'the most extreme version of the Esprit', came with a heightened sense of drama – the carbon-fibre rear wing was seriously over the top – even though little was changed mechanically. The engine was still rated at 350bhp and the gear ratios were the same. The brakes, though, were upgraded and the cabin – the best yet for the Esprit – embellished with carbon-fibre trim. But the old snags persisted, along with some new ones: stiffened suspension, for instance, did nothing for ride quality.

All the hype and ballyhoo surrounding the 3.5 twin turbo tended to overshadow what was perhaps the nicest, most engaging Esprit that Lotus ever made. It was not a V8. It was not even a 2.2. No, the 2.0-litre GT3, launched in 1996 as a new back-to-basics entry-level model, did 'only' 160mph and was shorn of the sibling V8's aerodynamic excesses. Its specification was relatively modest, too: the expensive Oz wheels, air-con, fancy seats, noise insulation, hi-fi and so on were relegated to the options list. But it was a quick, sweet and endearing car – an honest driving machine, pure and simple – that boasted 90 per cent of its superior's dynamic ability without the glaring drawbacks or high price tag. When this was written, late summer, 2000, the GT3 was nearly £10,000 cheaper than the regular V8. I know which I would have.

Specification	Lotus Esprit V8 (1999)
Engine	3506cc, V8, 4ohc, 32V
Engine layout	Longitudinal, mid
Power	350bhp at 6500rpm
Torque	295lb ft at 4250rpm
Gearbox	Five-speed manual
Drive	Rear wheel
Front suspension	Double wishbones, coils, anti-roll bar
Rear suspension	Double wishbones, coils, anti-roll bar
Steering	Assisted rack and pinion
Brakes	ABS-backed ventilated discs all round
Front wheels	Alloy 8.5Jx17
Rear wheels	Alloy 10Jx18
Front tyres	234-40ZR17
Rear tyres	285-35ZR18
Length	4370mm
Width	1885mm
Height	1150mm
Wheelbase	2420mm
Weight	1315kg (2899lb)
0-60mph (97kph)	4.2sec
0-100mph (161kph)	9.8sec
Top speed	175mph (282kph)
Fuel consumption	17-25mpg

Lotus 340R

Daringly different

Not a pretty sight. Bizarre 340R, based on Elise, has no doors, boot, side windows or roof. Styling adventurous but not to everyone's taste. Handling, cornering great.

It looked like a whimsical doodle by an imaginative art student. Surely it wasn't for real. Lotus was having some leg-pulling fun. Fun, yes, but it was deadly serious frivolity. Although the 340R appeared at the British NEC Motor Show as a kite-flying concept car, it was there to test public – and peer group – reaction. Reputations were on the line, and not just those of Lotus. *Autocar* magazine also had a say in how the car should look and be.

Styled by a team led by design chief Russell Carr (his predecessor, Julian Thomson, joined VW after penning the Elise), the 340R couldn't fail to attract attention with its exposed wheels and bizarre Star Wars bodywork. Was it pretty? No, it was stupendously ugly, like a buckled bathtub. As a balmy toy, as a street-legal pocket supercar to enjoy on track jollies, the 340R was out on its own. Or was it? Rivals like Caterham's Superlight 500 and Westfield's FW400 made the 340R look overweight and underpowered. Still, the message that Lotus received loud and clear from the car's NEC presence was simple: build it. Lotus did, and in double-quick time, starting late in 1999.

The radical 340R – the figure denoted the number of cars to be made and the quickie's target 340bhp/tonne power-to-weight ratio – was basically a tweaked Elise in a jock-strap. Stripped for action though it was, the high launch price of £35,000 underlined its standing, ability and exclusivity, even though the upstart rivals tried to spoil the launch party. Befitting a car of

Specification	Lotus 340R (2000)
Engine	1796cc, 4-cyl, dohc,16V
Engine layout	Transverse, mid
Power	177bhp at 7800rpm
Torque	126lb ft at 5000rpm
Gearbox	Five-speed manual
Drive	Rear wheel
Front suspension	Double wishbones, coils, anti-roll bar
Rear suspension	Double wishbones, coils
Steering	Unassisted rack & pinion
Brakes	Ventilated and drilled discs all round
Front wheels	Alloy 6Jx15
Rear wheels	8Jx16
Front tyres	195/50ZR15
Rear tyres	225-45ZR16
Length	3620mm
Width	1700mm
Height	1125mm
Wheelbase	2300mm
Weight	675kg (1488lb)
0-60mph (97kph)	4.7sec
0-100mph (161kph)	14.5sec
Top speed	130mph (209kph)
Fuel consumption	18-30mpg

visual and technical extremes, vital organs would be on display, not hidden by body panels. Thus the naked rump revealed the entire stainless steel exhaust system, even the engine if you removed its cover. The suspension, outboard of the slim composite bodywork, was also on show.

Through frosted panels you could see the driver's knees and torso (the original plan, to leave the sides open to the wind, was thwarted by problems with spray and draughts). To underline its competition heritage and intent, the 340R was bereft of soundproofing and trim. Why mask the engineering beauty of sculptured aluminium? Racing seats, twin roll hoops, a removable steering wheel, five-point harnesses and cross-drilled ventilated discs were also on the menu. A close-ratio gearbox, too, of course. Lotus listed as extras a comprehensive selection of competition options – fire extinguisher, engine cut-out and so on – to satisfy everyone's needs.

In the interests of weight reduction, the 340R had no doors, boot, side windows, roof (not even a canvas lid) or heater. Don't even ask about a radio. What it did have was track-fettled suspension, stiffer and lower than that of the regular Elise, embracing special coils and adjustable dampers. The car's special Yokohama boots looked more like grooved slicks than normal treaded tyres. Although they were road legal, Lotus conceded that they were less than ideal when negotiating standing water. Puddle dispersion was not a design priority. Dry grip and agility was.

Behind the cosy-for-two cockpit, slung transversely across the bonded aluminium chassis (see Elise), nestled Rover's K-series 1.8 twin-cam. Even

Minimalist cockpit of 340R bereft of decoration and equipment to keep down weight. You climb over sides to get in and out, you get wet if it rains.

though it had the regular engine's normal fixed-timing valve gear, tuning pushed up power to over 170bhp, giving a specific output of close to 100bhp per litre. While complying with noise regulations, the sound of the engine – growly induction, raspy exhaust – was amplified by the absence of insulation.

You didn't slide bum-first into a 340R. Oh no. You vaulted aboard, over its scalloped flanks that levelled with your shoulders when you settled down. The driving position, laid back and relaxed, was terrific. Fittings were reduced to bare essentials, with twin-pod Stack instruments and switchgear, including an old-fashioned starter button, deployed on a central girder-like structure. There was engineering beauty in the cockpit's elegant simplicity, so why mask it?

Although performance was great to 100mph, beyond which wind drag began to dull the car's enormous spirit, acceleration would have been sharper still had Lotus achieved its 500kg target, and the optimum 340bhp per tonne that went with it. In a defiant show of we-can-do-better, Caterham's street-legal featherweight, the 500R (for 500bhp per tonne), showed a clean exhaust pipe to the Lotus, suggesting that a 40-year development programme was not easily eclipsed. Truth is, the 340R – its road-hugging ability strengthened by downforce aerodynamics – steered, handled and gripped even better than it went in a straight line. Good job Lotus limited production to 340 (all pre-sold), otherwise 260R (for 260bhp per tonne) would have been a more appropriate name.

If there is a sequel to this book, Lotus's next car – the Renault V6-powered M250 – will be one of its stars.

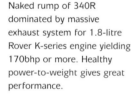

Naked rump of 340R dominated by massive exhaust system for 1.8-litre Rover K-series engine yielding 170bhp or more. Healthy power-to-weight gives great performance.

Marcos **Mantaray**

Lie back and **enjoy it**

The words 'Marcos' and 'modern' may not be in perfect sync, but who would deny a place for the Mantaray in these pages? To understand this car is to be familiar with Marcos's chequered history, and the qualities bequeathed by lusty forebears. First, then, the background.

Marcos (an amalgamation of its founders' names, Jem Marsh and aerodynamicist Frank Costin) emerged as a competitive sports car force in the Sixties. Jackie Stewart and Derek Bell, among other budding race drivers, cut their competition teeth in featherweight Marcos gullwings made out of lighter-than-steel marine ply (yes, wood). And devastatingly quick they were, too, as Jem Marsh himself could ably demonstrate on the track.

Marcos's first proper road car, also timber-based, was the Volvo-powered 1800, styled by Dennis Adams. It was from this dramatic-looking coupé that the Mantaray evolved through Mantura and Mantara iterations, both with steel frames, incidentally. Wood was fine technically but customer prejudice compelled Marcos to drop it.

While the legacy of the original 1800 was clearly seen in these evolutions of an old theme, it was hard to spot in the Mantaray. Sleek in visage as well as in rump, there was little to foster the image of a repro clinging to its past even though an Adams – this time Leigh, nephew of Dennis – was responsible for making the Mantaray look like the effective TVR-chaser it most definitely was.

The recipe was tried and trusted: steel spaceframe chassis (the only wood to be found in the Mantaray adorned the dash), glass-fibre bodywork (marred by wide and inconsistent panel gaps), all-independent suspension (classic coil-and-wishbone at the back), and a front-to-rear drivetrain. There

Specification	Marcos Mantaray (1999)
Engine	4554cc, Rover V8, ohv pushrod, 16V
Engine layout	Longitudinal, front
Power	250bhp at 4750rpm
Torque	275lb ft at 3600rpm
Gearbox	Five-speed manual
Drive	Rear wheel
Front suspension	MacPherson stuts, coils
Rear suspension	Double wishbones, coils
Steering	Power assisted rack and pinion
Brakes	Ventilated discs all round, no ABS
Front wheels	Alloy 7Jx15
Rear wheels	Alloy 7Jx15
Front tyres	205-55ZR15
Rear tyres	225-50ZR15
Length	4005mm
Width	1680mm
Height	1150mm
Wheelbase	2280mm
Weight	1100kg (2425lb)
0-60mph (97kph)	5.5sec
0-100mph (161kph)	14.8sec
Top speed	136mph (219kph)
Fuel consumption	20-30mpg

Ubiquitous Rover V8 engine good for 250bhp and stump-pulling torque. Swift acceleration accompanied by alluring exhaust rumble. GTS had 197bhp 2.0 Rover turbo.

was a choice of engines, starting with Rover's four-cylinder 2.0 for the GTS. The 197bhp turbocharged version actually yielded more horsepower than the in-between 3.9 V8. The engine to have, though, was the tweaked 4.6 V8, which gave 250bhp, stump-pulling torque at lazy revs, and one of the most addictive exhaust rumbles known to man. Only TVR dared to turn up the volume even more.

Geriatric it might have been, but ineffective the old pushrod V8 most definitely wasn't. Although it revved quite eagerly, mid-range wallop – call it in-gear flexibility – was the engine's most endearing quality. It endowed the Mantaray with the sort of lazy-giant performance that only a stonking V8 in a relatively light car can give.

Drive to the rear wheels was through a stiff-levered manual gearbox. What else? If shifting became too much effort – and it was quite demanding, taking into account the hefty clutch – you just gave up and let the tractable engine slog it out in a high cog. Well-sorted suspension, big boots and good weight distribution kept the Mantaray safe and honest on the twisty bits, though power-oversteer could catch the unwary in the wet. There was neither traction control to curb wheelspin, nor ABS to prevent skidding. You modulated the mighty AP brakes with a sensitive right foot, or suffered the consequences.

You didn't sit in a Mantaray – any Marcos for that matter – so much as lie in it, firmly gripped in slender recliner seats by the door sill on one side and the transmission tunnel that bisected the cockpit on the other. Being so laid back was great for relaxation and comfort. Another novelty, which Marcos pioneered (and Chrysler copied in the Viper), was adjustable pedals. Instead of sliding the seat to and fro to arrange a (perfect) driving position, you moved the powered pedal assembly by flicking a switch. The system worked so well that one wonders why it wasn't more widely flattered by imitation.

The **mad, mad** Mantis

Despite making fewer than 100 cars a year, Marcos approached the new millennium with three inter-related model lines. As well as the Mantaray, there was the 1994-released LM series, basis of Cor Euser's famous Porsche-humbling, Chevy powered LM600 in GT2 racing. Lesser LM 400 and LM 500 cars were powered by 4.0 and 5.0 Rover V8s.

The LM-based Mantis (which from 1998 starred in its own one-make championship), revived a name first used by Marcos for a mid-engined racer in the Sixties. Not for Marcos's flagship Mantis Spyder (and later GT) mere Rover V8 power, or even the hot Ford Mustang's 4.6 quad-cam, 32-valve V8 in standard form. What made the Ford's installation special in the Mantis was the presence up front of a belt-driven centrifugal Vortech supercharger that racked up power from 350 to an alleged 450bhp without compromising impressive refinement or reliability. Vortech supplied the blower and attendant hardware, while Marcos did the fitting at its humble Westbury premises in Wiltshire.

I have vivid memories of driving this monstrous machine up and down Cheddar Gorge and thinking that the Grand Canyon would have been a more fitting place for such a monstrous eyeful. Performance was prodigious provided you kept the revs up: let them drop below 2,500rpm and the engine's violence was subjugated by low-rev languor. Still, to rocket from rest to 100mph in 10 seconds flat was beyond the ability of a Viper, never mind Aston Martin's hugely powerful (but wretchedly heavy) Vantage. And neither could match the Mantis Spyder's bargain-basement price of around £50,000.

Not content with the 'regular' Mantis, Marcos later launched a lightweight variant based on the racer: up went the price (to £64,000) and power (over 500bhp); down came the weight (through the use of carbon-fibre body parts) and acceleration times (0-60mph in 3.8 seconds). Marcos was nothing if not bullish about its 180mph answer to the Dodge Viper.

Muscle-bound Mantis as strong as steroidal looks suggest. Beneath bizarre, bulging bodywork lurks quad-cam Ford V8 boosted by belt-driven Vortech blower to 450bhp. Instruments small, driving position laid back, finish sumptuous.

McLaren F1

Mega-cash, **mega-dash**

McLaren F1 styled by Peter Stevens to a Gordon Murray brief. Downforce achieved without aerodynamic addenda, spinal air intake feeds voracious engine. Car very light, compact.

Depending on your viewpoint, the McLaren F1 was either the craziest irrelevance on four wheels or the greatest sports car ever made. The *Daily Telegraph* subscribed to both views, it seemed. 'Few would argue that the F1 is the ultimate roadgoing car,' said one writer in a supplement about the world's best sportsters. 'The world's most amazing waste of money,' said the motoring editor in a round-up of the last Century's 100 worst cars. Let's see.

The ultimate roadgoing car? Well, the F1 was certainly the fastest and most powerful adrenaline pump I ever drove. Two memorable days on the loose in the wilds of Wales for a *Car* magazine drive story left me short on eulogies and totally gobsmacked. So addictive was the car's power – or more pertinently its record-shattering 550bhp per tonne power-to-weight ratio – that each through-the-gears 'fix' intensified the yearning for another.

What better crucible for purple prose than the F1? 'Squeeze the throttle and BMW's percussion section strikes up with a hard, hammering boom from a deep-seated echo chamber...docility gives way to ferocity as a brutal slug of raw torque wells the car forward...the huge muscle of its fabulous engine can be switched on and off like a light bulb...no Ferrari V12 gets close for aural uplift, never mind for sheer pulverising power.' Yes, I could wax lyrical at Olympic level about the McLaren F1.

The F40 was quick, the Jaguar XJ220 quicker still, but the F1's performance was not of this world. Nor, as you will gather, were the glorious, hair-raising sound effects of its monstrous 6.1-litre, 627bhp V12 BMW engine.

For the F1 to humble all previous slingshot exotics so decisively says much for the single-minded approach of the man who created it. McLaren's Gordon Murray had behind him a string of Formula 1 winners before he embarked on the ultimate (for which read fastest, most driver-satisfying) road car.

In a legendary 10-hour briefing to colleagues, he decreed that the F1 would be a cab-forward three-seater with the driver centrally placed (as in his diminutive Rocket) in a mid-engined featherweight with minimal overhangs and a very low centre of gravity. All the hefty bits would be contained within a long wheelbase to avoid dumb-bell weight distribution. Murray was obsessed with weight reduction (his target 1,000kg was not exceeded by much), so the F1 had to be compact, made of advanced carbon composites and have the absolute minimum of driver aids and equipment. Despite the huge power, there would be no traction control, no hydraulic assistance for the steering (a mistake in my humble opinion), not even a servo for the mighty brakes.

Dihedral doors that opened upwards rather than outwards, and a spinal backbone with a rooftop air intake to feed the voracious engine, were central to the design. So was wind-cheating penetration and fan-assisted ground-effect downforce. These and other aerodynamic considerations influenced how Peter Stevens (of Lotus fame) shaped a car that looked spot-on even though it was too small to match the imposing voluptuousness of Jaguar's XJ220.

Another edict was that the engine would be normally aspirated, not a lag-prone turbo as used in the Jag, F40 and Porsche 959. The F1 GTR's win at Le Mans rammed home the point that Murray's flexible, easy-to-drive road

World's best engine? Fabulous 6.1-litre BMW V12 makes 627bhp, glorious noise. Pushes F1 to over 230mph. Gold foil insulation in engine bay expensive but effective, exhaust complex.

McLaren

Passengers flank central
driver in F1 cockpit. Getting
in and out tricky, shutting
door awkward. Seats
comfortable, view ahead
unimpaired. Weight cut by
dispensing with equipment.

Specification	McLaren F1 (1992)
Engine	6064cc, V12, 4ohc, 48V
Engine layout	Longitudinal, mid
Power	627bhp at 7400rpm
Torque	479lb ft at 4000rpm
Gearbox	Six-speed manual
Drive	Rear wheel
Front suspension	Double wishbones, coils, anti-roll bar
Rear suspension	Double wishbones, coils, anti-roll bar
Steering	Unassisted rack & pinion
Brakes	Ventilated discs all round, no ABS
Front wheels	Alloy 9Jx17
Rear wheels	Alloy 11.5Jx17
Front tyres	235-45ZR17
Rear tyres	315-45ZR17
Length	4290mm
Width	1820mm
Height	1140mm
Wheelbase	2718mm
Weight	1130kg (2491lb)
0-60mph (97kph)	3.5sec
0-100mph (161kph)	6.5sec
Top speed	230mph (370kph)
Fuel consumption	14-23mpg

F1 quite small, ground clearance good. Ground effect downforce created by shape of body.

car was at heart a world-beating racer.

An amazing waste of money? Well, to all but the mega-rich, the F1 was certainly unthinkably expensive to buy and run. Priced at £630,000 with VAT, the F1 didn't just invoke the law of diminishing returns, it redefined it. For half-a-million less you could buy a nice Ferrari that was 90 per cent as much fun. What's more, you could park it without mounting a security guard on the engine-bay lining – 24-carat gold foil in the McLaren because it was the best insulation. And only the best would do for Gordon Murray's wacky wondercar.

By normal yardsticks, practicality was not a strong suit, either. Clambering into the central seat was almost as tricky as getting out of it, shutting the doors once ensconced an awkward stretch. Parking was a muscle-toning workout, and the tyres were kettle-drum noisy. Safety? Even allowing for massive crash protection, prodigious grip, tireless brakes and race-car handling that matched the performance, an F1 in the wrong hands didn't bear thinking about.

That it was essentially easy to drive – forward visibility was terrific, the driving position perfect, the width of manageable proportions, the shift fast but forgiving, the low-speed docility reassuring – tended to instil in the driver a false sense of mastery. It was almost too easy to access the car's power, to flex its mighty muscles. In the public domain, driving the F1 was first and foremost an exercise in humility and restraint. To explore the outer limits of its huge performance envelope was possible only on a closed circuit, such as that at Nardo where ex-GP driver Jonathan Palmer – who briefed me about driving the F1 before my two-day solo – established the car's staggering top speed of over 230mph.

The ultimate sports car? In my experience, no question about it. As to being a waste of money, what price a masterpiece, be it a Gordon Murray or a Vincent van Gogh? I know which I would sooner have.

McLaren

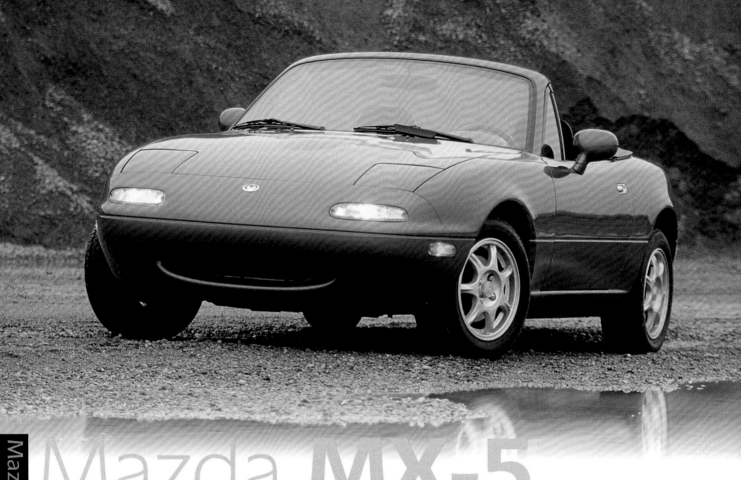

Mazda MX-5

The sports car **resurrected**

World's most popular sports car started with pop-up headlights. These gave way to fixed-lens ones in '97 facelift (bronze car overleaf). Changes conservative.

The era of the modern sports car starts right here, with the Mazda MX-5, the ragtop that rekindled the roadster boom. Known as the Miata in the USA, its main market, the MX-5 was a modern interpretation of the classic British sports car of the Sixties and Seventies. Austin-Healey (Sprite and 3000), MG (Midget and B/C), Sunbeam (Alpine) and Triumph (Spitfire, GT6 and TR) had long gone, while the best of the genre, Lotus's first Elan, fell victim of its maker's drive up-market. At mainstream level, then, only Fiat's dinky X1/9 and Alfa's dated Spider remained. None of the specialists – Caterham, Morgan, Reliant and TVR, for instance – could satisfy global demand for a simple, fun-to-drive, wind-in-the follicles roadster. Nor, across the Atlantic, could the Corvette, which had escalated in price, leaving the way open for crude pick-ups to masquerade as new-age sports cars. It was time for some action.

To say that Mazda saw the market opportunity and plugged it effectively would be to simplify the MX-5's tortured gestation. Former American motoring journalist Bob Hall (later a Mazda product planner) is credited with getting the Japanese interested in what became known internally as the LWS – lightweight sports. Hall, fluent in Japanese, was an enthusiast who had been nurtured on (and captivated by) British sports cars in the Sixties. He saw the need for a modern equivalent that would capture their spirit with modern underpinnings, that would be traditional in looks, layout and appeal, yet bang up-to-date in ability, reliability and practicality. Back to the future, as it were.

Although Mazda had in the past considered alternative layouts for a sort of junior RX-7, including front-wheel drive and a mid-engine configuration, Hall

Specification	Mazda MX-5 1.8S (1999)
Engine	1839cc, 4-cylinder, dohc, 16V
Engine layout	Longitudinal, front
Power	140bhp at 6500rpm
Torque	119lb ft at 4500rpm
Gearbox	Five-speed manual
Drive	Rear wheel
Front suspension	Double wishbones, coils, anti-roll bar
Rear suspension	Double wishbones, coils, anti-roll bar
Steering	Assisted rack and pinion
Brakes	Discs all round, ventilated at front
Wheels	Alloy 5Jx15
Tyres	195-50 R15
Length	3975mm
Width	1680mm
Height	1225mm
Wheelbase	2265mm
Weight	1030kg (2270lb)
0-60mph (97kph)	7.9sec
0-100mph (161kph)	23.0sec
Top speed	127mph (204kph)
Fuel consumption	25-32mpg

was adamant that 'his' car should have a traditional front-to-rear drivetrain. His guiding principle for the MX-5 was espoused by a simple acronym: KISS – keep it simple, stupid. Mazda did not stray far from that ethos.

In designer Tsutomu (Tom) Matano – Japanese by birth but international in outlook and experience – Hall found a kindred spirit, a man as passionate about the Miata concept as he was. Matano had worked for GM, Holden and BMW before joining Mazda. Soon he was heading the company's advanced product development studio at Irvine, California. It's part of motor industry folklore how these two single-minded, uncompromising men bullied and cajoled a sceptical Mazda into accepting the MX-5's viability, and then into making it. And what a phenomenal success the car has been. Since it broke cover at the Chicago show in 1989 (US sales started the same year, those in Britain in 1990), Mazda has made over half a million.

Simplicity was always the keynote to the MX-5's enduring success. So, to keep down costs, was the use of existing Mazda hardware wherever possible. Thus the 1.6 twin-cam 16-valve engine, driving the rear wheels through a close-ratio gearbox, came from Mazda's 323 1.6 hatchback, as did a number of other components. The steel monocoque chassis was specially made, though. Ditto the all-wishbone suspension that, along with 52/48 weight distribution, gave the MX-5 the agility of a true sportster. Several weight-reducing ploys were incorporated to ensure lively performance on modest power: for instance, the bonnet was of aluminium, the bumpers of plastic, the exhaust manifold of stainless steel. Even the battery was down-scaled to one of motorcycle proportions.

Working with Mark Jordan, son of Chuck, former head of GM design,

Facelifted MX-5 offered with two new four-cylinder engines – 1.6 and 1.8. Although performance lifted, still modest for sports car. Crisp, friendly handling greatest strength.

Matano drew inspiration for the MX-5's styling from the first Lotus Elan – the car that best epitomised what he and Hall were trying to achieve. Mazda actually bought an Elan for its engineers to drive, strip, appreciate and understand: what better way to get the 'feel' of the MX-5 spot on? As it happened, the Elan Sprint had a superior power-to-weight ratio than the MX-5, and therefore better acceleration – so no progress there. But the two cars had much in common in the handling department. Where the Mazda really scored, of course, was in build quality, safety and reliability – factors that helped initially make it practically depreciation-proof.

The Miata went on sale in the States early in the summer of 1989 at only $13,000 – about £7,400. Hopes that the MX-5 would be as keenly priced in the UK the following March were soon dashed. Market forces nearly doubled the price. Even so, there was no shortage of customers. Only one like-spirited rival – Reliant's unloved (and under-rated) Scimitar 1.8Ti, soon to be reskinned – undercut the new Mazda. TVR's rumbustious Ford V6-powered S2 cost over £2,000 more, the new Lotus Elan SE £5,600 more. Mind you, the turbocharged Lotus was decisively faster. The irony of Lotus going front-wheel drive just when Mazda introduced its Elan-inspired, rear-drive roadster was not lost on observers.

The back-to-basics MX-5 was launched to rave reviews around the world.

Fixed-lens headlights distinguish latest MX-5. Although similar to original (with pop-up lights) every panel different.

Everyone adored it. Although not very fast – a half-decent hot-hatch would comfortably out-drag it – the friendly little Mazda captured hearts with its neat, pert looks, superb handling and easy-to-live-with character. Though modest in power, the smooth, twin-cam engine answered the throttle with gutsy delivery and a satisfying snarl. Mazda also recognised the importance, as part of the overall driving experience, of a flickswitch gearchange that would encourage indulgent shifting. The MX-5 got one. Only on motorways, which rudely exposed the car's sprint gearing, was the little Mazda out of its depth. Top gear felt more like fourth when cruising, to the detriment of economy and range: the 10-gallon tank needed refilling every 250 miles or so. Short-haul fun the MX-5 provided in spades. Marathon motoring was never its forte.

Not that the little Mazda was uncomfortable. Far from it. Despite stiff suspension and a firm ride – the price paid for superb handling – the MX-5 had a no-frills, cosy-for-two cockpit that seemed to cocoon occupants, so low did they recline in supportive seats. There was no superfluous decoration, no embellishment, no gadgets to add weight, just a plain plastic dash carrying bare essentials. Among them were big-faced tacho and speedo, and eyeball vents. Small though it was, the MX-5 could accommodate beanpole drivers behind its low-set, fixed-position steering wheel, and the manual hood was a model up-and-over affair that could be swung in a matter of seconds without getting out. No need for electric motors here.

It was the MX-5's knife-edged handling, though, that made it a favourite with serious drivers. With power assistance, steering was quick (2.6 turns lock to lock), so you could flick through bends with wristy movements of the wheel. Pressing on, the car could be directed – aimed more like – to just the right degree on the throttle: lift off and the nose would tuck in; reapply power and it would run wide. No rival was more 'adjustable', to use a jargon word of the magazine road testers, than the MX-5. It had what the contemporary front-drive Elan ironically lacked: driver involvement. In short, Mazda had beaten Lotus at its own game.

Ignoring limited-edition specials, the Miata/MX-5 was five years old before its first proper makeover in 1994. The styling was left alone: why mess with a successful shape? On the face of it, Mazda answered criticisms of indifferent performance by increasing engine size from 1.6 to 1.8 litres, lifting power by 12bhp to 128bhp. Torque was up by a useful margin, too. More power, however, did not mean greater speed.

Trouble is, the revamped MX-5 was also heavier, so the net gain in performance was negligible. As if to acknowledge it, the UK importers offered a cut-price, stripped-out model without ABS, airbags, power steering, central locking, electric mirrors, alloy wheels, even a radio. Weighing in at under 1,000kg, this entry-level car, costing £3,000 less than the regular 1.8S, recaptured the no-frills spirit of the original 1.6. Pity the bigger engine was harsher and more raucous, though its exhaust note remained appealingly raspy.

One cause of the 1.8's weight increase was a body/chassis structure stiffened by several reinforcements, including a cockpit bar that linked the seat belt anchors. The all-disc brakes were upgraded and the suspension fine-tuned in the search for greater grip. If not quite so fine-edged as the original's, the 1.8's engaging handling was still brilliantly entertaining.

The Miata matures

By the mid-Nineties, when MX-5 sales worldwide were up to 350,000 (and running at 2,000 a month in the USA), Mazda was seriously considering a new look for its hugely successful seminal sports car. A hint of things to come appeared at the 1995 Chicago show in the shape of the muscular M Speedster, again penned by Tom Mantano's Californian design team. Nothing more than a concept car, they insisted. And so it proved. When the 'new' MX-5 broke cover at the 1997 Tokyo show, it was much more conservative, even disappointing. Some reviewers could see only retrogressive improvement.

Mindful of alienating existing Miata owners, Mazda chose a cautious evolutionary approach, so the new MX-5 didn't look radically different from the old one, even though every panel was altered. The most telling change was to replace the original's trademark pop-up headlights with fixed-lens ones that gave the car a smiling face. Among the advantages, Mazda asserted, were reduced drag and weight. As the body was slightly bigger – and the monocque stiffer – controlling weight was a design priority.

Until the release of a reported 1.5-litre turbocharged engine, said to yield 165bhp, the new MX-5 was offered with two normally aspirated engines – a 1.6 and a 1.8 with variable induction and six-speed gearbox. This time there really was a hike in performance, the new 1.6 out-performing the old 1.8, and the rejuvenated 1.8, good for nearly 130mph, setting new benchmarks for a car that had never been noted for outright zap.

While the déjà vu styling received lukewarm reaction, the car's fluent handling was acclaimed as better than ever. Ditto the gearchange, brakes and manual hood. Ten years before, the MX-5 had the sports car market virtually to itself. By the turn of the century, it was still ahead of the opposition it largely inspired. Some car.

Mazda RX-7
The rotary **wonder**

Third-generation RX-7, launched '91, best looking and fastest. Globular styling, bereft of edges, cheats the wind. No roadster derivative, new model on way.

The story of the RX-7 is the story of an engine. Dr Felix Wankel invented it, NSU pioneered it, and Mazda, after much soul-searching and expensive development, perfected it.

It was the gritty Japanese faithful who salvaged respect for the rotary after NSU, crippled by warranty claims for the doomed Ro80 saloon, had given it a bad name. Although several other manufacturers – GM, VW, Audi, Mercedes-Benz and Rolls-Royce among them – experimented with the Wankel, only Mazda stuck with it through thick and thin, not to mention the odd fuel crisis. Whatever else the Wankel may have been, economy was not a strength. It was uncannily refined, potent (Mazda won the Le Mans 24 Hours with a triple-rotor racer, remember), ultra-reliable (Mazda failures were virtually unheard of), and eventually clean. But the rotary's innate thirst, aggravated by the quest for low emissions, ruled it out for economy cars, if not high-performance ones.

Mazda's first rotary sportster was the low-volume Cosmo 110S coupé, which I remember performance testing for *Motor* in 1967. Costing £2,607 when an E-type fixed-head was only £2,068, the de Dion-axled Cosmo never stood a chance in Britain despite the novelty of a turbine-smooth engine that whooshed you to 60mph in an unremarkable 9.3 seconds. An overall fuel consumption of 18.7mpg underlined the car's Achilles' heel.

The Cosmo was followed by a series of undistinguished rotary-powered coupés – R100, RX-2, RX-3 and RX-4 (14.4mpg overall in *Motor's* test) – before the launch of the RX-7 in 1978. A year after I first glimpsed the new sportster on Mazda's test track near Hiroshima, I was being entertained by it on home ground. This time Mazda was on target with a strong contender,

Specification	Mazda RX-7 (1995)
Engine	1308cc, two rotors, twin Hitachi Turbos
Engine layout	Longitudinal, front
Power	237bhp at 6500rpm
Torque	218lb ft at 5000rpm
Gearbox	Five-speed manual
Drive	Rear wheel
Front suspension	Double wishbones, coils, anti-roll bar
Rear suspension	Double wishbones, coils, anti-roll bar
Steering	Assisted rack and pinion
Brakes	ABS-backed discs all round, ventilated at front
Wheels	Alloy 8Jx16
Tyres	225-50ZR16
Length	4295mm
Width	1750mm
Height	1230mm
Wheelbase	2425mm
Weight	1300kg (2866lb)
0-60mph (97kph)	6.0sec
0-100mph (161kph)	16.0sec
Top speed	158mph (254kph)
Fuel consumption	14-22mpg

if not an outright winner. Although the price in 1979 had risen through inflation to £8,549, the mainstream RX-7 was more competitive than the low-volume Cosmo had been.

The first RX-7, built only as a fixed-head coupé, got favourable crits from the motoring press despite its poor performance/economy ratio. The combination of heavy fuel consumption and indifferent acceleration was unacceptable unless the novel rotary engine's honey-smooth delivery transcended such objective disappointments. Mind you, the image of the RX-7 as a high-performance car was buoyed by competition success, not least by Win Percy's domination of Britain's saloon car championship – though quite how the cramped RX-7 ever qualified as a saloon remains a mystery.

Performance of the first-shape RX-7 was pepped up with development, but it was the launch of the second-generation series in 1986 that pushed Mazda into Porsche territory. The new car, reskinned from stem to stern – and made as an open roadster as well as a fixed-head coupé – even looked like a Porsche 924. What's more, its improved pulse-charge rotary engine, nominally rated at 2,254cc, yielded the same 150bhp as the 924S. Performance of the two cars was very similar; both would do 135mph and hit 60mph in just over 8 seconds. But to set against the Mazda engine's sweet hum were the usual innate flaws: 'hunting' like a two-stroke when part-throttle ambling, and lethargic pick-up with anything less than 3,000rpm on the tacho. It was, however, heavy fuel consumption that let the Mazda down most. Again.

No-one expected turbocharging to alleviate the problem, and it didn't – witness the awful thirst of the Turbo II (the lesser Turbo I was not sold in Britain), released in the late Eighties. Utilising a pair of twin-scroll Hitachi blowers, power was boosted by 35 per cent, torque by 44 per cent. Unfortunately, fuel consumption increased by a similar amount. With this 200bhp, 150mph streaker, Mazda entered the ranks of the junior supercar league with real authority. Porsche's new 944 2.7, well beaten on all-out performance, cost £4,000 more, BMW's M3 £2,500 more. However, both out-cornered the Mazda, criticised for its patchy handling and choppy ride.

The third-generation RX-7, which broke cover in 1991, was by far the best. As if to acknowledge that the quest for economy was a lost cause, Mazda went all-out for Porsche's jugular with a car of dazzling dynamic virtuosity. Sexy new globular styling boosted presence as effectively as it reduced drag. Power jumped to 237bhp, top speed to nearly 160mph. All right, so dazzling acceleration was accompanied by a less-than-thrilling hum from the turbine-smooth rotary – but, boy, did it go. Complementing the terrific powertrain was a chassis of great ability. Despite dull, power-assisted steering, the third RX-7 handled far better than any of its precursors.

The S3 RX-7 was withdrawn from the UK market in 1995 because low sales did not justify the expense of meeting upcoming European emission standards. It was never made as an open roadster.

Distinction of RX-7 is its rotary engine, to which Mazda remains uniquely loyal. In S3 guise – withdrawn from UK in '95 – twin-rotor turbo gave 237bhp with uncanny smoothness.

Mazda

Mercedes-Benz
SL500/600
Benchmark roadster

Merc SL 500 in its day
ultimate luxury sports. V8
engine less powerful than
V12, but car lighter than 600.

Like the honours graduate who worked on the dodgems, Merc's SL was over-qualified as a sporting funster. Over-endowed, too, you could say. But in the luxury roadster league, the SL was throughout the Nineties the car to beat, the car by which rivals – AC's Ace, Aston's DB7 Vantage and V8 Volante, and Jaguar's XK8/XKR included – were judged. They qualified for a place in this book on the coat-tails of the SL.

The mightiest of these mighty Mercs, which by the turn of the century had topped £100,000 in Britain, was the SL600, powered by a lazy 395bhp V12 engine that was the very embodiment of top-drawer refinement. Cars

with sporting aspirations came no smoother or more hushed. The best of the series from a driver's standpoint, though, was the lesser SL500 V8. Although it gave away four cylinders, a litre in displacement and 70bhp, it was marginally the quicker car and decisively the more wieldy.

The explanation is a familiar one: weight. Any power advantage enjoyed by the flagship V12 was

Specification	Mercedes SL600 (1993)
Engine	5987cc, V12, 4ohc, 48V
Engine layout	Longitudinal, front
Power	394bhp at 5200rpm
Torque	420lb ft at 3800rpm
Gearbox	4-speed automatic
Drive	Rear wheel
Front suspension	MacPherson struts, coils, adaptive damping, anti-roll bar
Rear suspension	Multi-link, coils, adaptive damping, anti-roll bar
Steering	Assisted recirculating ball
Brakes	ABS-backed ventilated discs
Wheels	Alloy 8Jx16/
Tyres	225-55ZR16
Length	4470mm
Width	1810mm
Height	1295mm
Wheelbase	2515mm
Weight	1960kg (4321lb)
0-60mph (97kph)	6.0sec
0-100mph (161kph)	15.0sec
Top speed	160mph (258kph)
Fuel consumption	15-20mpg

negated by additional mass. Even so, the 326bhp SL500 – at nearly 1,900kg one of the heaviest cars featured in this book – was still more sumo than sylph, especially with its standard-issue winter hardtop.

The sheer size of the SL dictated heavyweight status. So did all the systems it carried. The plush, press-button hood, for instance, required no fewer than 15 hydraulic cylinders to operate. Then there was all the ground-breaking safety gear, which included an ingenious spring-loaded roll-over bar designed to pop up in just 0.3sec when sensors detected imminent capsize. It also embraced ASR anti-skid control, operated from the brakes' ABS sensors.

Add automatic transmission to the list of performance-blunting features, and you might have expected the car to be a bit slow off the mark. Not so. The smooth, woofly quad-cam engine was as potent as it was discreet, the gearbox as eager to go as a get-set sprinter. It was the accessibility of so much effortless urge – and the ability of a great chassis safely to contain it – that made the SL500 such a worthy entertainer. It was in its day – and even beyond it – the best sports convertible than money could buy.

When this was penned, a new SL, due out in 2001, was subject to much rumour in the motoring press. Scoop pictures of disguised prototypes showed a sleek, wedge-nosed car with an SLK-based folding roof, not a soft-top like that of its illustrious predecessor. To keep down weight, the SL's old enemy, aluminium would figure prominently in the car's construction. High-tech systems, including active body control for the top models, were also on the menu, according to forecasts. So were V6, V8 and V12 engines, of course.

Mercedes

Luxurious cabin protected by pop-up roll over bar. Powered hood worked by 15 hydraulic cylinders, hardtop standard alternative.

Mercedes-Benz **SLK**

Sports of sorts

Seats well back in stub-tailed SLK which took roadster market by storm. Instead of soft-top, press-button steel roof pivots into boot well. Hoops give roll-over protection in crash.

Boulevard cruiser for the glitterati or serious driving machine for the card-carrying enthusiast? Truth is, the SLK – Merc's first half-affordable, four-cylinder, two-seater roadster since the 190SL was launched nearly 40 years before – tried to be both. Before its first makeover, it excelled at neither. Aimed squarely at Europe's other new-wave roadsters such as BMW's Z-series, Porsche's Boxster and the Alfa Romeo Spider, the SLK was a formidable contender in a class of high achievers. It brought to the market all the expertise and quality Mercedes could muster. What it failed to bring was a touch of magic – at least to begin with.

What distinguished the SLK from rivals – indeed, what made it unique – was its powered, press-button headgear. Not for this car a fabric lid supported by strips of metal. Instead, Mercedes meticulously engineered an all-steel affair operated by five hydraulic rams fed by a central pump. At the press of a console-mounted button, the roof would automatically unlock itself from the header rail, then swing back on arms to be swallowed in the boot. Now you see it, now (25 seconds later) you don't. It was the best kerbside party-trick in town, guaranteed to raise an envious eyebrow, even a laugh of appreciation. The only real snag, other than added weight, complication and cost, was that the boot more than halved in size when the roof panel was in occupation, limiting the car's use as long-term holiday wheels, especially as there was little space inside for odds and ends.

Based on a shortened C-class platform, the stub-tailed SLK had a traditional front-to-rear drivetrain, just like that of all other grown-up Mercs. Fancy multi-link rear suspension – the key to outstanding roadholding and user-friendly handling – was complemented up front by a double-wishbone

Specification	Mercedes-Benz SLK (2000)
Engine	2295cc, 4-cylinder, dohc, 16V, supercharger
Engine layout	Longitudinal, front
Power	190bhp at 5300rpm
Torque	206lb ft at 2500rpm
Gearbox	Five-speed auto
Drive	Rear wheel
Front suspension	Struts, coils, anti-roll bar
Rear suspension	Multi-link, coils
Steering	Assisted recirculating ball
Brakes	ABS-backed discs all round, ventilated at front
Front wheels	Alloy 7Jx16
Rear wheels	Alloy 8Jx16
Front tyres	205-55VR16
Rear tyres	225-55VR16
Length	3995mm
Width	1945mm
Height	1290mm
Wheelbase	2400mm
Weight	1340kg (2954lb)
0-60mph (97kph)	7.5sec
0-100mph (161kph)	20.0sec
Top speed	142mph (225kph)
Fuel consumption	21-30mpg

set-up. While there was talk of a V6 at the car's launch in 1995, the SLK went on sale in Europe with a selection of four-cylinder engines. In Britain, where a sales bonanza was anticipated – and confirmed by the hefty premiums paid to speculators by impatient must-haves – only the top engine was on offer. This was the supercharged 2.3 that had previously been received with lukewarm enthusiasm in the four-pot C230 Kompressor – never the sweetest of engines. Although it may have sounded less harsh and boomy in the SLK, it was still short on refinement, noise quality rather than volume offending sensitive ears, especially with the roof up. You could better savour the raspiness of the exhaust when motoring topless.

All-out performance did not feel as strong as test figures suggested, perhaps because there was no turbo-like thrust from the belt-driven blower. If there was, the five-speed automatic transmission effectively masked it. Self-changing gears? In a sports car? To deny the serious driver even the option of a do-it-yourself gearbox said a lot about the SLK's targeted customer. Sports of sorts, yes, red-blooded driving machine, no. Not until later, anyway, when a six-speed manual – and a slick-changing one at that – became available.

Although faster than the old 280SL, which cost thousands of pounds more, even the quickest Kompressor auto gave best to the 2.4-litre Boxster, never mind the subsequent 2.7 and 3.2S upgrades. Able though it was, the Merc was never half so entertaining or involving as the brilliant mid-engined Porsche, despite the rigidity of its massively cross-braced chassis, said to be as stiff as a tin-top saloon's. There was no scuttle shake, no hint of top-down dither, though the big tyres – 225/50s at the back – did tend to thunk and thwack, never mind roar, on stiffened-up suspension that made the ride harsh and jittery around town.

Although the assisted steering (not rack and pinion) lacked communicative tactility, you could hammer the SLK through corners – anything from hairpins to fast sweepers – safe in the knowledge that it would do nothing untoward, that it would always default to a play-safe game. Terrific grip, backed by traction control that could be switched off, made the SLK as skid-proof (and therefore as safe) as a sports car could be. Talking of safety, the novel pop-up roll-over bar on the SL was not deployed on the cheaper SLK. A reinforced screen surround and behind-the-seats hoops were deemed adequate protection. Other safety features included twin front and side airbags and standard-issue anti-lock brakes.

In the beginning I didn't take to the four-cylinder SLK autos. The first I drove disappointed so much that I concluded it was either a below-par sample (unthinkable) or I was having an off day. A second, longer stint a couple of years later would surely make amends. It didn't. I got no buzz out of driving this car, other than the unwanted one from the engine. Just as telling, perhaps, my wife was soon complaining about the harsh and crashy ride.

Objectively, the SLK auto just about delivered the goods. Subjectively, there were grounds for

First SLKs powered by take-it-or-leave-it four-cylinder 2.3-litre Kompressor (supercharger). Performance nothng special, refinement indifferent. Smooth, lusty 3.2 V6 came later.

Mercedes

disappointment in a soulless car with an uninspiring voice. What was needed – and delivered in 1999 – was Merc's sweet, super-refined 3.2-litre V6, which not only increased performance (power jumped to 218bhp) but replaced the 230 Kompressor's harsh sound effects with sonorously yowly ones. The extra two cylinders of the 18-valve SLK320 made all the difference. So did the optional, new-to-Britain six-speed gearbox, which proved that Mercedes could make a decent manual after all.

DIY gears transformed the SLK as a fun car. Even the two four-cylinder Kompressors, upgraded by fine tuning to yield 161 and 194bhp respectively, displayed a vitality that the previous 2.3 auto had lacked. At the third attempt, on a press launch for all three new variants, I found myself at last enjoying the four-cylinder cars and lusting after the V6. The best-value model of a trio that embraced cosmetic improvements, inside and out, as well as telling suspension changes, was undoubtedly the cheapest, the 200 Kompressor.

Regardless of what engine powered it, Merc's two-seater was arguably the most complete, most practical, most desirable roadster of its time. Its popularity was underlined by sales (160,000 before the first round of upgrades) that were almost double those of M-B's forecast. Britain (3,300 sales in 1999) was one of its best markets. Apart from the peerless headgear, it had dazzling good looks, huge presence and quality oozing from every pore. Tall drivers were comfortably accommodated in a classy cabin stripped on the Mk2 cars of its carbon-fibre decoration. If the fascia's new polished aluminium backing was not to your liking, timber embellishment was available instead.

Colourful cabin roomy for two, space for oddments poor. Initially, no alternative to automatic transmission. Six-speed manual came with first uplifting makeover.

Back to **the future**

MG RV8

By resurrecting the geriatric MGB, updated cosmetically and dynamically, Rover raked the ashes of nostalgia for all they were worth in the run-up to the MGF. Not that the 'new' B, renamed the RV8, would do much to satisfy groundswell demand for a modern world-beating MG that Britain could be proud of. Rover saw the low-volume RV8 as nothing more than a period toy for the well-heeled, as a stopgap retro appetiser for better things to come.

The RV8 was made possible only by the existence of British Motor Heritage's body-making facility at Faringdon, established to meet demand by MG restorers for replacement bodies and panels. BMH turned out the requisite 2,000 RV8 shells over a two-year period.

Conceptually, the RV8 was little different from the original B. It was a steel monocoque with a front-to-rear drivetrain and an antique cart-sprung rear axle. Visual changes centred around glass-fibre wings that fattened the haunches, and a new plastic nose with attractive inset headlights. The tail was cleaned up, too. Mechanically, the best news was the replacement of the original's 1.8 four-cylinder B-series engine (long since pensioned off) by Land Rover's 190bhp 3.9 V8, thus ensuring a decent turn of speed as well as lazy-giant lugging and an addictively burbly exhaust note.

Performance was adequately strong without being sensational; gutsy mid-range shove was what you exploited, not top-end fervour. While Rover made some telling chassis improvements, which included fitting fat low-profile tyres and decent telescopic dampers, they did not lift the RV8's handling out of the Dark Ages in which it was rooted. To its credit, the car did have communicative steering and strong brakes. It was also well made and tolerably comfortable, its cosy cockpit being nicely trimmed and equipped.

Specification	MG RV8 (1993)
Engine	3946cc, V8, ohv pushrod, 16V
Engine layout	Longitudinal, front
Power	190bhp at 4750rpm
Torque	234lb ft at 3200rpm
Gearbox	Five-speed manual
Drive	Rear wheel
Front suspension	Double wishbones, coils, anti-roll bar
Rear suspension	Live axle, leaf springs, anti-roll bar
Steering	Unassisted rack & pinion
Brakes	Ventilated front discs, rear drums, no ABS
Wheels	Alloy 6Jx15
Tyres	205-65VR15
Length	4010mm
Width	1695mm
Height	1320mm
Wheelbase	2330mm
Weight	1100kg (2425lb)
0-60mph (97kph)	7.0sec
0-100mph (161kph)	19.0sec
Top speed	138mph (222kph)
Fuel consumption	18-27mpg

MGF

The great **revival**

Slug-like MGF has long wheelbase, short overhangs, high waistline. Looks captivating rather than pretty. Unusual Hydragas suspension 'springs' evolved from those of Morris 1100.

Had Rover tried to revive, say, Wolseley, even Riley, in the mid-Nineties, it would have been laughed out of Longbridge. But MG was different. Despite the prosaic name, MG evoked strong feelings of affection, even passion, on both sides of the Atlantic. That it could be resurrected to global elation after so many years on ice says everything about the marque's enduring appeal, about the magic of a name.

True, there were MGs of sorts during the barren Eighties. Remember the badge-engineered Metros, Maestros and Montegos that kept MG alive, albeit on a dodgy life-support system, after the MGB's demise? As MGs have always been eclectic machines, borrowing heavily from related mainstream models, these family hacks (some of them scarily quick turbos) were not completely out of character. Didn't MG's founder Cecil Kimber establish the precedent for them with his fledgling Morris Garages? Kimber's first cars were nothing more than souped-up Morrises, after all.

Still, to take the fight to Japan, which had eclipsed Britain as the sports car world's epicentre, Rover would have to come up with something extra special. To beat the Japanese at their own game, nothing less than red-blooded roadster would do.

The dynamically challenged RV8, launched as a low-volume stopgap in 1993, was not the car for the job. Nor was it intended to be. Here, controversially, was nothing more than a home-spun appetiser for better

Specification	MGF 1.8VVC (2000)
Engine	1796cc, 4-cylinder, dohc, 16V
Engine layout	Transverse, mid
Power	143bhp at 7000rpm
Torque	128lb ft at 4500rpm
Gearbox	Five-speed manual
Drive	Rear wheel
Front suspension	Double wishbones, Hydragas springs, anti-roll bar
Rear suspension	Double wishbones, Hydragas springs, anti-roll bar
Steering	Electrically-assisted rack and pinion
Brakes	Discs all round, ventilated at front
Front wheels	Alloy 6.0Jx15
Rear wheels	Alloy 6.0Jx15
Front tyres	185-55VR15
Rear tyres	205-50VR15
Length	3915mm
Width	1780mm
Height	1260mm
Wheelbase	2375mm
Weight	1120kg (2469lb)
0-60mph (97kph)	7.8sec
0-100mph (161kph)	24.0sec
Top speed	128mph (206kph)
Fuel consumption	25-35mpg

things to come. The proper MG, the humdinger that would evolve into the F (even though D would have been a more logical sequence), would be a trendy mid-engined modernist like the Toyota MR2, not a retrospective car cast in the mould of the interim RV8. What's more, it would be entirely go-alone British, bereft of Honda input or hardware (BMW was not yet on the scene). It would also need to be the best-made MG ever – by a substantial margin.

The MGF's design cues were rooted in the stunning mid-engined EX-E concept car that Rover displayed at the Frankfurt show in 1985. It employed new 1.8 variations of Rover's acclaimed K-series engine, mounted amidships behind a plush two-seater cabin that emphasised the car's role as practical everyday wheels, rather than as a stark road-racer short on creature comforts. Rover did its homework assiduously – not least by absorbing magazine road tests of other sporting cars – and came up with a package intended to satisfy begoggled anoraks at one end of the scale and cloth-cap wrinklies recapturing their youth at the other. This meant creating a car that was more two-seater cabrio with strong sporting pretensions – a car for all reasons and seasons – rather than a pure-bred driving machine.

The mid-engined concept was chosen after late-Eighties prototypes with front-wheel drive and traditional front-to-rear drive had been rejected. Such a fashionable concept demanded up-to-date looks, not retro ones, though it was important for the car to have a traditional MG face. In line with the MGF's innate practicality, a decent boot (for those long-distance tours) was also a priority.

In the early Nineties, when Rover's in-house designers were fully stretched on other projects, styling proposals were commissioned from outside studios. That submitted by MGA (not part of MG, incidentally) was selected as a starting point, though the much-modifed final shape, which was prettier and more 'British', was evolved under Rover's Gerry McGovern.

MG

F's traditional cockpit smart but conventional, unadventurous. Regular car has five-speed manual gearbox. Steptronic, offering CVT or six-speed sequential shifting, costs extra.

Clutchless Steptronic
transmission an option on
MGF from 1999. In 'manual'
mode, driver has six speeds.

The wheelbase was long, the overhangs short, the waistline high, the lines endearingly chunky in a globular, almost slug-like way.

While the MGF drew heavily, as most MGs before it had done, on existing running gear, much of it from the Metro, it was based on a purpose-built, all-steel unitary structure, said to be as stiff as a typical three-door hatchback – no mean feat for a topless car. The F's solidity and integrity was rooted in its chassis. So was its crash-worthiness.

Hydragas suspension, originally developed for the Austin/Morris 1100 by Alex Moulton, provided the sort of ride/handling compromise that Rover's engineers sought. Basically a classic double-wishbone layout (the gas/fluid Hydragas units, connected front-to-rear, substituted for normal coil springs), the supple suspension gave an amazingly smooth ride, terrific grip and great user-friendly handling. Involving it was not, nor especially rewarding. For raw entertainment, for broad-grin, hands-on, bum-down tactility, the no-frills Mazda MX-5 had the sophisticated MG beaten. Even so, while reviewers were mindful of the MGF's limitations, they gave Rover's first all-in-house car since the Montego in 1984 a resounding thumbs-up. The MGF – soon a best-seller in its class – was just what the market wanted, its generous specification ensuring broad appeal within a niche sector.

Market research had indicated that straight-line performance was not of paramount importance, so the base 118bhp engine – Rover's four-cylinder twin-cam enlarged from 1.6 to 1.8 litres (beyond the limit originally envisaged for the K-series) – was up to the job. Relatively small engines served the Mazda MX-5, Toyota MR2 and new Fiat Barchetta well, so the MGF was in good company, especially as it weighed about the same as the foreign opposition.

For those who wanted more top-end performance, and were prepared to pay a premium to get it, there was a more powerful option, upgraded to 143bhp through the use of ingenious variable valve timing. VVC, rather than

MGF Super Sports, shown at
Geneva '99, powered by
supercharged engine giving
over 200bhp. Regular F has
118bhp, VVC 143bhp. Weight
blunts performance.

turbos or superchargers, had been found by Rover to be the most cost-effective way of boosting performance without running into cost, emission, economy or insurance problems. As it happened, VVC was not to everyone's liking as you had to work the peaky engine hard to extract any worthwhile advantage. The gutsy mid-range torque of the regular engine satisfied the needs of most customers perfectly well.

Drive to the back wheels was through a five-speed manual gearbox. Steptronic transmission became an expensive option (and then only with the base engine) in 1999, four years into the MGF's production life. Steel belt-and-pulley Steptronic gave the driver the option of fully automatic continuously variable transmission (CVT) – and the weird, constant, flat engine drone that came with it – or (and here's the good bit) six fixed-ratio gears selected sequentially, either by nudging the gear lever or pressing buttons mounted on the steering wheel. Technical overkill? Without doubt, but the system worked well and the shifts were seamlessly executed.

The arrival of Steptronic marked the first revamp of the MGF since its launch at the 1995 Geneva show. Addressing criticisms, such as they were, Rover sharpened the numb, electrically powered steering (but not by much) and smartened the cockpit with more aluminium embellishment, better seats and switchgear, height adjustment for the steering wheel, and so on. That so little was changed says much for the car's spot-on original specification, which included powered windows, all-disc brakes, decent audio and a neat, easy-to-work manual hood that kept noise levels down to coupé levels. With the optional hardtop, wind whoosh was even lower.

The MGF was always intended to have a long production life. And just as well, given the debacle early in 2000 of Rover's controversial disposal and break-up by BMW. Without profitable Land Rover in support, the MG brand assumed greater importance in the plans of Phoenix, the new owners. The MGF would need big injections of flair, feel and soul if it was to remain a sales success.

Morgan Plus 8

Time-warped funster

A Morgan Plus 8? In a book about modern sports cars? Why not? Morgan is alive and well and hand-making around 500 cars annually, which is fewer than required to satisfy a backlog of orders that has depositors waiting years for delivery. While archaic production methods still prevail at the labour-intensive Malvern factory where Morgans are assembled with much noisy hammering, all is not quite so Victorian as it looks: witness the presence of an ultra-modern paint shop. The switch from hand-beaten front wings to moulded aluminium ones, in the interests of efficiency and consistency, is another concession to modern cost-cutting practice.

Ubiquitous Rover V8 has powered Morgan Plus 8 since 1968. Once attached to four-speed Moss box, now Rover five-speeder. Engine has grown from 3.9 litres to 4.6.

For all that, traditional Stone Age Morgans, if not the new Aero 8, belong to the 21st century only as nostalgic freaks, as time-warped anachronisms of great vintage appeal. And vintage they are. The basic layout, the underlying style of the Plus 8 and its lesser 4/4 and Plus 4 siblings, has not changed

Specification	Morgan Plus 8 (1998)
Engine	4555cc, Rover V8, ohv pushrod, 16V
Engine layout	Longitudinal, front
Power	220bhp at 5000rpm
Torque	260lb ft at 3500rpm
Gearbox	Five-speed manual
Drive	Rear wheel
Front suspension	Sliding pillars, coils
Rear suspension	Live axle, leaf springs
Steering	Unassisted rack & pinion
Brakes	Ventilated front discs, rear drums, no ABS
Wheels	7Jx16
Tyres	205-55ZR15
Length	3990mm
Width	1500mm
Height	1290mm
Wheelbase	2490mm
Weight	980kg (2160lb)
0-60mph (97kph)	6.0sec
0-100mph (161kph)	16.0sec
Top speed	130mph (209kph)
Fuel consumption	16-23mpg

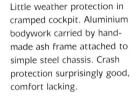

Little weather protection in cramped cockpit. Aluminium bodywork carried by hand-made ash frame attached to simple steel chassis. Crash protection surprisingly good, comfort lacking.

since the mid-Thirties when trike-specialist Morgan launched its first four-wheeler.

Morgan has always used proprietary engines (one-time ambitions to make its own were wisely shelved), so its powertrains have invariably been of contemporary stock. When the Plus 8 was launched in 1968, its ex-GM Rover V8 was already a decade old if not yet ubiquitous. Testimony to the dependability of this tough, muscular engine could by found in the 750,000 Buicks, Oldsmobiles and Pontiacs running around in North America at the time.

The first Plus 8 had a 3.5-litre 168bhp engine and a four-speed Moss gearbox noted more for agricultural strength than precision shifting. In 1990 the 3.5 was displaced by a 180bhp 3.9. Seven years on, in 1997, this was supplemented by the Range Rover's 4.6, tweaked by Rover's Powertrain Products to give 220bhp and 260lb ft of torque. Numerous other changes – wider doors, roomier cockpit, safety bracing, adjustable steering and so on – accompanied the larger engine, by now mated to a five-speed gearbox.

By modern standards, the Plus 8's chassis – a flimsy cross-braced Z-section affair that has more than a passing resemblance to a bedstead – was laughably crude. So was the suspension. Up front, Morgan still used a sliding pillar arrangement like that pioneered by H.F.S.Morgan, the company's founder, for his first three-wheelers. Every traditional Morgan since has been so equipped. Semi-elliptic cart springs suspended the live rear axle – as they did in most pre-war cars. While the use (from 1992) of

modern dampers did wonders for suspension control, the Plus 8's unpredictable handling, bronco-busting ride and heave-ho steering were not to everyone's liking.

Plus 8s could make short work of smooth circuits, but on public roads they were acutely surface-sensitive. Lumps, bumps and awkward cambers that a Lotus Elise shrugged aside with disdain could badly upset the equilibrium of a Plus 8. Masochists (me among them) asserted that it was all part and parcel of the Morgan magic. Critics who preferred to aim through corners, rather than wrestle their car round them, tended to disagree.

As you'd expect of a sportster with a power-to-weight ratio of over 220bhp per tonne, acceleration was terrific. Good old axle tramp (betrayed by yelp-yelp wheel patter) prevented a spectacular 0-60mph time. But in-gear pick-up, say from 50 to 70mph in fourth or fifth, was startling in a lazy-giant sort of way. Muscular engines didn't come much more flexible or effortless than this. Aerodynamically, cars didn't come much worse, either, which is why, with the drag coefficient rivalling that of St Paul's Cathedral, the Plus 8 was all out at 130mph, if you were lucky.

Although enlarging the cockpit improved access and civility, comfort was never in abundant supply. The seats were flat, the steering wheel too big, the elbows-out driving position flawed and the ride truly awful on anything but smooth asphalt. For all that, the Plus 8 was strong on character and rough-hewn charm. With the utilitarian hood (all press-studs and bracing strips) furled behind you, wind buffeting – there were no behind-your-neck draught excluders here – was strong enough to take your breath away. Great stuff.

All the fours

About half the cars Morgan made in the late Nineties were Plus 8s. The rest were either Ford Zetec-powered 1.8 4/4s (named after the first four-wheeled, four-cylinder car, launched in 1936 with a 34bhp Coventry Climax engine) or, until February 2000, when supplies of Rover's 2.0 twin-cam ran dry, Plus 4s (which kicked off with the 68bhp Standard Vanguard-engined 2.0 in 1950).

The Plus 4 had been dropped and resurrected before, so its absence was probably temporary. Not that its demise was such a tragedy. After all, the difference in performance between the 1.8 Zetec and the 2.0 T16 was less than suggested by the £4,520 that separated the two models on price at the turn of the century. What next for the model made famous by a series of Triumph TR pushrod fours?

Many different proprietary engines – from Coventry Climax, Ford, Fiat, Rover and Triumph – have driven Morgan's four-cylinder cars, most of them two-seaters. In the summer of 1999, though, Morgan re-introduced an old family favourite – the four-seater 4/4, new from the door hinges back. Gone was the old car's perched bench rear seat, to be replaced by two individual buckets, set 5in lower, that could be folded to create the largest luggage platform ever in a Morgan. Lengthening the doors also made access easier.

Before it was axed, the Plus 4, along with its 4/4 sibling, acquired the rack and pinion steering fitted for some years as standard equipment to the Plus 8. Unassisted, of course.

Morgan Aero 8

Mod Mog in period dress

Morgan's one previous attempt to modernise its cars was an abject failure. Although the bubble-topped Plus Four Plus coupé is now a coveted collector's item (only 26 were made), it was rejected as a misguided misfit in the Sixties. What buyers wanted – and were beginning to queue for – was the traditional vintage-style Morgan, not a trendy glass-fibre streamliner wrapped around a barrack-room bed-frame.

When developing its new Aero 8 – a modern sports car in period dress – Morgan didn't repeat the mistake. Mind you, it may in the process have perpetrated another.

The Aero 8 was the brainchild of Charles Morgan, grandson of founder H.F.S.Morgan, and boss (with his father Peter) of the Malvern-based family firm. It was junior who took what was for Morgan a revolutionary step and pushed the world's oldest privately owned car-maker into the 21st century. Morgan's new flagship supercar would still look 'traditional'. Under its aluminium skin, though, would be a high-tech, race-bred chassis and running gear. This time Morgan got its priorities right conceptually. But aesthetically? Perhaps not.

The Aero – the name evokes memories of a minimally screened sports three-wheeler of the inter-war years – grew from the GT2 racer that Charles Morgan campaigned in the 1997 FIA GT championship. Uncompetitive though it was against aerodynamically superior opposition (not least an upstart Marcos), the back-marker Morgan won many friends and admirers, if few accolades. More to the point, it laid the foundation for the Aero 8, unwrapped at the 2000 Geneva show. Production – of up to 200 cars annually – was due to start that summer.

Specification	Morgan Aero 8 (2000)
Engine	4398cc, BMW V8, 4ohc, 32V
Engine layout	Longitudinal, front
Power	286bhp at 5500rpm
Torque	322lb ft at 3700rpm
Gearbox	Six-speed manual
Drive	Rear wheel
Front suspension	Cantilever arms, lower wishbones, inboard coils, Rose joints
Rear suspension	Double wishbones, inboard coils, Rose joints
Steering	Assisted rack and pinion
Brakes	AP ventilated discs all round
Wheels	Mag alloy Oz 9Jx18
Tyres	225-40ZR18 run-flats
Length	4090mm
Width	1755mm
Height	1090mm
Wheelbase	2540mm
Weight	1000kg (2204lb)
0-60mph (97kph)	4.8sec (est)
0-100mph (161kph)	13sec (est)
Top speed	160mph (258kph) (est)
Fuel consumption	16-23mpg (est)

Morgan Aero 8 not to
everyone's taste aesthetically.
Lights give boss-eyed
appearance – but looks said
to grow on you.

At just under £50,000 it was the most expensive Morgan ever. The fastest, too, with a 286bhp, 4.4-litre BMW V8 engine under the bonnet. Unfortunately, it was by common consent Morgan's ugliest, too.

To develop the GT2 racer, and the road car it spawned, Morgan recruited as technical director Chris Lawrence, the former racing driver/engineer whose Lawrencetune Morgans were once the sports cars to beat. With co-driver Richard Shepherd-Barron, Lawrence won the 2.0-litre class at the 1962 Le Mans in a Plus 4 Supersports, and his SLR streamliners were sensationally quick giant-killers. Who better, then, to design and develop the Aero 8's chassis and suspension?

Forget the Plus 8's flimsy chassis and archaic sliding pillar suspension, both outdated when Morgan produced its first four-wheeler in 1936. Four years in the making, the hand-assembled Aero was based on a super-stiff tub made from coated laser-cut aluminium specially produced by Alcan in Germany for car construction. The structure's aluminium sections were bonded (ie glued, by Gurrit Essex adhesive) and (Bolhoff) riveted together to give 'exceptional' torsional rigidity – a first for a Morgan. Aluminium extrusions for the all-new suspension and brakes played their part in keeping the Aero's overall weight down to 1,000kg – appreciably less than that of, say, an MGF.

Jaguar's former engineering chief, Jim Randle, had a hand in the Aero's chassis design. So did the resources of Birmingham University. Inboard coil/damper units controlled the unique double-wishbone suspension – rose-jointed at both ends for precision control. Another first for Morgan was the use of power-assisted steering. Anchors came in the form of AP Racing ventilated discs all round – but without anti-lock.

A few years ago, when I asked him what engine would eventually replace the ubiquitous Rover V8, Peter Morgan gave a strong hint. 'I can't say, but Charles is very friendly with BMW's people.' The use of a 4.4-litre BMW V8

Aero 8's aluminium body carried by classy lightweight chassis and race-bred suspension developed from GT2 track car. BMW 4.4-litre V8 gives tremendous performance.

Cosy-for-two cockpit features ash frame as decoration.

engine in the Aero therefore came as no surprise. Engineers from BMW and Bosch Motorsport were seconded to Malvern Link to develop a bespoke engine management system. All 44 Morgan dealers world-wide were to receive full BMW service training, by the way.

Power was transmitted through a self-adjusting clutch and a six-speed Getrag manual gearbox to 18in Oz magnesium alloys shod with Dunlop foam-filled, run-flat tyres that did away with the need for a spare. This allowed Morgan to equip the Aero with a decent lidded boot big enough to carry the obligatory set of golf clubs.

When Charles Morgan said at the car's launch that he saw the Aero as a year 2000 equivalent of the 1968 Plus 8, was he being modest? Surely the Aero – the grandest development project ever undertaken by Morgan – represented a bigger leap forward than the crude Plus 8 had done over three decades before. In espousing modern technology, best seen in the chassis and drivetrain, Morgan created a car more international in flavour than any of its previous models. It stopped short, though, of commissioning an outside agency to update the aluminium bodywork – some of it still hand-beaten, the rest thermoplastically formed. A mistake, perhaps, given widespread criticism of the car's boss-eyed appearance. Not that the frontal treatment, dominated by the unfortunate lie of the headlights, was without merit.

The in-house styling team used CATIA software to address two incompatible goals: retaining traditional styling while improving aerodynamic efficiency. Flushing in the lights and raking back the windscreen helped reduce air resistance by 40 per cent, regardless of whether the hood – a multi-skinned manual affair – was up or down. With a drag factor of 0.39 (poor by normal yardsticks, outstanding for a Morgan), the Aero was reckoned to be good for 160mph. But would it be stable? Rear-end venturi, said to create negative lift, suggested that it would.

Venturi? On a Morgan? Ah, but there were also protruding door hinges, traditional bonnet catches and, of course, that familiar radiator grille to endorse the Morgan pedigree. Standard equipment included heated glass (to prevent misting up), a dash-mounted carry-all and Connolly leather, set off nicely by...guess what? Yes, polished ash, the hardwood that still frames the aluminium bodywork. Years ago, so the story goes, an engineering consultant's message to Morgan was quite simple: keep the ash. It did.

When this was written, Morgan had about 500 firm orders for the Aero 8, less than half of them from buyers on the waiting list for traditional models. The promise of a power-to-weight ratio that topped a Porsche 911 Turbo's was proving irresistible. The first customer cars were expected to leave Malvern in January, 2001.

Noble M10

The right stuff

Noble M10's fibreglass bodywork clothes race-bred spaceframe chassis that rides, handles well.

M10 powered by mid-mounted Ford Mondeo 2.5 V6, installed transversely. Performance matches that of Elise, exhaust note superior. Deep boot quite capacious.

The history of Britain's motor industry would be incomplete without a requiem to all those bullish specialists who have promised much and delivered little before vanishing into the ether, often in debt. If there's any justice in the uncertain world of car-making, Leicester-based Noble Moy Automotive won't be one of them. It will instead have progressed from promising newcomer when this book was proposed to fully fledged small-scale manufacturer by the time it was published. Grounds for optimism were fuelled by the astonishing M10, the tenth design from the pen of the prolific Lee Noble.

Lee Noble has to his credit several praiseworthy designs, race cars and replicas among them, including the Ultima (a scorchingly quick mid-engined sportster used by McLaren as a development mule for the F1) and the original Ascari supercar (said to be capable of 200mph). All told, self-taught Noble had made some 500 cars before he turned to creating a civilised mid-engined roadster, cast in the mould of the Lotus Elise. Amazed by its pace and ability, reviewers gave the resulting M10 a glowing endorsement. There was a new star on the block, deserving of success.

Although there was nothing especially advanced about the M10, it was clearly the work of people who knew their stuff. The race-bred tubular spaceframe chassis – a strong but comparatively light structure – was suspended at each corner by coil-sprung wishbones, wide-based at the back where a brake reaction arm was a Noble novelty. Unassisted rack and pinion steering and generous disc brakes all round were part of the package. So was a mid-mounted 2.5-litre Ford V6 mated, as in the Mondeo, to a five-speed gearbox. A canny rod-and-cable system ensured short-throw shifts.

Specification	Noble M10
Engine	2544cc, Ford V6, dohc, 24V
Engine layout	Transverse, mid
Power	168bhp at 6250rpm
Torque	162lb ft at 4250rpm
Gearbox	Five-speed manual
Drive	Rear wheel
Front suspension	Double wishbones, coils
Rear suspension	Double wishbones, links, reaction arm, coils
Steering	Unassisted rack & pinion
Brakes	Ventilated discs all round, no ABS
Front wheels	Alloy 7Jx15
Rear wheels	Alloy 7Jx16
Front tyres	205-55
Rear tyres	225-55
Length	3860mm
Width	1770mm
Height	1180mm
Wheelbase	2440mm
Weight	1000kg (2204lb)
0-60mph (97kph)	6.0sec
0-100mph (161kph)	17.0sec
Top speed	140mph (225kph)
Fuel consumption	20-32mpg

The products of small, cash-strapped manufacturers are often crucially flawed by their styling and finish. Not so the M10. If not the prettiest roadster ever made, the glass-fibre-bodied Noble had about it an air of competent professionalism that made it look like a mainstream car, not an eclectic 'bitsa' cobbled together in the garage. Inside and out, the workmanship impressed. At a launch price of around £30,000, it needed to, especially as the seats and driving position came in for criticism (they should, by now, have been improved).

Although heavier than the regular Lotus Elise, the M10 was a little more powerful, so the two cars were pretty evenly matched on acceleration. Tallish gearing didn't prevent the M10 from picking up strongly in fourth and fifth, or setting a high 140mph maximum – a clear 10mph advantage over the Lotus.

That the M10 should match or better the Elise on performance was no surprise, given its advantage in power and torque. That it made a nicer noise – a lovely guttural V6 wail – added an extra layer of icing to the cake. But here's the rub. The M10 also gave the Elise a good run for its money on ride and handling – a cracking endorsement of Noble's ability to deliver the goods. Cars ride and handle well only by design, never by accident. Hoods fold and erect easily, as did the Noble's, for the same reason.

Shortly before these pages closed for press, Noble was in the news again with an even more ambitious supercar. The dramatic M12 GTO coupé, priced at £45,000, was to be powered by a twin-turbo version of Ford's Duratec 2.5 V6 yielding over 300bhp. Classic double-wishbone suspension suspended the aluminium-reinforced spaceframe chassis.

Noble

Considering limited resources of fledgling makers, early M10 remarkably sophisticated, detailing good. Cabin smart, neatly trimmed. Flawed driving position was to be addressed.

Panoz
Esperante 2000
All-American **sophisticate**

Billed as BMW Z8 rival, Panoz
Esperante has classic long-
nose styling and Ferrari-like
visage. Pushrods feature in
rear suspension

Big-time international sports car racing has been enriched in the past few
years by the presence of a long-nosed oddball that looks like a fugitive
Batmobile. Don't laugh at the Panoz LMP. Or at the street-legal siblings that
bathe in its glory.

What made this radical American racer so unusual, and therefore all the
more welcome in a field of winged lookalikes, was that it flew in the face
of design convention. All the Prototype opposition – Audi, BMW, Ferrari,
Lola, Mercedes-Benz, Porsche, Joest, Riley and Scott et al – fielded
conventional racers with mid-mounted engines. The Panoz had its
thunderous Roush-built, Ford-based V8 ahead of the driver – as in Panoz's
road cars – if not up in the nose. Call it front mid-engined, on account of
the hefty bits, driver included, being set so far back in the carbon-fibre
chassis (take a bow, Reynard) that weight distribution was more that of a
mid-engined car than a front-powered one.

It worked. In the hands of ex-F1 drivers David Brabham and Jan
Magnussen, among others, the latest 6.0-litre, six-speed cars were super-
competitive against the best opposition during the 2000 season.

The competition wing of Panoz (pronounced 'Paynoze') was started by
wealthy business tycoon Don Panoz, whose background is in lucrative
pharmaceuticals. The success of his racers brought into sharper focus the
road-going sports cars that son Daniel had been building at Atlanta,

Specification	Panoz Esperante (2000)
Engine	4601cc, 4ohc, V8, 32V
Engine layout	Longitudinal, front
Power	320bhp at 6000rpm
Torque	317lb ft at 4750rpm
Gearbox	Five-speed manual
Drive	Rear wheel
Front suspension	Double wishbones, coils, anti-roll bar
Rear suspension	Double wishbones, pushrod-operated coil and dampers, anti-roll bar
Steering	Assisted rack and pinion
Brakes	ABS-backed ventilated discs all round
Wheels	Alloy 9Jx17
Tyres	255-55ZR17
Length	4478mm
Width	1859mm
Height	1295mm
Wheelbase	2692mm
Weight	1451kg (3200lb)
0-60mph (97kph)	5.1sec
0-100mph (161kph)	12.6sec
Top speed	155mph (249kph)
Fuel consumption	16-22mpg

Georgia, for some years.

Danny Panoz's first road car, launched in 1990, was based on a steel spaceframe chassis originally designed by the English engineer, Frank Costin. This later evolved into the current AIV (aluminium intensive vehicle) Roadster, built around a twin-tiered extruded aluminium chassis. Retro hot-rod in style (imagine a cross between a Cobra and a Caterham), the Roadster was a hand-built sports funster priced, following improvements to the leather-trimmed cockpit, at $62,500 for the 2000 model year. With ubiquitous 4.6 V8 quad-cam power from Ford's quick Mustang, Panoz claimed a 0-60mph time of 4.6 seconds. It also boasted 0.97g cornering power on Goodrich Comp TA rubber.

The subsequent Esperante, a more ambitious up-market luxury roadster – Panoz billed it as a BMW Z8 rival – was based on a Reynolds-extruded aluminium chassis bolted and bonded together, Lotus Elise style, to make an immensely rigid base structure. Although modern in appearance, the lightweight body, shaped in DZN's California studio, espoused classic design cues, including a long nose and a stubby tail (just like the racer). The provision of a two-golfbag boot was a design priority that dictated Merc SL-like dimensions.

Power was again Ford's 4.6-litre quad-cam, tuned to deliver 320bhp to the back wheels through a five-speed manual gearbox. A sequential automatic was planned as an option for 2001, and pushrod-activated rear dampers were a feature of the race-bred suspension. Sold through a US network of over 30 Panoz dealers, the Esperante was priced at around $80,000 – about £50,000.

It was the Esperante luxury roadster, its hood operated hydro-electrically, that spawned the tubular-framed, plastic-bodied GTS coupé designed for Sports Car Club of America (SCCA) competition. Come in 5.8 litres (and 385bhp) of bombproof pushrod power from Ford's motorsport division.

Panoz

First Panoz developed into AIV Roadster, yellow car, with central instruments in spartan cockpit. Subsequent Esperante, top left, with bonded aluminium chassis, has 320bhp.

Porsche 944 & 968

Great heart, dubious pedigree

Club Sport best of 968 series, evolved through 944 from Audi-built 924. Ancestry betrayed by outline of rear window.

Porsche's 944 just made it into the Nineties. It had evolved from the Porsche-badged, Audi-built 924, which in the first place was never intended to be a Porsche, and in the second never qualified as one according to purists – honest, marketing-led sportster though it was. Doubts about the 924's pedigree were partially dispelled by its 944 successor, which was a better, brawnier car with a pukka Porsche engine, albeit one with only four cylinders. Even though the Turbo derivative gave the 944 in its quickest form junior supercar status, real Porsches were built at Zuffenhausen and had air-cooled flat-six engines or sophisticated V8s. So said the pedants, anyway.

If the ghost of the 924 lingered on in the 944, it was largely exorcised by the confusingly named 968 – effectively an S3 944 even though 80 per cent of it was said to be new. The 968's arrival in the UK in the spring of 1992 was presaged by a 'sale' of old-stock 944s, which saw prices slashed by thousands of pounds. As there was no blown car in the 968 line-up (I'm discounting the later S and RS fixed-head racers), the outgoing 944 Turbo perhaps represented the zenith of Porsche's strain of ragtop fours, not to say a bargain for those who bought a sale-reduced one.

Although the 968 was an evolutionary car – the awkward outline of the rear window still betrayed its 924 ancestry – its fresh face, not universally loved, echoed the lines of the flagship 928 (complete with flushed pop-up headlights), all the better for spin-off prestige. What's more, the newcomer was built alongside 911s and 928s, consolidating its credibility as a real Porsche.

Beneath the bonnet was a fettled version of the 944's 16-valve twin-cam,

Specification	Porsche 968 Cabriolet
Engine	2990cc, 4-cylinder, dohc, 16V
Engine layout	Longitudinal, front
Power	240bhp at 6200rpm
Torque	225lb ft at 4100rpm
Gearbox	Six-speed manual
Drive	Rear wheel
Front suspension	Struts, lower wishbones, coils, anti-roll bar
Rear suspension	Semi-trailing arms, torsion bars, anti-roll bar
Steering	Assisted rack and pinion
Brakes	ABS-backed ventilated discs all round
Front wheels	Alloy 7.5Jx17
Rear wheels	9Jx17
Front tyres	225-45ZR17
Rear tyres	255-40ZR17
Length	4320mm
Width	1735mm
Height	1275mm
Wheelbase	2400mm
Weight	1460kg (3219lb)
0-60mph (97kph)	7.0sec
0-100mph (161kph)	16.5sec
Top speed	150mph (241kph)
Fuel consumption	17-25mpg

Four-cylinder 3.0 engine of 968 gives 240bhp, strong torque. Drive to rear wheels through six-speed Getrag manual. Cabin conventional, lacks flair – but beautifully finished, quality high.

its power increased by 14 per cent to 240bhp; at the time, no unblown production 3.0 yielded more. This healthy urge was delivered to the rear wheels through a six-speed, close-ratio Getrag gearbox or, at extra cost, Porsche's fancy new Tiptronic auto, which, by 'tipping' the selector back and forth, gave manual control. Trouble is, there were only four ratios, all on the tall side of sprint, which left the car struggling off the line, never mind out of uphill hairpins. Chassis, braking and suspension enhancements, not to mention cosmetic uplifts, completed the transformation from 944 to 968. Call it a junior 928 and you'd not be far wrong.

An ingeniously simple new variable valve system – dubbed Variocam, it altered the timing of the inlet cams by up to 15 degrees, boosting torque at low revs and power at high ones – was claimed to make the 968's engine as gutsy and flexible low down as it was raucously strong at the top. Hmm. Fact is, all-out performance was little if any better than the 944's. More humbling for Porsche, VW's much cheaper Corrado VR6 out-lugged the 968 with a smaller engine. Out-refined it, too. Not even the presence of counter-rotating balancer shafts, which smoothed away innate vibration, could make Porsche's lusty 'four' as sweet-running as the Corrado's classy V6. If not the slickest of manual shifts, that of the 968 never to my recollection discouraged indulgent shifting. Gear play was part of the fun – as it should be in any Porsche, four, six or eight.

If the 968's engine fell slightly short of expectations, eager though it was, its chassis surpassed them with handling that no sportster of comparable practicality and civility could better. Despite its front-mounted engine, the 968 had slightly rearward 48/52 weight distribution, all the better for traction and crisp turn-in. The secret? Slinging the hefty gearbox between the back wheels, Ferrari style (and never mind the convoluted, precision-blunting shift linkage that was a consequence of it). Meaningfully tactile steering, impeccable body control and sharp but not nervy responses inspired confidence in the 968's ability to zap through bends, better still a series of them, with alacrity.

It was the way the 968 cornered, gripped and braked, rather than the way it went, that made it such an exceptional driving machine. In stripped-down, rubbered-up, race-seated Club Sport guise, the 968 was truly memorable, one of the best – if not the best – sports cars of the decade. Trouble is, there was no roadster derivative of the CS, winner of *Autocar's* 'Performance Car of the Year' award in 1994. Only on the regular 968 could you get a powered hood.

Porsche
911 Cabriolet

The 911 goes **topless**

Porsche 911 20 years old before first cabriolet launched in 1983. Flush fitting powered hood of latest 996, above, based on Boxster's. Body reinforcements push up weight, engine 3.4 flat-six.

Porsche did not decapitate its 911 until the evergreen coupé was nearly two decades old. True, the Targa – first seen in 1966, three years after the 911 broke cover at the Paris Salon – had been around for ages. But lifting out a panel to let in a sun-soaked zephyr was not quite the same thing as embracing the sky. Targas were all right so far as they went, but to lovers of hair-tousling, breath-grabbing *al fresco* action, they weren't quite airy enough.

Actually, Porsche's first 911 Targa very nearly was a full convertible. With the roof off and its rear flexi-screen folded, only a reinforcing roll hoop remained above your head. The furling window soon gave way, though, to a body-bracing glass one, and by the mid-Nineties the Targa concept had evolved (some might say regressed) into something quite different. Instead of a removable hatch there was a see-through glass panel that, at the touch of a button, slid back and down inside the rear screen, leaving a hole above and a dim view aft.

The cabrio was first seen as a design study at the 1981 Frankfurt show. Public reaction was so positive that the car was rushed into production for the 1983 model year – the 20th birthday of the 911 – as an option on the 205bhp (180bhp in the USA) 3.0 SC. Porsche built 4,097 SC cabriolets before switching to the more powerful Carrera in 1984.

Since the first SC ragtop, the mainstream 911 has evolved through several

Specification	911 Cabriolet (1997)
Engine	3600cc, flat-six, air cooled, sohc, 12V
Engine layout	Longitudinal, rear
Power	272bhp at 6100rpm
Torque	252lb ft at 5000rpm
Gearbox	Six-speed manual
Drive	Rear wheel
Front suspension	Struts, coils, anti-roll bar
Rear suspension	Double wishbones, coils, anti-roll bar
Steering	Assisted rack and pinion
Brakes	ABS-backed ventilated discs all round
Front wheels	Alloy 7Jx17
Rear wheels	9Jx17
Front tyres	205-50ZR17
Rear tyres	255-40ZR17
Length	4245mm
Width	1735mm
Height	1300mm
Wheelbase	2720mm
Weight	1320kg (2910lb)
0-60mph (97kph)	5.2sec
0-100mph (161kph)	12.5sec
Top speed	160mph (258kph)
Fuel consumption	15-27mpg

Porsche

Roomy cabin of 996, fixed-head and cabriolet, big advance on previous model's. Steering wheel adjustable, centre console like Boxster's, seats enveloping, finish impeccable.

code numbers and stages, some more radical than others. After the 3.2 Carrera, which sired the beetle-browed, retro-look Speedster, came the re-platformed 964, officially known as the Carrera 2 and Carrera 4. Though these cars were said to be 87 per cent new, even if the concept wasn't, Porsche was working on even more drastic derivatives.

In 1994 came the 993 with a new chassis, wishbone rear suspension and a 3.6-litre, 272bhp engine. This interim car was displaced in '97 – with its début at the September Frankfurt show – by the clean-sheet 996 that will remain in production well into the 21st century.

As the theme of this book is modern sports cars, let's dwell on the 996 – the fifth-generation 911 – not least because it had so little in common with the previous four iterations other than in profile (which Porsche could have changed, but wisely chose not to) and the position and configuration of its rear-mounted flat-six engine.

For a start, the 996 had grown significantly – it was now somewhere between a traditional 911 and the defunct 928 in size – even though the fold-down rear 'seats' were still no more than kiddy perches, better used for stowing luggage. More GT than seminal sports, the 996's smooth new snout echoed that of the Boxster with which it shared components – headlights, mirrors, doors, even the front structure, for instance. So similar were the two cars from the front that it was difficult to tell them apart.

Such rationalisation underlined that the 996 was more closely associated with its mid-engined contemporary – the two cars had been developed in tandem and were produced on the same lines – than with the preceding 993. There was no need to rely on details (such as the deletion of front quarter lights) to tell the new 911 from the old, 996 from 993: one glance was enough. Inside, as without, the Boxster influence was stronger than the previous 911's. The dominating tacho, for instance, also displayed your speed digitally, Boxster-style, rendering the off-centre speedo largely redundant.

While the 911 in 996 guise no longer made a virtue of being ultra-compact (though small it still seemed when parked alongside, say, a Jaguar XK8), it was nothing if not lean, clean and hewn-from-an-ingot solid. Thanks in part to flush windows and a 'faster' windscreen – that of all previous 911s had been too upright aesthetically and aerodynamically – the drag coefficient dropped, for the fixed-head coupé, from 0.38 to 0.30, benefiting top speed (over 170mph) and fuel consumption (28mpg). Despite being longer, wider and stretched in wheelbase, all the better for crash safety and accommodation, the 996 was no heavier than its predecessor. The widespread use of aluminium (in the suspension components, for instance) explained that. For years, 911s had been putting on weight; time now to shed it.

Despite a drop in engine size, from 3.6 to 3.4 litres, output zapped to nearly 300bhp. The reason? A completely new Boxster-based flat-six 24-valve engine cradled by an aluminium subframe to reduce vibration. Four valves per cylinder, water cooling (all previous 911s had been air-cooled), an improved variable valve timing system (Variocam in Porsche-speak) and dry-sump lubrication were all part of what amounted to a revolutionary package. As a measure of the new engine's efficiency, specific output increased from 79 to 88bhp per litre. While water cooling undoubtedly suppressed noise, the quality of the engine's unique double-edged wail was largely unimpaired, thank goodness.

Power was delivered through a strengthened six-speed gearbox or a five-speed Tiptronic – a major advance on the old four-speeder. Push-button sequential shifting was on the menu, too. Great stuff. Ditto the handling, steering, braking and off-the-line traction, never mind the scorching performance. While softer and less agile, perhaps, than its smaller predecessors, the new 911 was still a great drive, still a thrilling experience, still as desirable as ever – especially (for sun-worshippers) as a Targa or cabriolet.

Bereft of the rattles and shakes, the super-stiff 996 ragtop, developed alongside the coupé, was equipped with a superb one-touch powered hood. Unlike that of its predecessor, this hood – a lightweight affair modelled on the Boxster's – disappeared from sight under a flush, body-coloured panel (on previous 911 cabrios, it sat untidily on the tail, back-pack fashion). As an expensive factory option, cabrio buyers could also specify a lightweight hardtop, easily manipulated by two pairs of hands. A Merc SL-style pop-up roll-bar came as standard along with other safety-related hardware.

Furled hood sat as ungainly backpack on earlier 911 cabrios. On later ones it disappeared under flush panel, smoothing deck.

Porsche
911 GT3 & Turbo

Fast, faster, **fastest**

If you want to get a buzz, get a roof. Whooshing along in a topless 911, slipstream massaging your brow, flat-six engine zinging behind your back, may be the embodiment of hedonistic travel, but it is unlikely to be the most exciting. Porsche's seriously addictive 911s have with few exceptions been fixed-head coupés, not ragtops.

Three limited-edition 911 tintops stand out in my memory. The first, beyond the scope of this book because it was made in 1973, is the classic 911RS Carrera 2.7, which, as a seminal funster of unparalleled intimacy, is a strong contender for the title of world's best sports car.

Power isn't everything, as the Carrera 2.7's modest 210bhp testifies. The Carrera 2-based RS of the early Nineties had 50bhp more but wasn't such unbridled fun to drive. I'd go further. It was the only 911 I've driven – and I've driven dozens and owned one – that I actually disliked. On a 400-mile pilgrimage to the Jim Clark museum in Duns, it was only on the last stretch of Scottish tarmac – freshly laid and challengingly twisty – that this thinly veiled racer showed its true mettle.

On super-smooth roads it was sensational: close-ratio gears, bum-pincher Recaros and Carrera Cup brakes heightened the driving experience. Elsewhere, lowered suspension – so stiff it turned your jowls to jelly – bequeathed a ride of intolerable jerkiness. As I wrote in *Car* in 1991: 'We grunt in unison, passenger and I, with every jaw-sagging bump. Even for

Specification	Porsche 911 Turbo (2000)
Engine	3600cc, flat-six, 4ohc, 24V
Engine layout	Longitudinal, rear
Power	414bhp at 6000rpm
Torque	413lb ft at 2700rpm
Gearbox	Six-speed manual
Drive	Rear wheel
Front suspension	MacPherson struts, coils
Rear suspension	Multi link, coils, anti-roll bar
Steering	Assisted rack and pinion
Brakes	ABS-backed ventilated discs all round
Front wheels	Alloy 8Jx18
Rear wheels	Alloy 11Jx18
Front tyres	225-40ZR18
Rear tyres	295-30ZR18
Length	4435mm
Width	1830mm
Height	1295mm
Wheelbase	2350mm
Weight	1540kg (3395lb)
0-60mph (97kph)	4.0sec
0-100mph (161kph)	9.0sec
Top speed	190mph (306kph)
Fuel consumption	14-22mpg

The ultimate driving experience? Latest 911 Turbo rockets to 60mph in 4.0 seconds, tops 190mph. Engine 414bhp, 3.6-litre, twin-turbo flat-six, drives through six-speed gearbox.

seriously addicted performance freaks, the buckling, rumbling motion of this unyielding car is not only hard to tolerate but a deterrent to quick driving.' The beneficial effects of more power (260bhp) and less weight (down by 10 per cent) went largely unnoticed as you braced yourself for the next onslaught of GBH.

The GT3 of the late Nineties wasn't a raw, race-bred, stripped-to-the-shell lightweight with a jitterbug ride and deafening road roar. Far from it. This fully equipped tearaway weighed a little more than the regular 911, hence the absence of the traditional RS (Renn Sport) epithet. Where the GT3 scored over its bloodline precursors was in uniting the feel and dynamic capabilities of a competition car with the creature comforts of a luxury one. It was a sensational combination.

Fearsome performance – from rest to 100mph in a little over 10 seconds – was rooted in a new naturally aspirated 3.6-litre, 360bhp engine evolved from Porsche's GT1 racer. Brakes, suspension and seats were fettled to sharpen responses and improve body control. And how. It all gelled for me at Goodwood's 1999 Festival of Speed hillclimb, despatched in a high-speed blur that started with a cloud of tyre smoke (no traction control here), progressed through a series of wristy flicks (strong steering feel, quick responses) and terminated with rib-crushing braking (after crossing the finish line on the silly side of fast). Sting-in-the-tail instability? Not a sign of it in this truly memorable car.

The last great 911 of the 20th century was Porsche's fifth-generation Turbo – the fastest-ever roadgoing 911. True, the 197mph limited-edition 959 of the late Eighties was a little faster all out. But the all-or-nothing

delivery of its peaky 3.0-litre, 450bhp engine, languid below 5,000rpm, was as challenging as it was exciting. The new Turbo's crushing acceleration was not only as strong against the clock but infinitely more accessible. Torque peaked at a lowly two-seven, then held steady till the tacho hit the red. Raw testosterone wasn't, however, delivered with the 911's characteristic double-edged wail. Here, muted by two intercooled KKK air pumps, was the quietest, most refined flat-six Porsche engine yet made.

GT3 cheaper than Turbo, almost as quick with 360bhp. Handles, goes, stops better that regular 911 on stiffer, lowered suspension. Cabin simply finished but not pared to bone.

Although the Turbo's twin-blower version of the dry-sump, 3.6, 24-valve engine yielded a monstrous 414bhp, its performance advantage over the GT3 was relatively modest. Blame it, as always, on extra weight, not least that imposed by viscous-coupled four-wheel drive and electronic stability control. On lavish equipment, too, just to underline the flagship role of a car that was only just on the right side of £100,000 when it went on sale in Britain in the summer of 2000. Price was unaffected by the choice of transmission: the six-speed manual (the preferred choice of serious drivers) cost the same as the five-speed Tiptronic (an experience-diluting press-button automatic).

Yet to break cover when this book went to press was Porsche's ultimate ragtop, the new 911 Turbo Cabriolet, said to share the same drivetrain as the coupé. Although there was talk of a folding hardtop, *à la* Merc SLK, for Porsche's answer to the BMW Z8, spy pictures in the motoring press depicted traditional canvas headgear.

The scene was set, then, for the ultimate cabriolet shoot-out: Porsche's open 911 Turbo pitched against Ferrari's 400bhp 360 Spider and AM's 420bhp DB7 Vantage V12 convertible.

Porsche Boxster

Quite simply the best

Boxster S addressed criticisms of indifferent performance from original 2.5, later upgraded to 2.7. Stiff chassis prevents scuttle shake, brilliant push-button hood stows neatly in well.

BMW had its Z3, Mercedes-Benz its SLK and, later on, Audi its TT. Topping them all, though, was Porsche's Boxster – in my estimation the best luxury roadster (as opposed to the best stripped-for-action one) of the Nineties, on the right side of silly money. My first encounter with this seductive car was so bewitching that I considered joining the Boxster's waiting list, safe in the knowledge that the car could be run for a year or so without losing value, perhaps even appreciating, given the crazy premiums being paid by must-have-nows. Alas, procrastination saw the queue stretch an overdraft too far. Just as well as there would have been no room for the dog.

The Boxster broke cover as a kite-flying concept car at the 1993 Detroit show – an appropriate venue to test public reaction, given the importance of the US market to Porsche. However, little but the concept – a mid-engined, open two-seater – survived the four-year gestation of the production Boxster, generally held to be less alluring than the squatter, cutely curvaceous original. Dream cars rarely translate into showroom ones without trauma.

Change for the worse aesthetically was evident in slab-sided flanks and long crumple-zoned overhangs – so long, in fact, that the twin-seat Boxster outstretched the outgoing 911, if not its fifth-generation replacement. Developed in tandem with the Boxster, the 996 version of the 911 shared with its cheaper sibling many components, parts of the body structure included. Engines, too – or rather the same new family of flat-six, water-cooled, four-valves-per-cylinder engines. Only in capacity and output did they differ.

In giving the two-boot Boxster a one-touch hood, decently civilised

Specification	Porsche Boxster 2.7
Engine	2687cc, flat-six, 4ohc, 24V
Engine layout	Longitudinal, rear
Power	220bhp at 6400rpm
Torque	192lb ft at 4750rpm
Gearbox	Five-speed manual
Drive	Rear wheel
Front suspension	Struts, coils, transverse arms, anti-roll bar
Rear suspension	Struts, coils, transverse arms, anti-roll bar
Steering	Assisted rack and pinion
Brakes	ABS-backed ventilated discs all round
Front wheels	Alloy 6Jx16
Rear wheels	Alloy 7Jx16
Front tyres	205-55ZR16
Rear tyres	225-50ZR16
Length	4315mm
Width	1930mm
Height	1290mm
Wheelbase	2415mm
Weight	1240kg (2734lb)
0-60mph (97kph)	6.5sec
0-100mph (161kph)	15.7sec
Top speed	150mph (242kph)
Fuel consumption	22-29mpg

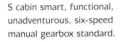

S cabin smart, functional, unadventurous, six-speed manual gearbox standard.

cockpit and at least one hold capable of swallowing golfbags, the car's practicality as everyday wheels was assured for singles and couples, if not families (or dog-owners). Built alongside the 911, there was never any question about quality, either. All right, so the Boxster was not as pretty as the show-stopper that sired it. To criticise the styling as bland, though, would be to ignore the car's terrific presence.

If Porsche erred it was not through incompetent styling but in denying the Boxster the performance of the 968 it effectively replaced – at least to begin with. The 3.0-litre, 240bhp 968 Club Sport would punch to 60mph in 6 seconds flat, comfortably out-sprinting the 2.4-litre, 204bhp Boxster. The new engine was smooth, sonorous, eager and willing to rev. All it lacked was sufficient muscle to do justice to a chassis clearly capable of handling a lot more. That said, the low-drag 140mph Boxster was no sluggard.

On the face of it, comparison with the defunct 968 showed the slower, pricier, less practical Boxster in a rather poor light. Bluntly, it was less car for more money. But wait. Any apparent inferiority paled to insignificance when weighed against the Boxster's two great strengths: its flat-six engine (which made it a real Porsche, not the offspring of a jumped-up Audi), and its mid-engined balance (which endowed the car with wonderfully fluent handling and cornering grip that not even the 968, ragged on the limit, could match).

Simply put, the Boxster went round corners like no previous production Porsche, certainly like no 911. With 48/52 weight distribution – against the 911's tail-heavy 36/73 – the Boxster had perfect inherent poise, with all the heavy bits confined between the wheels, not pendulously projecting beyond

Porsche

157

them. Flat-bottomed and shaped to hug *terra firma* – the boot spoiler popped up automatically at 50mph – the Boxster was aerodynamically stable, too.

Steering was not especially quick, but even with power assistance (considered unnecessary by some purists, given the relatively light loading of the front wheels) it was endearingly communicative, in the best Porsche tradition. It was the feeling of security, though, the impression of limitless cornering grip, that made the Boxster so sensational on the twisty bits. There was nothing uncertain about its handling, no sting-in-the-tail trickiness that made even its 911 contemporary – and blood brother – feel more of a handful when extended. The harder you drove the Boxster, the more it amazed.

In a feature for *Motor Sport* I found myself sitting aside 911 racer (and trader) Nick Faure, trying a Boxster for the first time. 'It seems to wipe the road...it gives you great confidence immediately...there's no learning curve at all – anyone could get in and drive it,' he said. Not like the 911, then.

Nick continued: 'I feel as though I've been driving it for 20 years...it's clearly been built by people who know what the feel of a car should be. The brakes are fantastic...' Amen to that.

Although Faure found the Boxster's performance adequate for the road, other reviewers were less charitable, complaining that performance could and should be better. Roll on the quickie, they said. In fact Porsche rolled on two – an uprated entry-level model (2.7 litres, 220bhp) and the Boxster S (3.2 litres, 240bhp), both introduced in 1999. Because the 2.7 cost very little more than the displaced 2.5 – even though it also boasted new 30-litre side airbags to protect your head and torso (a first in a roadster) – it struck me as the better buy, not least because the pricey six-speed S invoked the law of diminishing returns.

While the 2.7 – same bore, longer stroke, new engine management and drive-by-wire throttle – was still not supercar quick, it was decisively punchier

Production Boxster not as pretty as original show concept, but still an eye-catcher. Family resemblance to latest 911 strong – but engine amidships, not in tail. Original car had 2.5 'six'.

Boxster speedo dominated by central rev counter. On the move, speed also recorded digitally in tacho 'black hole'.

than the 2.5, especially when extended. Despite the presence of variable valve timing, the increase in torque, from 182 to 188lb ft, was more modest than the increase in power. Or so it felt on the road where the car's uncanny cornering ability still outshone its straight-line performance. On a closed track – former GP star Jonathan Palmer's thrilling Bedford Autodrome – I tried to unstick the tenacious Boxster by turning into chicanes hard on the brakes at silly approach speeds. No sweat. The laws of physics that can quickly unsettle a 911 were defied by the obedient Boxster.

Little in the way of ride comfort was sacrificed to achieve such precise, secure handling. If not exactly supple, the suspension – MacPherson struts up front, not classic double wishbones – coped well, albeit with a nutty knobliness, on pocked urban roads. It was at its best, though, when skimming briskly over rural ones.

You sat low in the intimate, roomy-for-two cockpit that broke with Porsche tradition in some ways (for instance, there were welcome hanging pedals, in place of awkward floor-hinged ones) and upheld it in others (simple, embellishment-free decor). One nonsense carried over from the 911 was to give the rev counter dominance over the all-important speedo. Actually, I found the speedo dial largely redundant because the duplicate digital read-out housed in the central tacho was much easier to read. Who else but Porsche would give you two speedos?

Unless geared-up with various options, a base Boxster (a rarity, I suspect) was hardly lavishly equipped for its price. Even the centre console bins and plastic wind deflector cost extra. However, given the engine's modest power and the tyres' huge grip, there was little need for traction control, and the pricey hardtop was hardly necessary given the excellence of the standard-issue electric hood. At the press of a button, the roof was up and over and furled from sight inside a lidded well in a scant 12 seconds. Ragtops came no better than this.

S for sufficient

Porsche had a fine line to tread with the go-faster Boxster S. On the one hand it had to be significantly quicker than the original 2.5-litre, 204bhp car to satisfy cries for a hike in performance. On the other it had to defer to the 3.4-litre, 300bhp 911 Carrera by being respectfully slower. It would never do to undermine the standing of the high-profit 911 with a junior upstart. Something midway between the two, something of around 2.9 litres and 250bhp, would do very nicely.

In the event, the S hit the road with a 3.2-litre engine yielding 252bhp. Bull's-eye on power, albeit briefly. Porsche knew (but the punters didn't at the time) that the base car was about to be upgraded anyway, with a 2.7, 240bhp engine. To bridge the gap between this motor and the 911's would have required 270bhp – easily achieved but too close to the Carrera for comfort.

The upshot of all this was that the 911 retained a healthy advantage over the Boxster S, but that the S's superiority over the base 2.7 was hardly dramatic. I drove both cars on the same day and concluded that the S was quicker by a margin that didn't really justify its high premium, even allowing for a six-speed gearbox. Pricey though it was, however, the S looked like something of a bargain at £30,000 less than the 911 Cabriolet, which is heavier and less aerodynamic than the fixed-head coupé and therefore not quite so quick.

Aside from its six-speed gearbox and bored and stroked engine – now with stronger crank (to allow a 7,200rpm limit), Bosch ME 7.2 electronics and a drive-by-wire throttle – the S differed from the regular Boxster in having a central drag-increasing air intake (the best visual giveaway), taller gearing, 17in alloys, some soft-touch decor and black-on-grey instruments. Cloth lining the hood not only covered the bracing bars but cut wind noise as well. With optional five-speed Tiptronic transmission came press-button gearchanging. Me? I preferred the slick-six manual.

159

Reliant Scimitar & Sabre

A promise unfulfilled

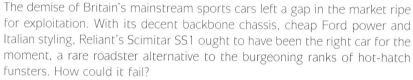

Scimitar SST styling, by the late William Towns, much cleaner than Michelotti's original, white car, below.

The demise of Britain's mainstream sports cars left a gap in the market ripe for exploitation. With its decent backbone chassis, cheap Ford power and Italian styling, Reliant's Scimitar SS1 ought to have been the right car for the moment, a rare roadster alternative to the burgeoning ranks of hot-hatch funsters. How could it fail?

Long faces and shuffling feet at the subdued 1984 press launch I attended foreshadowed an uphill struggle for the plucky little Scimitar. At first it was the car's fussy lines and indifferent finish that came in for criticism. So much for Italian style. Later road tests revealed able handling and agility but shortcomings in ride comfort, refinement, grip and performance. The four-speed 69bhp 1.3 was a no-hoper. Even with Ford's 96bhp CVH 1600 under the bonnet, the SS1 was no fireball.

Reliant's surprise adoption of the Nissan Silvia's 135bhp blown four-cylinder engine and five-speed gearbox was a stroke of genius that transformed the Scimitar. With a single belt-driven camshaft, eight-valve head and light-pressure turbocharging (the boost was limited to 7psi), the injected Nissan engine was nothing special technically. But it worked wonders. Acceleration to 60mph from rest tumbled from a tardy 12 seconds to around 7. Top speed leapt from under the ton to 125mph. Performance wasn't just tweaked, it was blasted on to a new plane. Only the very best tearaway hatchbacks, headed by Renault's 5GT Turbo, could

Specification	Reliant Scimitar Sabre
Engine	1809cc, 4-cylinder, sohc, 8V, turbocharger
Engine layout	Longitudinal, front
Power	135bhp at 6000rpm
Torque	141lb ft at 4000rpm
Gearbox	Five-speed manual
Drive	Rear wheel
Front suspension	Double wishbones, coils, anti-roll bar
Rear suspension	Semi-trailing arms, coils, anti-roll bar
Steering	Unassisted rack & pinion
Brakes	Discs at front, drums at rear, no ABS
Wheels	Alloy 6Jx15
Tyres	195-50ZR15
Length	3885mm
Width	1585mm
Height	1240mm
Wheelbase	2135mm
Weight	840kg (1859lb)
0-60mph (97kph)	7.2sec
0-100mph (161kph)	19.5sec
Top speed	130mph (209kph)
Fuel consumption	21-30mpg

live with the 1800Ti, which claimed several notable scalps in magazine tests. Porsche's 944, for instance, couldn't match the Reliant's terrific mid-range punch. As if the boost in performance was not enough, the Nissan engine was sweeter and more refined than the coarse CVH of the unwanted 1600. Being of Japanese manufacture, it could also be relied on to give long and trouble-free service.

Skilled extroverts found in the 1800Ti a hilariously tail-happy handler that could be flicked into outrageous oversteer with a deft right foot: if anything, the grip of modestly shod wheels carried by semi-trailing rear suspension was perhaps too easily relinquished on slippery tarmac. However, no-one now questioned the Scimitar's ability to entertain – the prime function of a sports car. The ride was still on the harsh side of jittery, and the strong-arm hood was awkward to secure and furl. With the Mazda MX-5's simple up-and-over now showing how it should be done, there was no longer any excuse for clumsy headgear.

There was nothing wrong with the Scimitar's packaging (mounting the spare wheel under the bonnet left a big uncluttered boot at the rear) but the wrapping still let it down badly. The late William Towns, who penned Aston Martin's DBS (and gruesome Lagonda) got the job of reskinning the Scimitar for the Nineties, of doing away with Michelotti's disliked excesses, particularly the 'layered-cake' swage lines. If not exactly pretty – Towns's hands were tied by several constraints – the SST was at least a cleaner, tidier car than the SS1 it displaced. Instead of a large number of small panels, which presented alignment problems during assembly, the SST had three large ones – floorpan, front section and rear section – all the better for fit and integrity.

The same 135bhp five-speed powertrain was carried over from the old car. And why not? It did a cracking job. In a straight line the SST could just about live with the quick version of the new front-drive Lotus Elan. Compared with the tail-happy Reliant, though, the safe, user-friendly Lotus was in another league when it came to cornering prowess.

On a performance-per-pound basis, the SST was of the right stuff. Poor detailing let it down, if you can call a cramped cockpit, heavy steering, unsupportive seats, a clumsy hood and poor hood-up ventilation mere details. Reliant stuck with it, though. After the company was bought from the receivers by Bean Industries in 1991, Towns had a second go at revitalising a bland shape. Literally tinkering round the

Interior smart, unadventurous. Power from 1.8 turbocharged Nissan 'four'.

edges, he gave the car flared wheelarches, sill extensions, a tail spoiler and colour-keyed bumpers (formerly black). Although the SST moniker was dropped in favour of Scimitar Sabre, demand remained very low.

Given more development, one felt that there was a better car in the 1800Ti/SST/Sabre trying to get out. Alas, it never emerged. There were troubled times ahead for Reliant, and the little Scimitar sports car didn't survive them.

Renault A610

Plastic **fantastic**

Renault's rear-engined GTA, the sub-supercar aimed at Porsche's jugular in the Eighties, found few buyers in Britain. Although the GTA went as well as it looked, neither tackiness nor left-hand drive helped its cause or cachet. Nor did the name, which hardly evoked the same coo-eh reaction as 'Carrera' or 'Esprit'. That the GTA came across as a Gallic upstart competing above its station did less than justice to a worthy car. The lack of image – crucial at this level – was as unfortunate as it was unfair. Denied its proper Alpine title in the UK (because Peugeot lay claim to it), the GTA was ostensibly robbed of a heritage burnished by competition winners. It was, after all, a descendant of the A110, which enjoyed cult status in France – and rightly so with two Monte Carlo Rally victories and a World Championship to its credit.

Dieppe-based Alpine – effectively the sporting wing of Renault – aimed to put the GTA's problems behind it with its 1992 successor. The A610 (also lumbered with an anonymous name) was 80 per cent new. It was also better made and finished, as well as faster and more equitably balanced. The steel chassis to which the composite body was bonded was stiffened up, the double-wishbone suspension tuned to good effect.

Of French idiosyncrasies – clap-hands wipers, funny door latches that weren't on the doors, floor-hinged pedals and bootless extremities, for example – there was still plenty of evidence, thank goodness: the A610 was no slave to fashion or convention. Should generous plus-two accommodation appear to disqualify Renault's fastest-ever car as a sportster, incidentally, remember that the occasional seating doubled as a boot: there was nowhere else to stow luggage.

Twin-turbo engine mounted behind rear axle, like Porsche 911's. Handling not upset by tail heaviness. Blown 3.0 V6 gives 250bhp, top speed of 160mph, vivid acceleration.

Specification	Renault Alpine A610
Engine	2975cc, V6, sohc, 12V, intercooled turbo
Engine layout	Longitudinal, rear
Power	250bhp at 5750rpm
Torque	258lb ft at 2900rpm
Gearbox	Five-speed manual
Drive	Rear wheel
Front suspension	Double wishbones, coils, anti-roll bar
Rear suspension	Double wishbones, coils, anti-roll bar
Steering	Assisted rack and pinion
Brakes	ABS-backed ventilated discs all round
Front wheels	Alloy 7Jx16
Rear wheels	Alloy 9Jx16
Front tyres	205-45ZR16
Rear tyres	245-45ZR16
Length	4415mm
Width	1760mm
Height	1190mm
Wheelbase	2340mm
Weight	1370kg (3020lb)
0-60mph (97kph)	5.9sec
0-100mph (161kph)	16.5sec
Top speed	165mph (266kph)
Fuel consumption	17-25mpg

The rear-mounted engine, pendulously mounted behind the back wheels, might also have been regarded as suspiciously oddball had Porsche not made such a layout technically respectable. By moving various components, including the spare wheel, from back to front, the A610's 43/67 weight distribution was an improvement on the GTA's 40/60. Press road testers concurred on one vital aspect of the A610: it handled well, without vice. Power steering may have robbed the helm of intimacy but it made for easier parking and greater agility.

Power came from a blown version of Renault's joint-venture PRV V6, increased in capacity from 2.5 litres (as in the GTA) to 3.0 litres, raising power by 50bhp to 250bhp. Torque was also muscled up. Just as important, it peaked at lower revs, so delivery was less lag-prone, more linear than the all-or-nothing GTA's. Pity that the engine betrayed its humble roots with undistinguished sound effects marked on the over-run by wastegate flutter.

Performance was almost a match for that of the contemporary blown Esprit SE. In a shoot-out against the Lotus for *Car* magazine, I fell for the striking French polymer in a big way. 'Despite its indifferent interior, which is neither traditionally opulent nor adventurously modern, the A610 grew in stature as the miles built up. If this isn't the world's most underrated supercar, never mind its most affordable, pray tell me what is...' Time hasn't dimmed that view.

Between February 1991 and early '95, when production ceased (to make way for the Spider), Renault made 849 A610s. This makes the last of the Regie's rear-engined sportsters more exclusive than a Ferrari 348.

Renault

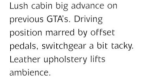

Lush cabin big advance on previous GTA's. Driving position marred by offset pedals, switchgear a bit tacky. Leather upholstery lifts ambience.

Renault Spider

The hefty lightweight

Zany Spider modern interpretation of Caterham (*née* Lotus) Seven. Wind deflector of first cars ineffective. Goggles essential to protect eyes. Proper glass screen came later.

If ever a car was upstaged by a superior rival, it was Renault's Spider. Launched to great acclaim at the spring 1995 Geneva show, the brave Spider was boldly conceived, audaciously shaped, superbly engineered and dynamically strong. As a high-style, street-legal racer for show-offs dedicated to hedonistic entertainment, it was a compelling dream come true, a latterday Lotus Seven in Gallic fancy dress. It would, Renault believed, be the ultimate in affordable driving machines. It wasn't.

Hand-built in hundreds, rather than thousands, the Spider was not a mainstream Renault profit-maker, but a zany, no-frills, look-what-we-can-do pocket rocket. Renault boring? Not us. There was, however, a spoiler in the plot. It turned out that anything the Spider could do, the cheaper Lotus Elise could do better. The Spider wasn't a bad car – I loved it and lusted after it – but the thunder-stealing Elise was a better one in most important respects, even if getting in and out wasn't one of them.

Both manufacturers – giant Renault and little Lotus – had in mind the seminal Seven when they conceived minimalist sports two-seaters worthy of the 21st century. Great minds being like thinkers, they came up with much the same formula: an aluminium-framed, composite-skinned, stylishly extravagant, starkly equipped road-hugger powered by an amidships transverse twin-cam four. Simplicity and lightness were common philosophies.

Renault's design chief, Patrick Le Quement, hatched the radical Spider with Christian Contzen, head of the company's motorsport division. The Spider was to be a real racer, with its own one-make circuit series, not merely a quasi one. Hence the involvement of Claude Fiore or Fiore

Specification	Renault Spider (1997)
Engine	1998cc, 4-cylinder, dohc, 16V
Engine layout	Transverse, mid
Power	150bhp at 6000rpm
Torque	140lb ft at 4500rpm
Gearbox	Five-speed manual
Drive	Rear wheel
Front suspension	Double wishbones, coils, anti-roll bar
Rear suspension	Double wishbones, coils, anti-roll bar
Steering	Unassisted rack & pinion
Brakes	Ventilated discs all round, no ABS
Front wheels	Alloy 8Jx16
Rear wheels	9Jx16
Front tyres	205-50VR16
Rear tyres	225-50VR15
Length	3795mm
Width	2200mm
Height	1250mm
Wheelbase	2345mm
Weight	950kg (2094lb)
0-60mph (97kph)	7.5sec
0-100mph (161kph)	24.0sec
Top speed	125mph (201kph)
Fuel consumption	25-34mpg

Concept, respected designers of competition cars, and Dieppe-based Alpine, who dropped the poor-selling (and under-rated) A610 coupé to clear its production lines for the new image-builder. But for problems with the Alpine name in Britain, the new sportster might have been called Alpine Spider rather than Sport Spider.

In the interests of weight-paring, the chassis was fabricated from aluminium extrusions to create a stiff monocoque structure said to be 40 per cent lighter than a comparable steel one. Rather than hide the welded seams, Renault left them exposed as a styling feature in a cockpit bereft of superfluous trim and equipment. Although the car had doors – they opened like insect wings to make getting in and out quite easy – there were no soft furnishings, no heater, no audio, no hood, not even a windscreen for the initial batch of cars. Instead, you peered over an arched wind-deflector, designed to sling airborne debris over your head. If it worked at all, it didn't work well enough to prevent dust, grit and stones, never mind bovine fall-out and spray, from peppering your face. I can tell you, it hurt. Without a helmet and visor you risked serious injury.

Double wishbone suspension (with racing-style rose joints and horizontal spring/damper units, just like Ferrari's F50) carried the stark, composite-clad sportster, while a 150bhp 2.0-litre twin-cam from the Clio Williams powered it through a five-speed manual gearbox. As the specification looked as tasty as the car's dramatic lines and bright colours, expectations ran high. With all that power and so little weight – under 800kg had been the target – performance would surely be staggering. It wasn't. Brisk, yes, Elise-beating, no. What no-one could fathom was how the aluminium-

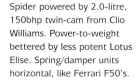

Spider powered by 2.0-litre, 150bhp twin-cam from Clio Williams. Power-to-weight bettered by less potent Lotus Elise. Spring/damper units horizontal, like Ferrari F50's.

based, stripped-to-the-metal Spider could weigh so much more than the little Lotus, even allowing for the proper windscreen that later cars (and all right-handed ones) were to get.

Traction was strong, the engine eager, but acceleration was always on the tame side of exciting. Although down on power, the 118bhp Elise was over 200kg lighter – and it showed. Only at top speed – about 125mph – were the two cars pretty evenly matched. Elsewhere, the lightness of the Lotus more than offset its power deficiency.

For outright cornering power, the well-shod Spider probably had the drop on the modestly tyred Elise. Only on a track could you safely probe the outer limits of its sensational roadholding. But there's more to fun-car entertainment than outright grip. Judged on other vital qualities – on ride comfort, communicative feedback, steering sensitivity, agility, adjustablity and fluency, for instance – the Elise had the Spider on the run. The Lotus also had the better gearchange, and its cockpit, though pretty basic, was not quite so stark as the Spider's. There was also the small matter of price. Why pay in Britain £25,950 for a topless Spider when you could buy an Elise, complete with (pathetic) hood, for £6,000 less?

As a fringe, flag-waving model rather than a big-volume mainstream one, the pricey Sport Spider was never going to flood the market like the Mazda MX-5. It was too finely focused to be of broad appeal, too specialised to sell in large numbers. In a three-year production span (from March 1996 to July '99) Dieppe-based Alpine made fewer than 2,000 Spiders, of which 100, as planned, were sold with right-handed controls in Britain, where the Lotus Elise stole the show.

No-frills cockpit devoid of trim and furnishings, exposed welded aluminium chassis interior feature. Winged seats strong on lateral support, helmet desirable.

Will the **real Cobra** please stand up?

Carroll Shelby, former pig farmer and Le Mans winner, was clearly miffed. 'For 20 years, I have watched others making knock-offs (of the Cobra),' he said on his Shelby American website. 'Would people rather have one of my CSX4000s...or one of those bootleg deals?' By the autumn of '99, 125 buyers of his reincarnated Cobra – the Anglo-American hybrid he created with AC's help in the Sixties – had answered the question. They preferred the real thing, each carrying Shelby's signature.

CSX is short for Carroll Shelby Export, which is how AC originally tagged the chassis destined for Shelby's Californian workshops, where bare bones received raw muscle. The revivals, stronger in chassis and better suspended without undermining authenticity, were sold either in component form or as 'rollers', less drivetrain. So much for the background.

Shelby's 'Son of Cobra', the Series 1, broke cover in 1999. Its muscular looks and brutal punch were clearly inspired by the Sixties classic, but don't be fooled by that. Here was a clean-sheet design, the first all-new car that Shelby had made at his Las Vegas headquarters. Squat and wide, the Series 1 (Ford still owns the Cobra name) sat on a lightweight aluminium chassis clothed in carbon-fibre bodywork said to weigh little more than 60kg. Suspension was race-bred, so the S1 was well equipped to excite.

Power came not from Ford – surprise, surprise – but from a fettled 4.0-litre Oldsmobile Aurora V8, tweaked to deliver 320bhp to the back wheels through a six-speed ZF gearbox. Quick steering (1.6 turns lock to lock), terrific performance (0-100mph in 11 seconds) mighty brakes (from the Corvette) and huge grip (315/40 rubber at the rear) backed the maker's claim that the S1 'is as close to a race car on the street as you can get.'

Specification	Shelby Series 1 (2000)
Engine	3998cc, 4ohc, V8, 32V
Engine layout	Longitudinal, front
Power	320bhp at 6500rpm
Torque	290lb ft at 5000rpm
Gearbox	Six-speed manual
Drive	Rear wheel
Front suspension	Double wishbones, coils, anti-roll bar
Rear suspension	Double wishbones, coils, anti-roll bar
Steering	Assisted rack and pinion
Brakes	Ventilated discs all round
Front wheels	Alloy 10Jx18
Rear wheels	Alloy 12Jx18
Front tyres	265-40ZR18
Rear tyres	315-40ZR18
Length	4292mm
Width	1943mm
Height	1194mm
Wheelbase	2405mm
Weight	1202kg (2650lb)
0-60mph (97kph)	4.4sec
0-100mph (161kph)	11.0sec
Top speed	170mph (2??kph)
Fuel consumption	15-25mpg

Strathcarron SC-5

Minimalist with the most

No doors, no roof, no trim, no basic creature comforts other than hip-hugging seats and a full-width screen. The Strathcarron was so finely focused on fun it made the Lotus Elise seem like an overweight softie.

Do not dismiss the Strathcarron as just another backyard special. As respected engineering consultants to the motor industry, Strathcarron identified a market niche for a simple mid-engined, race-bred sports lightweight. With firm parameters in mind, it went to race-car manufacturer Reynard to design and build the prototypes.

The result was an immensely stiff bonded composite monocoque assembled from panels of aluminium honeycomb. The structure was originally skinned in GRP. Production cars, would get bodywork made from aluminium-skinned plastic laminate. Cup-sized lights, stacked in threes gave the car its distinctive face.

In the interests of lightness, Reynard eschewed a customary car-sourced powertrain and opted instead for a superbike one from Triumph – a four-cylinder in-line twin-cam yielding 125bhp. In a car weighing around 560kg, this gave a fearsome 225bhp per tonne, and a claimed 0-60mph time of under 6 seconds. Direct steering, race-car handling, terrific agility and limpet grip were inbred.

De Dion-suspended rear wheels were driven through an underslung six-speed sequential gearbox and a special Hewland-built transaxle. Double wishbones suspended the front wheels, a quick, unassisted rack and pinion set-up steered them. Brembo disc brakes anchored the lithe lightweight. Sales were scheduled to start in September 2000, four years after the first SC-1 'clay'.

Specification	Strathcarron SC-4 (1999)
Engine	1180cc, 4-cylinder, dohc, 16V
Engine layout	Transverse, mid
Power	125bhp at 9700rpm
Torque	70lb ft at 6500rpm
Gearbox	Six-speed manual sequential
Drive	Rear wheel
Front suspension	Double wishbones, coils
Rear suspension	de Dion axle, control links, coils
Steering	Unassisted rack & pinion
Brakes	Ventilated discs all round
Front wheels	Alloy 6.5Jx16
Rear wheels	Alloy 7.0Jx17
Front tyres	195-60 16
Rear tyres	215-45 17
Length	3600mm
Width	1700mm
Height	1200mm
Wheelbase	2400mm
Weight	560kg (1235lb)
0-60mph (97kph)	5.5sec
0-100mph (161kph)	15.0sec (est)
Top speed	125mph (201kph)
Fuel consumption	25-35mpg

Suzuki Cappuccino
Small but **perfectly formed**

Suzuki's diminutive Cappuccino was the product of Japan's Kei Jidocha (small car) laws. Build 'em tiny (less than 130in long by 53in wide) and restrict their performance (with 660cc, 65bhp and 87mph limits) and micros like the Cappuccino were exempt from Draconian parking laws.

Small though it was, the wacky Cappuccino was a genuine sportster, a spiritual successor to the Austin-Healey Sprite and MG Midget. Under the bonnet was a three-cylinder, 12-valve, twin-cam turbo with the potential to deliver a lot more than the quoted 63bhp. Motorcycle ancestry explains a rev limit of over 9,000rpm, though no more than five-three was attainable in fifth, before the regulator cut in at around 85mph – no great handicap in '70 mph' Britain. Acceleration was nippy, no more: Mazda's full-size MX-5, not noted for straight-line fireworks, was appreciably quicker. It was the eagerness of the revvy little engine, and the slickness of its short-throw gearchange, that made the Cappuccino feel so feisty. Economy was also good – outstanding, even, if you suppressed the engine's willingness to scream its head off.

With quick steering (surprisingly power-assisted) and firm suspension, the little Suzuki handled more like a kart than a car. Agility was its forte, back-doubles its speciality, city streets its natural habitat. The ride, mind, was jittery around town and the cockpit cramped for six-footers. Toy-like dimensions, if not dynamics, effectively restricted usage to people of average height or below.

Equipment was quite generous – UK cars even had air-conditioning – but there was little in the way of luggage space, especially when the headgear filled the boot. You travelled light, or not at all, in a Cappuccino.

Specification	Suzuki Cappuccino (1994)
Engine	657cc, 3-cylinder, dohc, 12V, turbocharger
Engine layout	Longitudinal, front
Power	63bhp at 6500rpm
Torque	63lb ft at 4000rpm
Gearbox	Five-speed manual
Drive	Rear wheel
Front suspension	Double wishbones, coils, anti-roll bar
Rear suspension	Multi link, coils, anti-roll bar
Steering	Assisted rack and pinion
Brakes	Ventilated front discs, solid rear discs, no ABS
Wheels	Alloy 5Jx14
Tyres	165-65HR14
Length	3295mm
Width	1395mm
Height	1185mm
Wheelbase	2060mm
Weight	665kg (1466lb)
0-60mph (97kph)	11.5sec
Top speed	83mph (134kph) (governed)
Fuel consumption	35-50mpg

Toyota MR2

The Targa goes soft

Latest back-to-basics roadster aims to eclipse Mazda MX-5.

According to some observers, the era of the modern sports car starts right here, with the Toyota MR2. Although targa-topped, and therefore not fully open to the elements – not, in fact, a genuine roadster at all – the 1984 original had impeccable credentials as a pure-bred driving machine years before Mazda launched its all-conquering MX-5.

Something of a 'bitsa' visually, the first MR2 (standing for Midships Recreational 2-seater) was dynamically right on target. Dull Toyota could muster a little flair after all. Weight blunted performance of the raucous 122bhp 1.6 twin-cam four (the 4A-EG as used in the Corolla GT) that screamed away behind your ears, but the things that mattered to serious drivers – steering, gearchanging, handling, agility, cornering – were all of top-drawer quality.

Fiat's mid-engined X1/9 (also targa-roofed) had been around since 1972 as a template, so the MR2, Japan's best sports car since the Datzun 240Z, was hardly original in concept. Its execution, though, was something of a revelation. Not that Japanese dependability and build quality prevented demand-led production declining from over 42,500 in 1985 to fewer than 18,200 in '88, the Mk1's last full year of production.

Specification	Toyota MR2 (2000)
Engine	1794cc, 4-cylinder, dohc, 16V
Engine layout	Transverse, mid
Power	138bhp at 6400rpm
Torque	127lb ft at 4400rpm
Gearbox	Five-speed manual
Drive	Rear wheel
Front suspension	MacPherson struts, coils, anti-roll bar
Rear suspension	Multi-link struts, coils, anti-roll bar
Steering	Assisted rack and pinion
Brakes	Ventilated discs all round
Front wheels	Alloy 6Jx15
Rear wheels	Alloy 6.5Jx15
Front tyres	185-55VR15
Rear tyres	205-50 VR15
Length	3885mm
Width	1695mm
Height	1240mm
Wheelbase	2450mm
Weight	970kg (2138lb)
0-60mph (97kph)	7.0sec
0-100mph (161kph)	23.0sec
Top speed	130mph (209kph)
Fuel consumption	28-37mpg

As a product of the Eighties, the original MR2 is outside the scope of this book. Its second-generation replacement, which was bigger, heavier, plusher and, with a 2.0-litre twin-cam engine, faster than the raw-boned 1.6 it succeeded, was less distinctive, less focused as a driver's plaything. Less secure in its handling, too, until modified to address an oversteer problem. If you wanted your hair ruffling, only the GT T-bar variant, with two removable roof panels, could oblige – just. Strong sellers though they were in the early years, the undistinguished MR2s that spanned the Nineties were not sports cars of the top-down, jowl-creasing, eye-watering variety.

With the back-to-basics third-generation MR2, which broke cover as a production car at the 1999 Frankfurt show (though it had been 'scooped' in the motoring press as early as '97 and had previously appeared as a concept at Chicago), Toyota rediscovered the plot through a 'renegade' engineering team that pursued its goal after the MR2 programme had been officially halted.

Here at last was classic roadster entertainment. On sale by the end of 1999, the Mk3 iteration of Toyota's global two-seater retained the mid-transverse engine layout of its predecessors. However, space for a furled hood was created by placing the powertrain further back – a move that also benefited crash safety and insulation from the noisy bits. Lengthening the wheelbase made for better handling balance, too.

At £24,000 in Britain, the outgoing MR2, more coupé than sportster, was in a kind of limbo-land, neither one thing nor the other and expensive with it. By the turn of the century, sales had slumped to a trickle. There were potentially richer pickings downmarket in the land of fun that Mazda had milked so well. Everyone else, it seemed, was cashing in on the MX-5's runaway success, so why not Toyota?

The focus of the re-invented MR2 was so different that to inherit the old one's name hardly seemed appropriate. Hence MRS (for Mid-engined Recreational Spyder), which the newcomer was called in Japan. To think of the MRS as a cheap Porsche Boxster – even as a Lotus Elise with a few more creature comforts – was to get the basics more or less into perspective. With the MGF as a targeted rival, Rover took the new Toyota very seriously.

It used to be unwritten industry lore that new models would be bigger, heavier and more expensive than the ones they succeeded. Not the MRS, which was 294mm (nearly a foot) shorter and marginally narrower than the outgoing car. Weight was down to around 1,000kg (less than that of the original MR2), allowing the use of a smaller 1.8 all-aluminium Celica engine boasting lightweight internals and 'intelligent' variable valve timing. Even so, power was down from the 2.0 MR2's 173bhp to an unremarkable 138bhp. Off came the roof, helping to save weight, to be replaced by a simple up-and-over manual hood, complete with heated glass rear window, that stowed neatly

First MR2, bottom left, messily styled but dynamically strong. Its bigger, heavier, plusher successor, below, less focused as a driver's car. Neither was made as an open roadster.

without tonneau or rigid lid.

With terrific traction and a respectable power-to-weight ratio of 146bhp per tonne, the MR2 went as well as the more powerful outgoing 2.0 car. By Lotus Elise standards, though, acceleration was nothing special. Not so economy, which ranged from good to outstanding, depending on how you drove. As variable valve timing gave an even flow of power, shifting gears – the change was as switch-like as ever – was more of an indulgence than a necessity. The MRS was introduced with a five-speed manual gearbox. By the time you read this, though, the two-pedal sequential 'box featured on the concept show car may well have reached production.

The MRS went on sale in Britain, badged MR2, in the spring of 2000, priced at under £18,500, which was competitive with Mazda's MX-5 1.8 and the regular MGF. Toyota forecast that it would sell 3,500 cars in the first full year, making the UK one of the MR2's best European markets. But was such optimism warranted, given the strength of the opposition and the weaknesses of the MR2? There was nothing amiss with its prowess as a funster, but the cramped cockpit was a bit low-rent, the styling unimaginitive, even a tad drab, and the absence of a boot amazing. Restricting luggage space to behind-the-seats cubbies and a tiny under-bonnet bin (also housing the space-saver spare) greatly reduced the MR2's practicality as everyday wheels, and virtually ruled it out as holiday transport. UK buyers did, however, get anti-lock brakes, twin airbags, even a CD. A factory-fitted hardtop to supplement the decent (though crease-prone) hood cost an extra £1,500.

Air scoops feed mid-mounted 138bhp transverse engine. Pert, minimalist styling, hardtop pricey extra.

Toyota had promised a pure, simple, lithe sports car with quick reflexes and ample pizzazz – and that's what it delivered. Whether it eclipsed the more practical MX-5, a decade its senior yet still radiating the bloom of youth, is an ongoing debate.

TVR S & V8S

Angles out, curves in

TVR took off after Peter Wheeler took over. Before 1982 the Blackpool-based sports car maker produced many worthy funsters – Vixens, Tuscans, Tasmins and Ms – that attracted enthusiast buyers bored by mainstream alternatives. In a TVR they found individuality, if nothing quite so exotic or well-made as a Porsche or Ferrari. What Wheeler, proprietor and boss, brought to TVR was style, flair and prestige. TVRs had always been exclusive and fast. Wheeler gave them glamour too.

There was nothing wrong with the basic TVR template – established by founder Trevor Wilkinson in 1957 – of sturdy tubular steel chassis, front-to-rear drivetrain, low-slung glass-fibre bodywork and plenty of proprietary power. Through good times and bad since, TVR has consistently espoused this formula. Technical overkill, like a mid-mounted engine or four-wheel drive, never mind traction control, anti-lock brakes or four-wheel steering, was not in the script. Wheeler did go on to make his own engines (of which more later), not to mention ambitious Ferrari-threatening supercars, but he stuck in the main to the traditional plot, relying on gut reaction for guidance, just as Sir William Lyons once did at Jaguar, and Colin Chapman at Lotus.

Wheeler's revival of the old M-series, renamed the S, may have seemed retrogressive at the time, but with hindsight it can be seen as a turning point in TVR's fortunes. For a start, it underlined Wheeler's taste (clearly shared by his customers) for voluptuously curvy cars rather than chisel-edged ones – and they didn't come much more angular than the wedge-shaped Tasmins or the big 350/390/420 two-seaters he inherited. It also validated an old American adage: for maximum thrills, a small, lightweight car is best served

Specification	TVR V8S (1992)
Engine	3950cc, V8, ohv pushrod, 16V
Engine layout	Longitudinal, front
Power	240bhp at 5750rpm
Torque	275lb ft at 4200rpm
Gearbox	Five-speed manual
Drive	Rear wheel
Front suspension	Double wishbones, coils, anti-roll bar
Rear suspension	Semi-trailing arms, coils
Steering	Unassisted rack & pinion
Brakes	Ventilated front discs, solid rear discs, no ABS
Wheels	Alloy 6.5Jx15
Tyres	205-60ZR15
Length	3960mm
Width	1670mm
Height	1225mm
Wheelbase	2285mm
Weight	1029kg (2248lb)
0-60mph (97kph)	5.3sec
0-100mph (161kph)	14.0sec
Top speed	150mph (242kph)
Fuel consumption	19-27mpg

Fearsome TVR V8S spawned by Ford V6-powered S series, revival of M-series. Curvy lines were back in, chisel edges out. Bonnet bulge needed to clear machinery.

by a stonking great engine.

The TVR S started life in 1987 with just sufficient power – 160bhp from Ford's ancient, all-iron 2.8-litre pushrod V6 – to make it interesting. Lots of accessible torque, emphasised by a fruity exhaust (a TVR speciality), may have made the rumbustious S seem quicker than it actually was, but it handled well, gripped tenaciously and looked and felt the part of a serious sports car. It seduced me into buying one, though my tenure of a scarlet one-previous-owner S2 was short-lived.

In some respects – performance, looks, handling, sound effects, even practicality – the big-booted S fulfilled its promise. I loved its rakish profile, elegant five-spoke alloy wheels, flat cornering and canny headgear – neither hood nor targa but something in between that gave the best of both worlds. I tolerated the general lack of sophistication – the crude dash, awkward doors, choppy ride, pathetic mirrors, inefficient demisting and wretched ground clearance.

The all-important driving experience, though, was flawed in my car by squadgy seats, heavy steering and a sticky gearshift. Worse still, my trust in the car was undermined by a serious engine malfunction that left me stranded, though whether this was down to Ford or TVR is open to debate. I should have avoided the S2 and gone instead for a 2.9 168bhp S3, which in several key ways – performance, accessibility and comfort among them –

TVR

174

Fettled 4.0-litre Rover V8 gives lightweight TVR S huge performance. Like-priced Elan couldn't keep up. Care needed in wet if limitations of spaceframe chassis not exceeded.

Cabin tidy but ergonomically flawed. Instruments small and poorly sited, switchgear basic, centre divide fouls gear-changing elbow. TVR's adventurous interiors came later in Nineties.

was a superior car. Better still, I should have waited for the formidable V8S.

Sired by the S3, the V8 united for the first time all the ingredients – slinky looks, light weight and huge muscle – that were to become the hallmarks of Wheeler's subsequent TVRs. The inspiration for the Millennium Dome could have been the huge bonnet bulge needed to accommodate the 4.0-litre Rover V8 from the 400SE. It did the styling no favours. Given the size of the engine, 240bhp and 275lb ft of torque were nothing special. In a car weighing just on a tonne, though, these outputs lifted performance to a new plane, way beyond that of the V8's Ford-engined precursors.

Quick though the like-priced Lotus Elan was, it was soundly trounced by the TVR. Ditto Porsche's 944 convertible, costing very nearly twice as much. In the V8S TVR had a civilised roomy-for-two roadster that could match the acceleration of Caterham's cramped Seven HPC – and beat its top speed by 20mph. Here, half-forgotten a decade on, was the first of TVR's modern supercars, capable of humbling a Ferrari Testarossa in a straight 0-60mph sprint.

There were inevitable snags. For a start, the presence of so much horny power exposed the limitations of the S's spaceframe chassis and tyres. Driven with circumspection, the V8 was forgiving enough, not least because of communicative steering and surprisingly supple suspension. The only traction control on slippery roads was that exercised by a delicate right foot. If wheelspin and whoopsie oversteer were not to test the driver's opposite-lock skills, caution was the watchword, especially in the wet. This was no car for the faint-hearted or the inept.

Then there was the noise, which, even by TVR's standards, was over the top. The big V8 massaged your hearing apparatus with a thumping throb when ticking over, stirring the neighbours as much as adrenalin. Blip the throttle and the fettled howitzer barked like a Can-Am racer. Goose-pimply though it may have been to petrolheads out in the sticks, the blaring exhaust was excessive in noise-conscious suburbia. On motorways, too, given that wind roar added to the cacophony. Still, for those who wanted stupendous performance in a two-seater roadster that offered more than peripheral civility and practicality, the V8S was hard to beat in the early Nineties.

TVR Griffith

The beautiful **brute**

Long-running Griffith, launched '92, soon eclipsed older S3 and S V8. Gorgeously clean, smooth, flowing lines epitomise TVR styling at its best.

They do things the old way at TVR, by hand, experience and intuition. And it works. Thus the Griffith – the first truly stunning TVR, with knock-out looks worthy of Pininfarina at its best – wasn't shaped on a computer screen. Overseen by Peter Wheeler, it was sculpted from foam blocks with file, scraper and blade, working to a simple principle: if it looked right, it was right; if it didn't, it wasn't. The plus-two Speed Eight, shown alongside the prototype Griffith at the 1990 NEC show, clearly didn't shape up and was dropped. The same fate, thank goodness, had befallen an earlier proposal for a four-door fixed-head.

Within weeks of its 1992 launch, the Griffith had eclipsed its TVR siblings, S3 and V8S, in popularity, and was accounting for 80 per cent of all orders. For the first time in the company's history, annual production pushed into four figures, endorsing a simple sales pitch: style with speed was a winning combination, and TVR had cracked it.

Uniting elements of the V8S and the 1988-released Tuscan racer (Tuscan road cars belonged to a previous era), the Griffith conformed to TVR's established formula – stiff triangulated spaceframe chassis, big-hearted up-front V8 engine, and glass-fibre bodywork that caught the eye. That it also cheated the wind and was bereft of the surface rippling that marred previous big-banger TVRs were important bonuses. So was the adoption of race-bred double-wishbone rear suspension – a significant advance on the V8S's semi-trailing arrangement.

The Griffith inevitably called to mind the first Jaguar E-type, lauded for its looks, performance and great value for money. It was just these qualities that set the new TVR apart from rivals. Rivals? What was to challenge the

Specification	TVR Griffith 500 (1995)
Engine	4997cc, V8, ohv pushrod, 16V
Engine layout	Longitudinal, front
Power	340bhp at 5500rpm
Torque	350lb ft at 4000rpm
Gearbox	Five-speed manual
Drive	Rear wheel
Front suspension	Double wishbones, coils, anti-roll bar
Rear suspension	Double wishbones, coils
Steering	Unassisted rack & pinion
Brakes	Ventilated front discs, solid rear discs. No ABS
Front wheels	Alloy 7Jx15
Rear wheels	Alloy 7.5Jx16
Front tyres	205-55VR15
Rear tyres	225-50ZR16
Length	3895mm
Width	1945mm
Height	1205mm
Wheelbase	2280mm
Weight	1060kg (2337lb)
0-60mph (97kph)	4.4sec
0-100mph (161kph)	10.4sec
Top speed	165mph (266kph)
Fuel consumption	15-21mpg

160mph Griffith, priced at just over £27,000 in its most powerful 4.3-litre form (the lesser 4.0 cost £2,500 less)? Ferrari's Testarossa was faster all out. So was Porsche's 911 Turbo. But neither could live with the Griffith to 100mph through the gears.

Prepared by TVR Power, the company's Coventry-based engine division, the 4.3 engine was tweaked to give 280bhp and 304lb ft of torque. In a car that tipped the scales at barely a tonne, genuine supercar performance was there for the taking. Never mind the party-trick 0-60mph time of under 5 seconds, even the 0-100mph one of 11. It was the blink-and-you've-missed-it in-gear times with which the 4.3 despatched every 20mph increment from 20 to 120mph that made the Griffiths so awesomely quick. It wasn't just a case of tapping into massive torque. It was instant access to that torque – and the ground-trembling exhaust rumble that went with it – that had the hairs on your neck standing on tiptoe. Dynamically as well as aurally, sports two-seaters came no more thrilling than this.

You took wet-road liberties at your peril in the Griffith, which had neither traction control nor anti-lock brakes – Wheeler's dislike of electronic aids is legendary. It didn't even have power steering – and you knew it when close-quarter manoeuvring. Once properly on the move, steering effort dropped to a manageable level. More to the point, it gave decent communicative feedback – no, make that kickback – which is just as well, given the ease with which traction could be broken on slippery roads. On dry ones, the Griffith put down its power with impressive alacrity, squirting from second-gear corners like a dragster.

TVR was quick to address early criticisms of poor back-end damping but

Classic TVR Griffith true to form with GRP bodywork wrapped round steel spaceframe chassis.

was happy to continue without electronic aids. If you wanted pansy safety equipment, the message was clear: look elsewhere. Traction control, for instance, was provided by the driver's right foot.

The Griffith's cockpit – opulence personified in leather trim – was light years on from that of the S2 that had frustrated me. There was no need to twist an ankle or splay your legs. The driving position was great. Stubby gear lever, chunky wheel and pedals that encouraged fancy footwork made the Griffith feel right as soon as you slid into its embracing seat. Even the dash – a problem area for all specialist manufacturers – looked good. Unidentified switches teased newcomers, but there was little wrong with the instruments. TVRs had come of age. They had finally escaped from their 'plastic special' image.

The grand plan was to boost performance of the Griffith still further by displacing its old pushrod Rover engine with TVR's own Al Melling-designed AJP V8. This was the most ambitious and expensive project in TVR's history, and essential to Wheeler if TVR was to take its place alongside Ferrari and Porsche. However, teething problems with the potent AJP prompted a rethink. The performance advantage of the Griffith over the new Chimaera – a slightly larger, less overtly sporting version of the Griffith – was achieved by enlarging the 4.3 Rover V8 to 5.0 litres. With 340bhp on tap, the mighty Griffith 500 was, as intended, faster than the 4.3, witness its amazing 0-100mph time of 10 seconds dead. On the open road, the 500 was nothing short of awesome. Around town, low-rev collywobbles made for jerky progress. Being faster and pricier did not make the 500 necessarily better, merely scarier.

Best looking TVR of them all? Griffith eclipsed V8S with stunning looks. Roof panel braced into place by over-centre struts.

TVR Chimaera

Stretcher case

For a specialist manufacturer producing only a thousand or so cars a year, you might have thought that two model lines – the S/V8S and Griffith – were more than sufficient. Ambitious TVR, growing bolder and more innovative by the year, reckoned otherwise, hence the launch of the Griffith-based Chimaera in 1993. Slightly bigger and less aggressive than the car that sired it, the Chimaera (the name was taken from that of a mythical monster), didn't quite recapture the breathtaking lines of the sexy Griffith. But then TVR's third model was more hot cruiser than out-and-out sports – in Ferrari terms, more Mondial than 348 – even though it was still a two-seater with braced-panel headgear like that of sibling models.

A Rover V8 engine would power the Chimaera, not the AJP 4.2 that was intended for the faster, pricier Griffith and upcoming Cerbera. (In the event, the Cerbera was the first recipient, after the Tuscan racer, of the AJP8, its production so long delayed that told-you-so sceptics were mustering for a field day when the 185mph Cerbera, its 4.2-litre AJP engine even better than TVR promised, finally went on sale in 1996 and proved the doubters wrong.)

The Chimaera, meanwhile, became TVR's mainstay model, offering more of the same traditional fare – the same stupendous muscle (initially from a 235bhp 4.0 or a 280bhp 4.3, later from a 4.5 and 5.0), the same he-man controls (still no standard power steering, though it was listed as an option), the same coo-eh presence (who needed expensive styling studios?), the same sort of uplifting driving experience. Some reviewers were still less than enthusiastic about the Chimaera's handling when pressing on, just as they had been about that of the Griffith. But for the money, TVR's luscious 160mph sports-tourer was a class act visually and dynamically.

Stretched Chimaera not as sporty as Griffith, but more practical. Retains 'braced panel' headgear.

Specification	TVR Chimaera
Engine	3950cc, V8, ohv pushrod, 16V
Engine layout	Longitudinal, front
Power	240bhp at 5250rpm
Torque	270lb ft at 4000rpm
Gearbox	Five-speed manual
Drive	Rear wheel
Front suspension	Double wishbones, coils, anti-roll bar
Rear suspension	Double wishbones, coils, anti-roll bar
Steering	Assisted rack and pinion
Brakes	Ventilated discs front and rear, no ABS
Front wheels	Alloy 7Jx15
Rear wheels	7Jx16
Front tyres	215-50ZR15
Rear tyres	225-50ZR16
Length	3990mm
Width	1935mm
Height	1280mm
Wheelbase	2500mm
Weight	1020kg (2249lb)
0-60mph (97kph)	5.0sec
0-100mph (161kph)	12.0sec
Top speed	160mph (258kph)
Fuel consumption	18-26mpg

TVR Cerbera

New engine, old magic

Mighty Cerbera was first production recipient of TVR's own V8. Later Speed Six variant pictured. Car styled in house. High-sill, low-roof cabin accessed through handleless doors.

Stretching the wheelbase and adding rear seats, albeit vestigial plus-twos, seems more likely to diminish sporting prowess than enhance it. Had the 1996 Cerbera been Rover-powered, it would have been a lesser car dynamically than its smaller, lighter siblings. But it wasn't. Here, at last, to confound the sceptics, was the first showing in a road car of TVR's long-awaited, Al Melling-designed AJP8 engine. And what a formidable powerhouse it was.

TVR came of age with the Cerbera as a fully fledged, card-carrying member of the supercar set. Peter Wheeler's previous offerings had been none the worse (some might say all the better) for their bought-in Rover engines, but they weren't pure-breds. The Cerbera, with its own unique, race-bred V8, was the first pedigree TVR. More than that, it leapt into the car world's most exclusive arena with real authority, toting performance that very few rivals could beat, regardless of cost. Enter price into the equation and the Cerbera 4.2 (never mind the later 4.5) left the most illustrious opposition playing catch-up on a bangs per buck basis.

Think of the Cerbera (named after a mythical multi-headed dog that guarded the gates of Hell) as a Chimaera with a long wheelbase, racing engine, fixed-head coupé bodywork and trick equipment and you'd not be far from the mark. Under the voluptuous skin (again, a curvy in-house design strongly influenced by the Chimaera's) was a well-sorted spaceframe chassis and double-wishbone suspension that imbued the Cerbera with better, more trustworthy manners than those possessed by any previous TVR. It wasn't the unusually good ride/handling compromise that made the headlines, though. It was the new V8 engine.

Specification	TVR Cerbera 4.5 (1999)
Engine	4475cc, V8, 1ohc, 16V
Engine layout	Longitudinal, front
Power	420bhp at 6750rpm
Torque	380lb ft at 5500rpm
Gearbox	Five-speed manual
Drive	Rear wheel
Front suspension	Double wishbones, coils, anti-roll bar
Rear suspension	Double wishbones, coils, anti-roll bar
Steering	Assisted rack and pinion
Brakes	Ventilated discs front and rear, no ABS
Front wheels	Alloy 8Jx17
Rear wheels	Alloy 8Jx17
Front tyres	235-40ZR17
Rear tyres	255-40ZR17
Length	4280mm
Width	1865mm
Height	1220mm
Wheelbase	2565mm
Weight	1170kg (2579lb)
0-60mph (97kph)	4.2sec
0-100mph (161kph)	9.0sec
Top speed	185mph (298kph)
Fuel consumption	16-24mpg

Although Melling's AJP8 was unusually light and compact, there was little about its basic specification – single overhead camshafts, two valves per cylinder, fixed timing and straightforward induction – to suggest exceptional performance. But the spec deceived only to flatter, witness an honest if rather uncouth 350bhp at 6,500rpm, and 320lb ft of torque. With its flat-plane crank, Melling's narrow-angle V8 didn't produce the characteristic exhaust waffle of the Rover-engined cars – or of any big-bang Yank V8 for that matter. It screamed like a Ferrari.

Very few cars outside a small clutch of mega-streakers could crack 0-60mph in under 4 seconds, or break 10 seconds to the ton. Top speed was estimated at 185mph, which was about 25mph more than achieved by Porsche's contemporary 911 Carrera 2 costing over £20,000 more. Just as impressive as the engine's all-out delivery was its lusty flexibility and seamless punch. Light in flywheel and therefore low in inertia, the engine 'blipped' like the racer it was. It also exposed the less-than-snappy shift of the five-speed Borg Warner T55 gearbox.

Although tolerably quiet when cruising, the snarling, rough-idling Cerbera was raucously noisy when extended through the gears. Mechanical mayhem at the 7,000rpm limit, to which gear-driven camshafts contributed, underlined that this was no hush-hush car. Engine refinement was not a priority. Nor was fancy equipment like traction control, ABS, airbags or assisted steering. Without optional PAS, mind, you heaved hard at the wheel.

I wasn't alone in feeling snug to the point of being claustrophobic in the Cerbera's high-silled, low-roof cabin, accessed through handle-less doors,

Instruments clustered round steering wheel. Push-button switches for wipers, main-beam and horn also set into chunky wheel. Electric door openers and keyless ignition controversial.

opened electrically when buttons in the mirror pods were pressed. Give me a solid key any day. Can't say I was too keen on the long, access-hindering doors or the finely calibrated instruments festooned around the overloaded steering wheel, either. However, while some of the Cerbera's electrickery and detailing smacked of gimmickry, nothing got in the way of the car's animal-raw aggression and awesome performance.

Unbelievably, there was more to come. The V8 was joined in 1998 by a 4.0 straight-six that Wheeler saw as the Rover V8's eventual successor. Although originally conceived by Al Melling, TVR's second own-brand powerhouse was developed by in-house engine guru John Ravenscroft. The engine of the subsequent Cerbera Speed Twelve was Ravenscroft's own work. What next? Surely it would have to be a flat-16?

TVR

TVR Tuscan
Speed Six **sets the pace**

Cheese-grater grille and tiny headlights give swoopy, big-booted Tuscan Speed Six dramatic visage. Bonnet bulged to clear 360bhp, twin-cam engine. Huge performance matched by intoxicating sound effects. Chassis shortened version of Cerbera's, steering sharp.

Was there no end to prolific TVR's creativity and imagination? Not content with a three-model range, boss Peter Wheeler added to his existing Griffith/Chimaera/Cerbera line-up a fourth model – the Tuscan – early in 2000. TVR's first Tuscan was a hot coupé made in the late Sixties. Since 1989 raw-boned racers of that name have entertained us in a one-make race series that's had repercussions for all Blackpool's road cars: hands-on Wheeler was a regular competitor; the AJP8 engine gained maturity through track competition; and TVR's spaceframe chassis was regularly crash-tested.

The new roadgoing Tuscan, which went on sale in the spring of 2000, owed virtually nothing to its racing namesake. Although cast in the mould of all Wheeler's previous cars – set-back front engine, tubular backbone chassis, rear-wheel drive and so on – it was in detail if not in concept the most innovative TVR yet, and arguably the best looking.

The origins of the new Tuscan, which split the Rover-engined Griffith/Chimaera from the Cerbera on price and sophistication, lay in the 1997 Griffith Speed Six show car, which had attracted so much groundswell interest that TVR was inundated with deposits long before production. What prospective buyers saw, though, was not what they eventually got. To avoid confusion (bad enough

Specification	TVR Tuscan Speed Six
Engine	3996cc, straight-six, 2ohc, 24V
Engine layout	Longitudinal, front
Power	360bhp at 7000rpm
Torque	320lb ft at 5250rpm
Gearbox	Five-speed manual
Drive	Rear wheel
Front suspension	Double wishbones, coils, anti-roll bar
Rear suspension	Double wishbones, coils, anti-roll bar
Steering	Assisted rack and pinion
Brakes	Ventilated discs front and rear, no ABS
Front wheels	Alloy 8Jx18
Rear wheels	Alloy 8Jx18
Front tyres	235-35ZR18
Rear tyres	255-35ZR18
Length	4160mm
Width	1910mm
Height	1180mm
Wheelbase	2360mm
Weight	1060kg (2337lb)
0-60mph (97kph)	4.2sec
0-100mph (161kph)	9.6sec
Top speed	180mph (290kph)
Fuel consumption	Figures unavailable – call it heavy

already) the name, other than the Speed Six epithet, was subsequently changed from Griffith to Tuscan. Dissatisfied with the show car's appearance, designer Damian McTaggart and boss Peter Wheeler – by now recognised as a gifted stylist in his own right – also changed the shape.

One interesting feature of the new car was a rigid lift-out roof panel that stowed in the generous boot without stealing much luggage space; the rear window could be dispensed with as well. Another was a two-layer bonnet, comprising a top nose section giving access to consumable liquids, and a load-bearing aft one bolted over the engine: between the two was a gap to expel spent cooling air. The prominent bonnet hump (echoed at the rear) was not designer whimsy but a necessity to accommodate TVR's new straight-six engine, first seen in the Cerbera in 1998.

Unlike the AJP V8, which had a single gear-driven camshaft per bank and only two valves per cylinder, the lightweight straight-six had two chain-driven camshafts operating four valves per cylinder via fingers. To reduce oil-swirl power losses, it also had dry-sump lubrication, allowing low-set cradling in the chassis – the usual backboned, double-wishbone affair based on that of a cut-down Cerbera's. Why a straight-six and not a more compact V6? One emotional reason was that in-line sixes make such a lovely noise, witness Aston Martin's DBs, Jag's E-type and all Big Healeys.

Like its fancy lights – tiny inset Hellas up front, high-set units in the roll hoops at the back – the Tuscan's dash was a novelty zone. The extravagant ring of instruments that festooned the Cerbera was replaced by a giant arc-shaped speedo carrying an LCD digital display for additional selectable info, revs included. There was no wood embellishment, but plenty of brass and

aluminium in a cockpit effectively divided into two tight-fitting capsules by a carpeted, elbow-high backbone carrying a tall, short-throw gearlever that looked like a BTCC sequential shifter, but wasn't.

With 360bhp to propel a lightweight two-seater, the Tuscan Speed Six promised to be TVR's fastest car – faster even than the 4.5 Cerbera in terms of lap times where braking and cornering counted for as much as straight-line huff. That it was also designed for comfort and practicality – neither traditional TVR strengths – suggested that Europe's grandees had a real fight on their hands from what was shaping as TVR's best-ever car.

Or was it? While praising the new Tuscan's performance, powertrain and presence (not to mention its build quality, adventurous styling and funky instrumentation), the hotshots of *Evo* magazine had misgivings about the car's handling. 'The sharp steering and soggy suspension are an unhappy combination...the rear...feels out of sync, one step behind the front, almost as if the tyre pressures were wildly out.' *Autocar* concurred, especially about super-sharp steering (1.7 turns lock to lock) that was over-sensitive. 'On a typically bumpy British B-road...the steering is a liability.' With fine tuning – notably a 'slower' rack and firmer rear suspension – both magazines reckoned the Tuscan was a winner. 'One of the most thrilling and satisfying engines currently in production,' said *Autocar* of the Speed Six.

Sorting out the TVRs

Year	Model	Engine	Power
1991-94	V8S	3,950cc (Rover)	240bhp
1992-93	Griffith 400	3,950cc (Rover)	240bhp
1992-93	Griffith 430	4,280cc (Rover)	280bhp
1993-94	Chimaera 4.3	4,274cc (Rover)	280bhp
1993-99	Chimaera 4.0	3,950cc (Rover)	235bhp
1993 to date	Griffith 500	4,988cc (Rover)	320bhp
1994-96	Chimaera 4.0HC	3,950cc (Rover)	275bhp
1994 to date	Chimaera 5.0	4,988cc (Rover)	320bhp
1996 to date	Chimaera 4.5	4,546cc (Rover)	285bhp
1996 to date	Cerbera 4.2	4,280cc (AJP8)	360bhp
1997 to date	Cerbera 4.5	4,475cc (AJP8)	420bhp
1998 to date	Cerbera Speed Six	3,996cc (TVR straight-six)	350bhp
2000 to date	Tuscan Speed Six	3,996cc (TVR straight-six)	360bhp
2000 to date	Cerbera Speed Twelve	7,700cc (TVR V12)	800bhp

Confused by TVR's range since the early Nineties? You aren't alone. Arranging its models in chronological order isn't easy as overlaps and false trails cloud the picture. Who better than TVR, then, to provide an accurate summary? Here, especially for this book, is Blackpool's own potted guide to the last decade of the 20th century. By the spring of 2000 TVR was still making the Rover-engined Griffith and Chimaera, as well as the own-label Cerbera and Tuscan Speed Six. The first use of the AJP8 engine, other than in the Tuscan racer (not to be confused with the Tuscan Speed Six), was in the 1996 Cerbera. Note that TVR now refers to its engines as Speed Sixes, Speed Eights or Speed Twelves. Nothing confusing about that.

Ah yes, the Cerbera Speed Twelve, scourge of the supercar set. When Blackpool's mega-trackstar surfaced in the spring of 2000 – the press launch was at the Croft race track – the sheer audacity of the thing ruffled the establishment. Described by TVR's tireless boss Peter Wheeler as a racing car with number plates, the Speed Twelve was no luxury express for well-heeled playboys, no Aston Martin DB7 V12. Far from it. Here was a serious competition machine for the committed hotshot. Here was TVR's contender for GT racing honours, starting with Britain's national championship (it was a winner by June) and graduating to the FIA GT category, dominated by Lister, Chrysler and Porsche.

Basis of the Speed Twelve racer, designed by Neill Anderson, was a combination monocoque/spaceframe chassis of steel and aluminium – a simple structure that would appeal to privateer racing teams. Power came from a 7.7-litre, 90-degree, 48-valve V12 – effectively two canted straight-sixes on a common nitrided crankshaft – claimed to develop an outrageous 800bhp in roadgoing form, nearer 900bhp unrestricted, which put the Speed Twelve in line to eclipse the McLaren F1 as the world's fastest 'production' car. Top speed would have to exceed 240mph if the brawny lightweight – it tipped the scales at 1,100kg – was to steal the F1's crown. At £160,000 apiece – which included a full roll cage, six-speed sequential Hollinger 'box and AP racing brakes – the Speed Twelve was three times the price of the Cerbera 4.5. I've yet to discover whether it is thrice as exciting.

Ultima GTR

200mph on a budget

The fastest car you've never have heard of could well be the Ultima GTR. When this was written, Ultima Sports Ltd had just despatched to an American client a 780bhp, 240mph projectile that had spent some time in MIRA's wind tunnel. 'At that sort of speed, you need to get the aerodynamics right,' said Ultima's boss Ted Marlow. Even Marlow's lesser GTR demonstrator, powered by an Edelbrook-injected 6.3-litre Chevrolet V8 was capable of over 200mph.

The original Ultima was the product of the prolific Lee Noble (see Noble M10) who created a Group C-inspired mid-engined road-racer powered by a Renault engine. Noble sold a clutch of tricky-to-make replicas before the Ultima's name and manufacturing rights were bought in 1990 by Ted Marlow. Since then, the car has been developed, refined and productionised.

The upgraded GTR joined the existing Mk4 Sports and open Spyder in 1999. All three were based on a spaceframe chassis with classic double-wishbone suspension at both ends. While a 355bhp Chevy 5.7 V8 was the favoured engine, other powertrains – Rover V8, Jaguar V8 and variously configured Fords – were also on the menu. So was Porsche's G50 five-speed transaxle. Most cars were sold as component packages at prices from £20,000, but fully assembled cars, costing from £45,000, could also be supplied. Where else can you buy so much performance for so little? Dramatic race-inspired GRP bodywork that made the squat, bubbled-canopied, be-winged Ultima look like an escapee from Le Mans ensured that you never went unnoticed. Nor did you go unrewarded: hustling an Ultima came close to the ultimate driving experience. What else, given a power-to-weight ratio close to that of a McLaren F1's?

Specification	Ultima GTR
Engine	6300cc, V8, ohv pushrod, 16V
Engine layout	Longitudinal, mid
Power	534bhp at 5900rpm
Torque	528lb ft at 4800rpm
Gearbox	Five-speed manual
Drive	Rear wheel
Front suspension	Double wishbones, adjustable coils
Rear suspension	Double wishbones, adjustable coils
Steering	Unassisted rack & pinion
Brakes	Ventilated discs front and rear, no ABS
Front wheels	Alloy 9Jx18
Rear wheels	13.5Jx18
Front tyres	235-35ZR18
Rear tyres	335-30ZR18
Length	4000mm
Width	1850mm
Height	1070mm
Wheelbase	2560mm
Weight	990kg (2183lb) (with Chevy V8)
0-60mph (97kph)	3.5sec
0-100mph (161kph)	8.5sec
Top speed	204mph (328kph)
Fuel consumption	Heavy

Vauxhall VX220

GM turn to Lotus magic

Vauxhall VX220 has same lightweight chassis as Lotus Elise, built at same plant. VX heavier, better equipped; but 2.2-litre, 145bhp from Astra Coupe larger, more powerful.

GM's Speedster raised more eyebrows than sniggers when it broke cover at the '99 Geneva show. An Opel/Vauxhall sports car? Why not? There were precedents from both bloodlines. Opel could point to its 1968-73 GT, a fixed-head two-seater evolved from a concept first seen at the '65 Frankfurt show. Vauxhall's pretty Panther Lima-based Equus of the late Seventies didn't make it into production, but the brainchild of Vauxhall's one-time design chief Wayne Cherry (who went on to greater things within

the GM empire) did serve as a reminder that Vauxhall's roots lay in sporting thoroughbreds of the grandest kind. Remember the great 30/98 of the Twenties? And the uppercrust Prince Henry of the previous decade?

A year on, at Geneva 2000, concept dream had evolved into production reality with little visible change. Although the Speedster tag was retained by Opel, it was replaced on the Vauxhall by VX220 – VX reviving memories of a previous strain of go-faster Vauxhalls that were less successful as image builders than the 220 promised to be despite an excruciating ad campaign that featured a bearded heretic in his underpants. It was what the VX220 stood for – flair, imagination, excitement, fun – that mattered, not its fiscal contribution to GM's coffers.

The grp-bodied VX220 was based on the bonded aluminium chassis of the Lotus Elise and the classy double-wishbone suspension that carried it. There were, however, telling differences between the two even though they were made alongside each other at Lotus's Hethel headquarters near Norwich in a new plant dedicated for the job. Fewer than nine out of ten component parts were interchangable, according to GM, so to regard the VX220 as an Elise with a new powertrain would be to sell it short. For a start it was bigger: length, width and wheelbase were all up on those of the daintier, lighter Elise. The side sills were slimmer (but still awkward to straddle), spring and damper rates recalibrated (to the benefit of ride comfort), wheels and tyres changed (in the interests of user-friendliness), the brakes backed by a servo, never mind ABS (safety first).

Fears that Lotus – once owned by GM, of course – would be shooting

Spartan cockpit comfortable but tricky to access. Trim and furnishings simple, aluminium structural as well as decorative. Steering wheel tiny.

VX220 styling, quite different
from that of Elise, the work
of ex-Audi Martin Smith. Twin
tailpipes stacked vertically.

Specification	Vauxhall VX220 (2000)
Engine	2198cc, 4-cylinders, 2ohc, 16V
Engine layout	Transverse, mid
Power	147bhp at 5800rpm
Torque	150lb ft at 4000rpm
Gearbox	5-speed Getrag manual
Drive	Rear wheel
Front suspension	Double wishbones, coils, anti roll bar
Rear suspension	Double wishbones, coils
Steering	Unassisted rack & pinion
Front wheels	Alloy 5.5Jx17
Rear wheels	Alloy 7.5Jx17
Front tyres	175-55WR17
Rear tyres	225-45WR17
Length	3790mm
Width	1884mm
Height	1113mm
Wheelbase	2330mm
Weight	875kg (1929lb)
0-60mph (97kph)	5.5sec
0-100mph (161kph)	14.5sec (est)
Top speed	135mph (225kph)
Fuel consumption	25-35mpg

itself in the foot by sharing the brilliant Elise with a rival were dismissed. The VX220 would be less the raw-boned, street-legal, back-to-basics toy, more the complete funcar sophisticate for the everyday enthusiast. The spec didn't extend to power steering, air-con, powered windows or central locking, but it did include a driver's airbag (housed in a tiny steering wheel) and half-decent headgear. Lotus might have got away with a joke hood, but GM could not. Nor could it allow an aurally uplifting exhaust note, more's the pity.

Being better equipped and more civilised than the Elise, the VX220 was also 100kg heavier – a problem addressed by increasing power. As the Elise's Rover engine was a non-starter for a GM product, into the modified aluminium tub, slung transversely behind the cockpit, went a torquey 2.2-litre, 16-valver yielding 147bhp and 150lb ft of torque. This lightweight twin-cam from the new Astra Coupe could, according to rumour, be supplemented later by a 190bhp 2.0 turbo. Although the regular 2.2 – the L850 in GM speak – had a horsepower advantage over the 1.8 Elise 111S, the crucial power-to-weight ratio was inferior.

Prior to the press launch, which took place after this book's copy deadline, the guess was that all-out performance would be down on that of the regular Elise. It wasn't. Vauxhall's performance claims – 0-60mph in 5.6ec, 136mph top speed – suggested that the VX220 would show a clean exhaust pipe (actually two of them, vertically stacked) to the regular Elise, never mind Toyota's much cheaper MR2.

Twin counter-rotating balancer shafts promised a smooth delivery to generously-shod rear wheels through a five-speed manual gearbox. As the front tyres were of curiously modest dimensions (and therefore grip) compared with those at the back, there was little likelihood of the VX200 readily swapping ends – an inclination of early Elises, as I once discovered when testing at Thruxton. Sharp responses and agility were design priorities gifted by Lotus, but user-friendliness was high on the agenda, too. The VX220 would understeer safely, protecting the unskilled from a wagging tail, and corrective action.

GM planned to make 3000 of its new sports car a year, a third of them badged Vauxhalls for the UK market. As production would end in 2003, the final tally was likely to be on the short side of 10,000, ensuring exclusivity. The VX220, to be sold in the UK through 50 selected Vauxhall dealers, was not expected to rob the like-priced Elise of sales so much as expand the burgeoning roadster market. Its targeted competitors were not from Hethel so much as Alfa Romeo, BMW, Honda, Mazda, MG and Toyota.

Strong, distinctive visage gives VX220 more presence than Elise. Bold styling fore-shadows that of future Vauxhalls.

Airy alloys carry skinny front tyres to induce safe understeer when cornering. Grip still strong, ABS-backed brakes terrific.

Vauxhall

Westfield FW400

The wonders of carbon-fibre

Baby supercar. Westfield FW400 employs carbon-fibre chassis to reduce weight to minimum. Tuned Rover K-series engine gives Ferrari-humbling acceleration. Fine grip, handling, brakes.

Only a handful of cars can rocket to 60mph from rest in under 4 seconds. Westfield's 190bhp FW400 is one of them. The secret of Ferrari-humbling, head-dunking acceleration is in the name: FW for featherweight, 400 for the target in kilograms (though the actual weight was a little higher). That's light, astonishingly light given that a Lotus Elise, powered by basically the same Rover K-series engine, weighs nearly twice as much. A power-to-weight ratio of some 475bhp per tonne (375bhp per tonne for the lesser 150bhp car) explains the FW400's ability to reach 100mph in 10 seconds flat. Anything beyond the ton, though, and oomph-to-poundage is overruled by air drag – and whatever else it might have been, Westfield's minimalist supercar was no wind-cheater.

To know Westfield's background is to understand its flagship car. Chris Smith and his Westfield team had been building sportsters for nearly two decades before the FW400, the company's most ambitious project to date, broke cover at the 1998 British Motor

Specification	Westfield FW400 (2000)
Engine	1796cc, 4-cylinder, 2ohc, 16V
Engine layout	Longitudinal, front
Power	190bhp at 7000rpm
Torque	150lb ft at 5750rpm
Gearbox	Five-speed manual
Drive	Rear wheel
Front suspension	Double wishbones, coils, anti-roll bar
Rear suspension	Double wishbones, coils
Steering	Unassisted rack & pinion
Brakes	Ventilated discs front and rear, no ABS
Front wheels	Alloy 6Jx13
Rear wheels	Alloy 7Jx13
Front tyres	185-60
Rear tyres	205-60
Length	2340mm
Width	1640mm
Height	1035mm
Wheelbase	2340mm
Weight	430kg (948lb)
0-60mph (97kph)	4.5sec
0-100mph (161kph)	10.5sec
Top speed	140mph (225kph)
Fuel consumption	25-34mpg

Westfield SEight

This book would be incomplete without mention of the Westfield SEight, which, on a bangs-per-buck basis, was the most excitingly scary hotrod I drove in the Nineties. All Westfield's previous Lotus-inspired sports cars had been propelled by four-cylinder engines of modest displacement – Ford 1.6s and 1.8s (in two states of tune) were on offer at the end of the Nineties, though Westfield had also used 150bhp 2.0 Vauxhall power to good effect.

For the daring SEight (get the name?), Westfield bravely shoe-horned into the spaceframe chassis the ubiquitous 3.9 Rover V8 engine that sounded like thunder and went like lightning. The engine of the car I drove – an early Westfield demonstrator – had been fettled (with high-lift cams and four Dell'Orto carburettors) to give 270bhp, but there was, it seems, an even hotter 330bhp version. Even with the standard 200bhp Westfield listed nine years on at the turn of the century, the SEight was awesomely quick and much cheaper than the FW400.

Four things about the SEight I drove are fixed in my memory: acceleration that was plain scary, ear-wilting sound effects from the side exhaust, power-oversteer you could trigger at will, and a ludicrously short range that had you diving into a garage forecourt every 80 miles or so (the SEight's fuel tank was later enlarged from 6.25 to 11 gallons, extending the range to a half-respectable 150 miles, more if you took it easy).

Show. Once into junk shops and classic cars, Smith entered the replicar business by building disarmingly realistic MG Midget-based reproductions of Colin Chapman's little streamlined racer, the Lotus Eleven. I remember rushing one round the West Midlands countryside and thinking between smiles: 'These people know what they're doing. Let's have more.'

The market for sports-racers like the Eleven being limited, Smith soon took to building Lotus Seven lookalikes (again Midget-based) for a wider kit-car clientele. Before long he had exceeded Morgan's annual output of 500.

When sales took off, Caterham – owner of the Lotus Seven's imprint and design – took legal action, forcing Westfield (the name came from Smith's house) to drop its Seven and introduce the substantially altered Westfield SE, styled by Roger Tucker of RT Designs. The SE not only got Caterham's nod of approval but was the first car of its sort in factory-built guise to gain low-volume type approval.

While price and performance differed according to engine (and engine tune), the SEs shared basically the same spaceframe chassis and GRP bodywork. Originally all Westfields had live rear axles. Traction, grip and ride were all improved with the introduction of double-wishbone rear suspension – Westfield's own – as an option.

Self-assembly was denied buyers of the sophisticated FW400 – the first Westfield without a conventional tubular spaceframe chassis. Instead, ex-F1 designer Martin Ogilvie was commissioned to build a carbon-fibre/Nomex honeycomb alternative. Without its quick-release GRP clothing, the tub weighed a mere 50kg. With this radical weight-saving ploy came new styling,

notable for the presence of cowled wind deflectors instead of a screen, forcing occupants – two at a squeeze – into full-face helmets. At your peril did you drive without one.

Chris Smith saw in the FW400 an exciting, uncompromised funster for road and track. Its race-bred credentials were underlined by a five-speed, dog-box Hewland transaxle that helped to give slightly rearward weight distribution. It also cut power losses with its straight-cut gears.

The harder you drove, the better the FW400 felt – gentle progress betrayed transmission snatch – so it was as a let-it-rip track star that Westfield's little streaker excelled on funky tyres and suspension set for maximum grip.

At a smidgeon under £40,000, the 190bhp FW400, its Janspeed-built engine tweaked by Rover's Powertrain Products to VHPD (very high performance derivative) spec, was, er, pricey, demand limited.

191